Frommer's®

PORTABLE

San Francisco

1st Edition

**by Erika Lenkert and
Matthew R. Poole**

Macmillan • USA

ABOUT THE AUTHORS

A native San Franciscan, **Erika Lenkert** worked for HarperCollins before becoming a freelance writer. She has contributed to dozens of travel guides and is currently seeking her fortune in both San Francisco and Hollywood. Her Siamese cats are along for the ride.

Combining the only three things he's good at—eating, sleeping, and criticizing—**Matthew R. Poole** has found a surprisingly prosperous career as a freelance travel writer. A native Northern Californian and author of nearly a dozen travel guides to California and Hawaii, he's looking forward to retiring at 30 but fears he won't be able to tell the difference. He currently lives in San Francisco and has no intention of writing a novel.

Erika and Matthew also contribute to Frommer's *California* and *California from $60 a Day* guides.

MACMILLAN TRAVEL

A Simon & Schuster Macmillan Company
1633 Broadway
New York, NY 10019

Find us online at **http://www.mgr.com/travel** or
on America Online at Keyword: **Frommer's**

ISBN 0-02-861424-0
ISSN 1090-5480

Editor: Douglas Stallings
Design by Michele Laseau
Digital Cartography by John Decamillis & Ortelius Design
Maps copyright © by Simon & Schuster, Inc.

SPECIAL SALES

Bulk purchases (10+ copies) of Frommer's and selected Macmillan travel guides are available to corporations, organizations, mail-order catalogs, institutions, and charities at special discounts, and can be customized to suit individual needs. For more information write to Special Sales, Macmillan General Reference, 1633 Broadway, New York, NY 10019.

Manufactured in the United States of America

Contents

List of Maps

ACKNOWLEDGMENTS

Matthew and Erika would like to thank Dawn Stranne, Meredith Post, Elaine Sosa, and Shirley Fong-Torres.

AN INVITATION TO THE READER

In researching this book, we discovered many wonderful places. We're sure you'll find others. Please tell us about them, so we can share the information with your fellow travelers in upcoming editions. If you were disappointed with a recommendation, we'd love to know that, too. Please write to:

Erika Lenkert and Matthew R. Poole
Frommer's Portable San Francisco, 1st Edition
Macmillan Travel
1633 Broadway
New York, NY 10019

AN ADDITIONAL NOTE

Please be advised that travel information is subject to change at any time, and this is especially true of prices. We therefore suggest that you write or call ahead for confirmation when making your travel plans. The authors, editors, and publisher cannot be held responsible for the experiences of readers while traveling. Your safety is important to us, however, so we encourage you to stay alert and be aware of your surroundings. Keep a close eye on cameras, purses, and wallets, all favorite targets of thieves and pickpockets.

WHAT THE SYMBOLS MEAN

✪ Frommer's Favorites

Hotels, restaurants, attractions, and entertainment you should not miss.

⑤ Super-Special Values

Hotels and restaurants that offer great value for the money.

The following abbreviations are used for credit cards:

AE	American Express	EU	Eurocard
CB	Carte Blanche	JCB	Japan Credit Bank
DC	Diners Club	MC	MasterCard
DISC	Discover	V	Visa
ER	enRoute		

1

The San Francisco Experience

*Y*ou are standing on the corner of Powell and Geary streets at San Francisco's famed Union Square, pausing a moment to catch your breath. Bags in hand bear the rewards of a memorable day of shopping. It's about four in the afternoon on a summer Sunday; a stiff, cool breeze from the west mocks the cloudless skies. Above the din and traffic you hear the clang of a bell, and moments later a cable car—precariously overloaded with wide-eyed tourists—approaches from behind, groaning its way up yet another steep hill. A steady stream of chattering pedestrians passes by, few of whom seem to speak English as a first language. Across the way a bellhop hails a taxi for an older couple, both men dressed in black. Though the sun is out, glimmering skyscrapers block any hope of a warm ray. "Should've dressed warmer," you reply to a shiver as you head back to your hotel to get ready for dinner. As you round the corner, an old man selling flowers on the street corner smiles and hands you a rose—a fitting end to a thoroughly enjoyable day.

Welcome to San Francisco.

Consistently rated one the top tourist destinations in the world, San Francisco is awash with multiple dimensions: Its famous, thrilling streets go up, and they go down; its multifarious citizens—along with their native cultures, architectures, and cuisines—hail from San Antonio to Singapore; and its politics range from hyper-liberalism to an ever-encroaching wave of conservatism. Even something as mundane as fog takes on a new dimension as it creeps from the ocean and slowly envelops San Francisco in a resplendent blanket of mist.

The result is a wee bit o' heaven for everyone: In a city so multi-faceted, so enamored with itself, it's truly hard not to find what you're looking for. Feel the cool blast of salt air as you stroll across the Golden Gate. Stuff yourself on a Chinatown dim sum. Browse the Haight for incense and crystals. Walk along the beach, pierce your nose, see a play, rent a Harley—the list is endless. Like an eternal world's fair, it's all happening in San Francisco, and everyone's invited.

There are, however, three things you should know before coming to San Francisco. First, don't call it 'Frisco. Locals are horribly proud of their city and are surprisingly tolerant of tourists, but even a hearty, "I sure love 'Frisco!" will undoubtedly be met with a cool reply. Second, dress warm. Bob Hope once remarked that San Francisco is the city of four seasons—every day. Temperatures can drop darn quickly within minutes, so be prepared. And finally, arrive with an open mind. There are so many diverse cultures and lifestyles crammed within this tiny peninsula that exercising tolerance and politeness isn't just a courtesy but a necessity. San Francisco's a crazy city, no doubt, but we wouldn't want it any other way.

1 Frommer's Favorite San Francisco Experiences

Cafe-Hopping in North Beach: One of the most pleasurable smells of San Francisco is the aroma of roasted coffee beans wafting down Columbus Avenue. Start the day with a cup of Viennese at Caffè Trieste (a haven for true San Francisco characters), followed by a walk in and around Washington Square, lunch at Mario's Bohemian Cigar Store (à la focaccia sandwiches), book browsing at City Lights, more coffee at Caffè Greco, and dinner at L'Osteria del Forno or Moose's. Finish off the day with a little flamenco dancing at La Bodega or a nightcap at Tosca's.

A Visit to MOMA: Ever since the new MOMA opened in 1995, its been the best place to go for a quick dose of culture. Start by touring the museum, then head straight for the gift shop (oftentimes more entertaining than the rotating exhibits). Have a light lunch at Caffè Museo, where the food is a vast improvement from most museums' mush, then finish the trip with a stroll through the Yerba Buena Gardens across from the museum.

A Walk Along the Coastal Trail: Walk the forested coastal trail from the Cliff House to the Golden Gate Bridge, and you'll see why San Franciscans put up with living on a fault line. Start at the parking lot just above Cliff House and head north. On a clear day you'll have incredible views of the Marin Headlands, but even on foggy days it's worth the trek to scamper over old bunkers and relish the crisp, cool air. Dress warm.

An Adventure to Alcatraz: Even if you loathe tourist attractions, you'll like Alcatraz. The rangers have done a fantastic job of preserving The Rock—enough to give you the heebie-jeebies just looking at it—and they give excellent guided tours (highly recommended).

A Stroll Through Chinatown: Chinatown is a trip. We've been through it at least 100 times, and it's never failed to entertain us. Skip the crummy camera and luggage stores and head straight for the outdoor markets, where a cornucopia of the bizarre, unbelievable, and just plain weird sits in boxes for you to scrutinize (one day we saw an armadillo for sale, and it wasn't meant to be a pet). Better yet, take one of Shirley Fong's Wok Wiz tours of Chinatown for the full effect.

A Date in the Haight: Though the flowers of power have wilted, the Haight is still, more or less, the Haight: a sort of resting home for aging hippies, dazed Deadheads, skate punks, and an assortment of rather pathetic young panhandlers. Think of it as visiting a "people" zoo as you walk down the rows of used clothing stores and leather shops, trying hard not to stare at that girl (at least we *think* it's a girl) with the pierced eyebrows and shaved head. End the mystery tour with a plate of mussels at Cha Cha Cha, one of San Francisco's top restaurants.

A Walk Across the Golden Gate Bridge: Don your windbreaker and walking shoes and prepare for a wind-blasted, exhilarating walk across San Francisco's most famous landmark. It's simply one of those things you have to do at least once in your life.

A Cruise Through the Castro: The most populated and festive street in the city is not just for gays and lesbians (though the best cruising in town is right here). While there are some great shops and cafes—particularly Café Flore for lunch—it's the people-watching that makes the trip a must. And if you have the time, catch a flick at the beautiful 1930s Spanish colonial movie palace, the Castro Theatre.

A Day in Golden Gate Park: A day at Golden Gate Park is a day well spent. Its arboreal paths stretch from the Haight all the way to Ocean Beach, offering dozens of fun things to do along the way. Top sites are the Conservatory of Flowers, Japanese Tea Garden, Asian Art Museum, and the Steinhart Aquarium. The best time to go is Sunday, when portions of the park are closed to traffic (rent skates or a bike for the full effect). Toward the end of the day, head west to the beach and watch the sunset.

An Early Morning Cable Car Ride: Skip the boring California line and take the Powell-Hyde cable car down to Fisherman's Wharf—the ride is worth the wait. When you reach the top of Nob Hill, grab the rail in one hand and hold the camera with the other, because you're about to see a view of the bay that'll make you a believer. Oh, and don't call it a trolley.

2

Planning a Trip to San Francisco

*R*egardless of whether you chart your vacation months in advance or travel on a whim, you'll need to do a little advance planning to make the most of your stay. This chapter will help you with all the logistics.

1 Visitor Information

The **San Francisco Convention and Visitors Bureau,** P.O. Box 429097, San Francisco, CA 94142-9097 (☎ **415/391-2000**), is the best source for any kind of specialized information about the city. Even if you don't have a specific question, you may want to send them $2 for their 100-page magazine, *The San Francisco Book,* which includes 50 pages of lodging information, a three-month calendar of events, city history, shopping and dining information, and several good, clear maps. The bureau only highlights members' establishments, so if they don't have what you're looking for, it doesn't mean it's nonexistent.

You can also get the latest on San Francisco at the following on-line addresses:

- *Bay Guardian,* the free weekly's web site:
  http://www.sfbayguardian.com
- **Hotel accommodations**, reserve on-line:
  http://www.hotelres.com/
- **Q San Francisco,** for gays and lesbians:
  http://www.qsanfrancisco.com/
- **SF Gate,** the city's combined *Chronicle* and *Examiner*
  newspapers: http://www.sfgate.com

2 When to Go

If you're dreaming of convertibles, Frisbee on the beach, and tank-topped evenings, change your reservations and head to Los Angeles.

Contrary to California's sunshine-and-bikini image, San Francisco weather is mild and can often be downright fickle—it's *nothing* like that of neighboring Southern California. While summer is the most popular time to visit, it's also often characterized by damp, foggy days, cold windy nights, and crowded tourist destinations. A good bet is to visit in spring, or better yet, autumn. Every September, right about the time San Franciscans mourn being gypped (or fogged) out of another summer, something wonderful happens: The thermostat rises, the skies clear, and the locals call in sick to work and head for the beach. It's what residents call "Indian summer." The city is also delightful during winter, when the opera and ballet seasons are in full swing, there are fewer tourists, many hotel prices are lower, and downtown bustles with holiday cheer.

SAN FRANCISCO CALENDAR OF EVENTS

January
- **San Francisco Sports and Boat Show,** Cow Palace. Draws thousands of boat enthusiasts over a nine-day period. Call the Cow Palace Box Office (☎ **415/469-6065**) for details. Mid-January.

February
✪ **Chinese New Year.** In 1997, the year of the ox, public celebrations will again spill onto every street in Chinatown. Festivities begin with the crowning of "Miss Chinatown USA" pageant parade, and climaxes a week later with a celebratory parade of marching bands, rolling floats, barrages of fireworks, and a block-long dragon writhing in and out of the crowds. Make your hotel reservations early.

　　Where: Chinatown. **When:** New Year is February 7; festivities go from February 15 to 23; New Year Parade is on February 22. **How:** Arrive early for a good viewing spot on Grant Avenue. For information call ☎ **415/982-3000.**

March
- **St. Patrick's Day Parade.** Almost everyone's honorarily Irish at this festive affair starting at 12:30pm at Market and Second streets and continuing past city hall. But the party doesn't stop there. Head down to the Embarcadero's Harrington's bar after work hours and celebrate with hundreds of the Irish-for-a-day as they gallivant amidst the closed-off streets and numerous pubs. Call ☎ **415/391-2000** for details. The Sunday before March 17.
✪ **San Francisco International Film Festival.** Started 40 years ago, this is one of America's oldest film festivals featuring more than

100 films and videos from more than 30 countries. Tickets are relatively inexpensive, and screenings are very accessible to the general public. Entries include new films by beginning and established directors.

Where: The AMC Kabuki 8 Cinemas, at Fillmore and Post streets and many other locations. **When:** mid-April through early May. **How:** For a schedule or information call ☎ **415/931-FILM.**

April

- **Cherry Blossom Festival,** Japantown. Meander through the arts and crafts and food booths aligning the blocked-off streets; watch traditional drumming, sumo wrestling, flower arranging, origami, or a parade celebrating the cherry blossom and Japanese culture. Mid- to late April.

May

- **Cinco de Mayo Celebration,** Mission District. This is the day the Latino community celebrates the victory of the Mexicans over the French at Puebla in 1862. Mariachi bands, dancers, food, and a parade fill the streets of the Mission. May 5.

○ **Bay to Breakers Foot Race.** Even if you don't participate, you can't avoid this run from downtown to Ocean Beach that stops morning traffic throughout the city. About 80,000 entrants gather—many dressed in wacky, innovative, and sometimes X-rated costumes—for the approximately $7^1/_2$-mile run. If you're feeling lazy, join the throng of spectators who line the route in the form of sidewalk parties, bands, and cheerleaders of all ages to get a good dose of true San Francisco fun.

  Where: Golden Gate Park. **When:** Third Sunday of May. **How:** The event is sponsored by the *San Francisco Examiner* (☎ **415/777-7770**).

○ **Carnival.** The San Francisco Mission District's largest annual event, Carnival, is a two-day series of festivities that culminates with a parade on Mission Street over Memorial Day weekend. One of San Franciscans' favorite events, more than half a million spectators line the route, and the samba musicians and dancers continue to play on 14th Street, near Harrison, at the end of the march.

  Where: Mission Street, between 14th and 24th streets, and Harrison Street, between 15th and 21st streets. **When:** Memorial Day Weekend. **How:** Just show up. Phone the Mission Economic and Cultural Association (☎ **415/826-1401**) for more information.

June

- **Union Street Fair,** along Union Street from Fillmore to Gough streets. Stalls sell arts, crafts, food, and drink. You'll also find a lot of great-looking young, yuppie cocktailers packing every bar and spilling out into the street. Music and entertainment are on a number of stages. Call ☎ **415/346-4446** for more information. First weekend of June.

- **Haight Street Fair.** Featuring alternative crafts, ethnic foods, rock bands, and a healthy number of hippies and young street kids whooping it up and slamming beers in front of the blaring rock 'n' roll stage. The fair usually extends along Haight between Stanyan and Ashbury streets. For details call ☎ **415/661-8025.** Usually the second Sunday in June.

- **Lesbian and Gay Freedom Day Parade,** Market Street. A prideful event drawing up to half a million participants. The parade's start and finish has been moved around in recent years to accommodate road construction, but traditionally it begins at Civic Center Plaza and ends with hundreds of food, art, and information booths and sound stages. Call ☎ **415/864-3733** for information. Usually the third or last weekend of June.

- **Stern Grove Midsummer Music Festival.** Pack a picnic and head out early to join thousands who come here to lie in the grass and enjoy classical, jazz, and ethnic music and dance in the Grove at 19th Avenue and Sloat Boulevard. These free concerts are held every Sunday at 2pm. Either show up with a lawn chair or blanket, or clamor by phone to reserve one of the envied picnic tables—they're free, but they go quickly, so call Parks and Recreation one week before the performance on Monday morning at 9am at 415/666-7027 or 415/666-7035. There are food booths if you forget snacks, but you'll be dying to leave if you don't bring warm clothes—the Sunset district can be one of the coldest parts of the city. Call ☎ **415/252-6252** for listings. Mid-June through August.

July

- **Fourth of July Celebration and Fireworks.** This event can be somewhat of a joke, since more often than not, like everyone else, fog comes into the city on this day to join in the festivities. Sometimes it's almost impossible to view the million-dollar fireworks from Pier 39 on the northern waterfront. Still, it's a party and if the skies are clear, it's a damn good show.

- **San Francisco Marathon.** One of the largest marathons in the world. For entry information, contact the USA Track and Field Association (☎ 415/391-2123). Usually second weekend in July.

September

- **San Francisco Fair.** There are no tractor pulls or monster trucks at San Francisco's rendition of an annual county fair. This sophisticated urban party is attended by thousands and includes restaurant and winery booths, street artists, fine artists, and high-quality local entertainment. The fair is held at the Fort Mason Center each Labor Day weekend. For information call ☎ 415/391-2000.

✪ **San Francisco Blues Festival.** The largest outdoor blues music event on the West Coast celebrates its 25th anniversary in 1997 and will again feature both local and national musicians performing back-to-back during the three-day extravaganza.

    Where: On the grounds of Fort Mason. **When:** Usually in late September. **How:** You can charge tickets by phone through BASS TicketMaster (☎ 510/762-2277). For schedule information ☎ 415/826-6837.

- **Castro Street Fair.** Celebrates life in the city's most famous gay neighborhood. Usually third weekend in September.

✪ **Sausalito Art Festival.** A juried exhibit of more than 180 artists. It is accompanied by music—provided by Bay Area jazz, rock, and blues performers—and international cuisine, enhanced by wines from some 50 different Napa and Sonoma producers. Parking is impossible; take the Red and White Fleet (☎ 415/546-2628) ferry from Fisherman's Wharf to the festival site.

    Where: Sausalito. **When:** Labor Day weekend, early September. **How:** For more information call ☎ 415/332-3555.

October

- **Columbus Day Festivities.** The city's Italian community leads the festivities around Fisherman's Wharf celebrating Columbus's landing in America. The festival includes a parade along Columbus Avenue and sporting events, but for the most part, it's just a great excuse to hang out in North Beach and people-watch. For information call ☎ 415/434-1492. Sunday before Columbus Day.

- **Halloween.** A big night in San Francisco. A fantastical parade is organized at Market and Castro, and a mixed gay/straight crowd revels in costumes of extraordinary imagination. October 31.

- **San Francisco Jazz Festival.** This festival presents eclectic programming in an array of fabulous jazz venues throughout the city. With close to two weeks of nightly entertainment and dozens of performers, the jazz festival is a hot ticket. Past events have featured Herbie Hancock, Dave Brubeck, the Modern Jazz Quartet, Wayne Shorter, and Bill Frisell. For information call ☎ **415/864-5449** or 800/627-5277. End of October, beginning of November.

December

- **The Nutcracker,** War Memorial Opera House. Performed annually by the San Francisco Ballet (☎ **415/776-1999**). Tickets to this Tchaikovsky tradition should be purchased well in advance.

3 Safety

San Francisco, like any large city, has its fair share of crime, but unlike New York and Los Angeles, most folks here don't have firsthand horror stories. There are some areas where you need to exercise extra caution, particularly at night—notably the Tenderloin, the Western Addition, the Mission District, and around the Civic Center. In addition, there are a substantial number of homeless people throughout the city with concentrations in and around Union Square, the theater district, the Tenderloin, and Haight Street, so don't be alarmed if you're approached for spare change. Basically, just use common sense.

See "Fast Facts: San Francisco" in chapter 3 for city-specific safety tips. For additional crime-prevention information, phone San Francisco SAFE (☎ **415/553-1984**).

4 Tips for Travelers with Special Needs

FOR PEOPLE WITH DISABILITIES

Most of San Francisco's major museums and tourist attractions are fitted with wheelchair ramps. In addition, many hotels offer special accommodations and services for wheelchair-bound and other visitors with disabilities. These include extralarge bathrooms and ramps for the wheelchair-bound and telecommunication devices for deaf people. The San Francisco Convention and Visitor Bureau (see section 1, "Visitor Information," above) has the most up-to-date information.

Travelers in wheelchairs can secure special ramped taxis by calling **Yellow Cab** (☎ **415/626-2345**), which charges regular rates for the service. Disabled travelers may also obtain a free copy of the "MUNI Access Guide," published by the **San Francisco Municipal Railway,** Accessible Services, 949 Presidio Ave., San Francisco, CA 94115 (☎ **415/923-6142**). Call this number Monday through Friday from 8am to 5pm weekdays.

FOR GAY MEN & LESBIANS

If you head down to the Castro—an area surrounding Castro Street near Market Street that's predominantly a gay and lesbian community—you'll understand why the city is a mecca for gay and lesbian travelers. Since the 1970s, this unique part of town has remained the colorfully festive gay neighborhood teeming with "outed" city folk who meander the streets shopping, eating, partying, or simply cruising. If anyone feels like an outsider in this part of town, it's heterosexuals, who, although warmly welcomed in the community, may feel uncomfortable or downright threatened if they harbor any homophobia or aversion to being "cruised." For many San Franciscans, it's just a fun area (especially on Halloween) with some wonderful shops.

It is estimated that gays and lesbians form one-fourth to one-third of the population of San Francisco, so it's no surprise that in recent years clubs and bars catering to them have popped up all around town. Although lesbian interests are concentrated primarily in the East Bay (especially Oakland), a significant community resides in the Mission District, around 16th Street and Valencia.

Several local publications are dedicated to in-depth coverage of news, information, and listings of goings-on around town for gay and lesbians. *Bay Area Reporter* has the most comprehensive listings, including a weekly calendar of events and is distributed free on Thursdays. It can be found stacked at the corner of 18th and Castro streets and at 9th and Harrison streets, as well as in bars, bookshops, and various stores around town. It may also be available in gay and lesbian bookstores elsewhere in the country.

FOR WOMEN

Women's services are often lumped together in the lesbian category, but there are resources geared toward women without regard to sexuality. The **Bay Area Women and Children's Center,** 318 Leavenworth St. (☎ **415/474-2400**), offers specialized services and city information to women. **The Women's Building,** 3543 18th St. (☎ **415/431-1180**), is a Mission-area space housing feminist art shows and political events and offering classes in yoga, aerobics, movement, and tai chi chuan. The **Rape Crisis Hotline** (☎ **415/ 647-7273**) is staffed 24 hours daily.

FOR SENIORS

Seniors regularly receive discounts at museums and attractions and on public transportation; such discounts, when available, are listed in this guide, under their appropriate headings. Ask for discounts everywhere—at hotels, movie theaters, museums, restaurants, and attractions. You may be surprised how often you'll be offered reduced rates. When making airline reservations, ask about a senior discount, but find out if there is a cheaper promotional fare before committing yourself.

The **Senior Citizen Information Line** (☎ **415/626-1033**) offers advice, referrals, and information on city services. The **Friendship Line for the Elderly** (☎ **415/752-3778**) is a support, referral, and crisis-intervention service.

5 Getting There

BY PLANE

THE MAJOR AIRLINES   San Francisco is serviced by the following major domestic airlines: **American Airlines,** 433 California St. and 51 O'Farrell St. (☎ 800/433-7300); **Delta Airlines,** 433 California St. and 124 Geary St. (☎ 800/221-1212); **Northwest Airlines,** 124 Geary St. and 433 California St. (☎ 800/225-2525); **Southwest Airlines,** at the airport (☎ 800/I-FLY-SWA); **TWA,** 595 Market St., Suite 2240, at the corner of 2nd Street (☎ 415/ 864-5731 or 800/221-2000); **United Airlines** (☎ 800/241-6522), 433 California St., 124 Geary, and Embarcadero One; and **USAir,** 433 California St. (☎ 800/428-4322).

THE MAJOR AIRPORTS   Two major airports serve the Bay Area: San Francisco International and Oakland International.

San Francisco International Airport   San Francisco International Airport, located 14 miles south of downtown directly on U.S. 101. Travel time to downtown during commuter rush hours is about 40 minutes; at other times it's about 20 to 25 minutes.

The airport offers a toll-free hotline available weekdays from 8am to 5pm (PST) for information on ground transportation (☎ **800/ 736-2008**).

A cab from the airport to downtown will cost $25 to $30, plus tip.

SFO Airporter buses (☎ **415/495-8404**) depart from outside the lower-level baggage claim area to downtown San Francisco every 15 to 30 minutes from 6:20am to midnight. They stop at several Union Square–area hotels, including the Grand Hyatt, San Francisco Hilton, San Francisco Marriott, Westin St. Francis, Parc Fifty Five, Hyatt Regency, and Sheraton Palace. No reservations are needed. The cost is $9 one way, $15 round-trip; children 2 to 16 (accompanied by an adult) pay $5 each way, and children under 2 ride for free.

Other private shuttle companies offer door-to-door airport service, in which you share a van with a few other passengers. **SuperShuttle** (☎ **415/558-8500**) will take you anywhere in the city, charging $10 per person to a hotel; $11 to a residence or business, plus $8 for each additional person; and $38 to charter an entire van for up to seven passengers. **Yellow Airport Shuttle** (☎ **415/282-7433**) charges $10 per person. Each shuttle stops every 20 minutes or so and picks up passengers from the marked areas outside the terminals' upper level. Reservations are required for the return trip to the airport only and should be made one day before departure. Keep in mind that these shuttles demand they pick you up two hours before your flight, three during holidays.

Oakland International Airport   Located about 5 miles south of downtown Oakland, at the Hagenberger Road exit of Calif. 17 (U.S. 880), Oakland International Airport (☎ **510/577-4000**) is used primarily by passengers with East Bay destinations. Some San Franciscans, however, prefer this less-crowded, accessible airport when flying during busy periods.

Again, taxis from the airport to downtown San Francisco are expensive, costing approximately $45, plus tip.

If you make advance reservations, the **AM/PM Airporter,** P.O. Box 2902, Oakland, CA 94609 (☎ **510/547-2155**), will take you from the Oakland Airport to your hotel any time of the day or night. The price varies, depending on the number of passengers sharing the van, but is usually $35 to $45 or less per person; get a quote when you call.

The cheapest way to downtown San Francisco is to take the shuttle bus from the airport to BART (Bay Area Rapid Transit, ☎ **510/464-6000**). The **AirBART** shuttle bus (☎ **510/562-8428**) runs about every 15 minutes Monday through Saturday from 6am to midnight, Sunday from 8:30am to midnight, stopping in front of Terminals 1 and 2 near the ground transportation signs. The cost is $2, for the 10-minute ride to BART's Coliseum terminal. **BART** fares vary, depending on your destination; the trip to downtown San Francisco costs $2.15 and takes 20 minutes once onboard. The entire excursion should take around 45 minutes.

RENTING A CAR   All the major companies operate in the city and have desks at the airports. Call their 800 numbers before leaving home and shop around for the best price. Currently you can secure a compact car for a week for about $150, including all taxes and other charges.

Some of the national car-rental companies operating in San Francisco include: **Alamo** (☎ 800/327-9633); **Avis** (☎ 800/331-1212); **Budget** (☎ 800/527-0700); **Dollar** (☎ 800/800-4000); **Hertz** (☎ 800/654-3131); **National** (☎ 800/227-7368); and **Thrifty** (☎ 800/367-2277).

In addition to the big chains, there are dozens of regional rental places in San Francisco, many of which offer lower rates. These include **A-One Rent-A-Car,** 434 O'Farrell St. (☎ 415/771-3977) and **Bay Area Rentals,** 229 7th St. (☎ 415/621-8989).

BY CAR

San Francisco is easily accessed by several major highways: Interstate 5, from the north, and U.S. 101, which cuts south-north through the peninsula from San Jose and across the Golden Gate Bridge to points north. If you drive from Los Angeles, you can either take the longer coastal route (437 miles and 11 hours) or the inland route (389 miles and 8 hours). From Mendocino, it's 156 miles and 4 hours; from Sacramento it's 88 miles, $1^{1}/_{2}$ hours; and from Yosemite it's 210 miles or 4 hours.

PACKAGES & TOURS

Tours and packages combining transportation, hotel accommodations, meals, and sightseeing are sometimes available to San Francisco. Sometimes it's worth signing onto a tour package just to secure the savings that operators can achieve by buying travel services in bulk. Often you'll pay much less than if you had organized the same trip independently, and you can always opt out of the preplanned activities. Before signing up, however, read the fine print carefully and do some homework. Most of the airlines listed above, along with many other tour companies, offer both escorted tours and on-your-own packages. Discuss your options with a travel agent and compare the prices of each tour component with those in this guide.

3

Getting to Know San Francisco

*H*alf the fun in becoming familiar with San Francisco is wandering around and haphazardly stumbling upon great shops, restaurants, and viewpoints that even locals may not know exist. But you'll find that although metropolitan, San Francisco is a small town and you won't feel like a stranger for long. If you get disoriented, just remember that downtown is east, Golden Gate Bridge is north, and even if you do get lost, you probably won't go too far since three sides of the city are surrounded by water. The most difficult challenge you'll have, if traveling by car, is mastering the maze of one-way streets.

1 Orientation

VISITOR INFORMATION

Once in the city, visit the **San Francisco Visitor Information Center,** on the lower level of Hallidie Plaza, 900 Market St., at Powell Street (☎ **415/391-2000**), for information, brochures, discount coupons, and advice on restaurants, sights, and events in the city. They can provide answers in German, Japanese, French, Italian, and Spanish, as well as English, of course. To find the office, descend the escalator at the cable-car turnaround.

The office is open Monday through Friday from 9am to 5:30pm, on Saturday from 9am to 3pm, and on Sunday from 10am to 2pm. It's closed on Thanksgiving Day, Christmas Day, and New Year's Day.

Dial **415/391-2001** any time of day or night for a recorded message about current cultural, theater, music, sports, and other special events. This information is also available in German, French, Japanese, and Spanish.

Pick up a copy of *The Bay Guardian.* The city's free alternative paper lists all city happenings—their kiosks are located throughout the city and in most coffee shops.

CITY LAYOUT

San Francisco occupies the tip of a 32-mile-long peninsula between San Francisco Bay and the Pacific Ocean. Its land area measures about 46 square miles. Twin Peaks, in the geographic center of the city, is more than 900 feet high.

San Francisco may seem confusing at first, but it quickly becomes easy to negotiate. The city's downtown streets are arranged in a simple grid pattern, with the exception of Market Street and Columbus Avenue, which cut across the grid at right angles to each other. Hills appear to distort this pattern, however, and can seem disorienting. But as you learn your way around, these same hills will become your landmarks and reference points.

MAIN ARTERIES AND STREETS **Market Street** is San Francisco's main thoroughfare. Most of the city's buses travel this route on their way to the Financial District from the outer neighborhoods to the west and south. The tall office buildings clustered downtown are at the northeast end of Market; one block beyond lie the Embarcadero and the Bay.

The Embarcadero curves along San Francisco Bay from south of the Bay Bridge to the northeast perimeter of the city and terminates at Fisherman's Wharf, the famous tourist-oriented pier. Aquatic Park, Fort Mason, and the Golden Gate National Recreation area are located farther on around the Bay, occupying the northernmost point of the peninsula.

From the eastern perimeter of Fort Mason, **Van Ness Avenue** runs due south, back to Market Street. The area we have just described forms a rough triangle, with Market Street as its southeastern boundary, the waterfront as its northern boundary, and Van Ness Avenue as its western boundary. Within this triangle lie most of the city's main tourist sights.

NEIGHBORHOODS IN BRIEF

Union Square   Union Square is the commercial hub of the city. Most major hotels and department stores are crammed into the area surrounding the actual square, and there are a plethora of upscale boutiques, restaurants, and galleries tucked between the larger buildings.

Financial District   East of Union Square, this area bordered by the Embarcadero, Market, Third, Kearny, and Washington streets is the city's business district and stomping grounds for many major corporations. The pointy TransAmerica Pyramid, at Montgomery and

San Francisco at a Glance

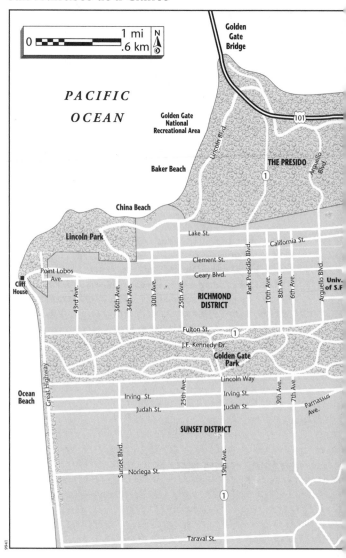

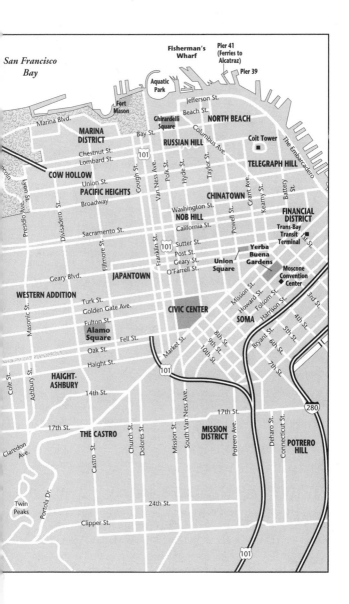

San Francisco Bay

Fisherman's Wharf
Pier 41 (Ferries to Alcatraz)
Pier 39

Aquatic Park
Fort Mason
Ghirardelli Square
Jefferson St.
Beach St.
NORTH BEACH
Marina Blvd.
MARINA DISTRICT
Bay St.
RUSSIAN HILL
Columbus Ave.
Coit Tower
Chestnut St.
Lombard St.
TELEGRAPH HILL
The Embarcadero
COW HOLLOW
Union St.
PACIFIC HEIGHTS
Broadway
CHINATOWN
Washington St.
NOB HILL
FINANCIAL DISTRICT
Trans-Bay Transit Terminal
Sacramento St.
California St.
Sutter St.
Post St.
Geary St.
O'Farrell St.
Union Square
Yerba Buena Gardens
Moscone Convention Center
JAPANTOWN
WESTERN ADDITION
Geary Blvd.
Turk St.
Golden Gate Ave.
Fulton St.
Alamo Square
Fell St.
CIVIC CENTER
SOMA
Mission St.
Howard St.
Folsom St.
Harrison St.
Bryant St.
Oak St.
Haight St.
Market St.
HAIGHT-ASHBURY
14th St.
17th St.
THE CASTRO
17th St.
MISSION DISTRICT
POTRERO HILL
Twin Peaks
24th St.
Clipper St.
Presidio Ave.
Divisadero
Fillmore St.
Masonic St.
Cole St.
Ashbury St.
Claredon Ave.
Portola Dr.
Lyon St.
Gough St.
Van Ness Ave.
Polk St.
Hyde St.
Taylor St.
Franklin St.
Powell St.
Grant Ave.
Kearny St.
Battery St.
Church St.
Dolores St.
Mission St.
South Van Ness Ave.
Potrero Ave.
Dehara St.
Connecticut St.
8th St.
9th St.
10th St.
7th St.
6th St.
5th St.
4th St.
3rd St.
101
101
280

Clay streets, is one of the district's most conspicuous architectural features.

Chinatown   The official entrance to Chinatown is marked by a large red and green gate on Grant Avenue at Bush Street. Beyond lies a 24-block labyrinth, bordered by Broadway, Bush, Kearny, and Stockton streets, filled with restaurants, markets, temples, and shops—and of course, a substantial percentage of San Francisco's Chinese residents.

North Beach   The Italian quarter, which stretches from Montgomery and Jackson to Bay Street, is one of the best places in the city to grab a coffee, pull up a cafe chair, and do some serious people-watching. Night life is equally happening; restaurants, bars, and clubs along Columbus and Grant avenues bring folks from all over the Bay Area here to fight for a parking place and romp through the festive neighborhood. Down Columbus toward the Financial District are the remains of the city's Beat generation landmarks. Telegraph Hill looms over the east side of North Beach, topped by Coit Tower.

Fisherman's Wharf   North Beach runs into Fisherman's Wharf, which was once the busy heart of the city's great harbor and waterfront industries. Today, it is a tacky tourist area with little if any authentic waterfront life, except for recreational boating and some friendly sea lions.

Nob Hill/Russian Hill   Bounded by Bush, Larkin, Pacific, and Stockton streets, Nob Hill is the genteel, well-heeled district of the city, still occupied by the major power brokers and the neighborhood businesses they frequent. Russian Hill extends from Pacific to Bay and from Polk to Mason. It is marked by steep streets, lush gardens, and high-rises occupied by both the monied and the more bohemian.

Civic Center   Although millions of dollars have been expended on brick sidewalks, ornate lampposts, and elaborate street plantings, the southwestern section of Market Street remains downright dilapidated. The Civic Center, at the "bottom" of Market Street, is an exception. This large complex of buildings includes the domed City Hall, the Opera House, Davies Symphony Hall, and the city's main library.

Cow Hollow   Located west of Van Ness Avenue, Cow Hollow is largely residential and occupied by the city's Young and Yuppie. Its two primary commercial thoroughfares are Lombard Street, known for its many relatively inexpensive motels, and Union Street, a flourishing shopping sector filled with restaurants, pubs, cafes, and shops.

Marina District   Created on landfill for the Pan Pacific Exposition of 1915, the Marina boasts some of the best views of the Golden Gate. Streets are lined with elegant Mediterranean-style homes and apartments, which are inhabited by the city's well-to-do singles and wealthy families. Here too, is the Palace of Fine Arts, the Exploratorium, and Fort Mason Center. The main street is Chestnut between Franklin and Lyon, which is lined with shops, cafes, and boutiques.

Pacific Heights   The ultra-elite, such as the Gettys and Danielle Steele—and those lucky enough to buy before the real estate boom—reside in the mansions and homes that make up Pacific Heights. When the rich meander out of their fortresses, they wander down to Union Street, a long stretch of boutiques, restaurants, cafes, and bars.

Japantown   Bounded by Octavia, Fillmore, California, and Geary Boulevard, Japantown shelters only about 4% of the city's Japanese population, but it's still a cultural experience to explore these few square blocks and the shops and restaurants within them.

SoMa   The area is officially demarcated by the Embarcadero, Highway 101, and Market Street, with the greatest concentrations of interest located near Yerba Buena Center, along Folsom and Harrison streets between Steuart and 6th, and Brannan and Market. Along the waterfront are an array of restaurants. Farther west, around Folsom between 7th and 11th streets, is where much of the city's night clubbing occurs.

Mission District   The Mexican and Latin American populations, along with their cuisine, traditions, and art, make the Mission District a vibrant area to visit. There's a substantial community of lesbians around Valencia Street, several alternative arts organizations, and most recently the ultimate in young hipster nightlife. New bars, clubs, and restaurants are popping up on Mission between 18th and 24th streets and Valencia at 16th Street. Don't be afraid to visit this area, but do use caution at night.

The Castro   One of the liveliest streets in town, Castro is practically synonymous with San Francisco's gay community. Located at the very end of Market Street, between 17th and 18th streets, Castro supports dozens of shops, restaurants, and bars catering to the gay community.

Haight-Ashbury   Part trendy, part nostalgic, part funky, the Haight, as it's most commonly known, was the soul of the psychedelic and free-loving 1960s and the center of the counterculture movement. Today, the neighborhood straddling upper Haight Street on the eastern border of Golden Gate Park is more gentrified, but the commercial area still harbors all walks of life. The food, shops, and bars cover all tastes. From Haight, walk south on Cole Street, to a more peaceful and quaint neighborhood.

2 Getting Around

BY PUBLIC TRANSPORTATION

The **San Francisco Municipal Railway,** 949 Presidio Ave., better known as **Muni** (☎ 415/673-6864), operates the city's cable cars, buses, and Metro streetcars. Together, these three public transportation services crisscross the entire city, making San Francisco fully accessible to everyone. Buses and Metro streetcars cost $1 for adults, 35¢ for ages five to 17, and 35¢ for seniors over 65. Cable cars cost a whopping $2 ($1 for seniors from 9pm to midnight and from 6 to 7am). Needless to say, they're packed primarily with tourists. Exact change is required on all vehicles except cable cars. Fares quoted here are subject to change.

If you plan on making extensive use of public transportation, you may want to invest in a comprehensive route map ($2), sold at the San Francisco Visitor Information Center and in many downtown retail outlets.

Muni **discount passes,** called "Passports," entitle holders to unlimited rides on buses, Metro streetcars, and cable cars. A Passport costs $6 for one day, and $10 or $15 for three or seven consecutive days. As a bonus, your passport also entitles you to admission discounts at 24 of the city's major attractions, including the M. H. De Young Memorial Museum, the Asian Art Museum, the California Academy of Sciences, and the Japanese Tea Garden (all in Golden Gate Park); the Museum of Modern Art; Coit Tower; the Exploratorium; the zoo; and the National Maritime Museum and Historic Ships (where you may visit the U.S.S. *Pampanito* and the S.S. *Jeremiah O'Brien*). Among the places where you can purchase a Passport are the San Francisco Visitors Information Center, the Holiday Inn Civic Center, and the TIX Bay Area booth at Union Square.

BY BUS   Buses reach almost every corner of San Francisco, and beyond—they travel over the bridges to Marin County and Oakland. Some buses are powered by overhead electric cables;

others use conventional gas engines; and all are numbered and display their destinations on the front. Stops are designated by signs, curb markings, and yellow bands on adjacent utility poles, and most bus shelters exhibit Muni's transportation map and schedule. Many buses travel along Market Street or pass near Union Square and run from about 6am to midnight, after which there is infrequent all-night "Owl" service. If you can help it, for safety purposes avoid taking buses late at night.

Popular tourist routes are traveled by bus nos. 5, 7, and 71, all of which run to Golden Gate Park; 41 and 45, which travel along Union Street; and 30, which runs between Union Square and Ghirardelli Square.

BY BART   BART, an acronym for Bay Area Rapid Transit (☎ 415/992-2278), is a futuristic-looking, high-speed rail network that connects San Francisco with the East Bay—Oakland, Richmond, Concord, and Fremont. Four stations are located along Market Street (see "San Francisco Municipal Railway," above). Fares range from 90¢ to $3.55, depending on how far you go. Tickets are dispensed from machines in the stations and are magnetically encoded with a dollar amount. Computerized exits automatically deduct the correct fare. Children four and under ride free. Trains run every 15 to 20 minutes, Monday through Friday from 4am to midnight, on Saturday from 6am to midnight, and on Sunday from 8am to midnight.

BY TAXI

This isn't New York so don't expect a taxi to suddenly appear right when you need one. If you're downtown during rush hours or leaving from a major hotel it won't be hard to hail a cab—just look for the lighted sign on the roof that indicates if one is available. Otherwise, it's a good idea to call one of the following companies to arrange a ride: **Veteran's Cab** (☎ 415/552-1300), **Desoto Cab Co.** (☎ 415/673-1414), **Luxor Cabs** (☎ 415/282-4141), **Yellow Cab** (☎ 415/626-2345), **City** (☎ 415/468-7200), and **Pacific** (☎ 415/986-7220). Rates are approximately $2 for the first mile and $1.80 for each mile thereafter.

BY CAR

You don't need a car to explore downtown San Francisco, and in fact, in central areas, such as Chinatown, Union Square, and the Financial District, a car can be your worst nightmare, especially if you ever need to park it somewhere. But if you want to venture outside of the city, driving is the best way to go. If you need to rent a car, see the car rental information in chapter 2. Before heading outside of the city, especially in winter, call for California road conditions (☎ 415/557-3755).

BY FERRY

The **Golden Gate Ferry Service** fleet, Ferry Building (☎ 415/923-2000), operates between the San Francisco Ferry Building, at the foot of Market Street, and downtown Sausalito (30 minutes).

To/From Sausalito   Service to Sausalito is frequent, departing at reasonable intervals every day of the year except New Year's Day, Thanksgiving Day, and Christmas Day. Phone for exact schedule information. The ride takes a half hour and costs $4.25 for adults and $3.20 for kids aged 6 to 12. Senior and physically disabled passengers ride for $2.10; children five and under ride free.

The **Blue and Gold Fleet,** Pier 39, Fisherman's Wharf (☎ 415/705-5444 or 510/522-3300), operates daily from the Ferry Building and Pier 39 to Oakland, Alameda, and Vallejo. Fares are $3.75 adult, $1.50 children, and $2.50 seniors to Oakland; $7.50, $4, and $6 respectively to Vallejo. This service will also take you to Marine World Africa USA on a package trip that includes boat, bus shuttle, and admission. Call for prices.

The **Red and White Fleet,** Pier 41 and 43^1/$_2$ (☎ 415/546-2700 or 800/229-2784) operates from Pier 43^1/$_2$ to Sausalito and Tiburon. Ferries also operate to Angel Island daily in summer and weekends only in winter. On weekdays ferries operate from Tiburon to the Ferry Building.

Round-trip fares to Angel Island are $9 adult and seniors, $8 children 12 to 18, $4.50 children 5 to 11, and free for children under five. Sausalito/Tiburon fares are $11 adults and seniors, $5.50 children. At press time, the Blue and Gold Fleet had just purchased the Red and White Fleet and schedule changes were yet to be determined. Call either number for updated schedules and fare changes.

FAST FACTS: San Francisco

Airport   See "Getting There" in chapter 2.

American Express   For travel arrangements, traveler's checks, currency exchange, and other member services, American Express has an office at 295 California St., at Battery Street (☎ 415/536-2686), and at 455 Market St., at 1st Street (☎ 415/536-2600) in the Financial District, open Monday through Friday from 9am to 5pm and Saturday from 9am to 2pm. To report lost or stolen traveler's checks, call 800/221-7282. For American Express Global Assist call 800/554-2639.

Area Code   The area code for San Francisco and the peninsula is 415; Oakland, Berkeley, and much of the East Bay use the 510 area code. All phone numbers in this book are in San Francisco's 415 area code, but there's no need to dial it if you're within the city limits.

Baby-Sitters   Hotels can often recommend a baby-sitter or child-care service. If yours can't, try Temporary Tot Tending (☎ 415/355-7377 or 415/871-5790 after 6pm), which offers child care by licensed teachers by the hour for children from three weeks to 12 years of age. It's open Monday through Friday from 6am to 7pm (weekend service is available only during convention times).

Business Hours   Most banks are open Monday through Friday from 9am to 3pm. Several stay open until about 5pm at least one day a week. Many banks also feature ATMs for 24-hour banking (see section 1, "Visitor Information," in chapter 2).

Most stores are open Monday through Saturday from 10am to at least 6pm, with restricted hours on Sunday. But there are exceptions: Stores in Chinatown, Ghirardelli Square, and Pier 39 stay open much later during the tourist season, and large department stores, including Macy's and Nordstrom, keep late hours.

Most restaurants serve lunch from about 11:30am to 3pm and dinner from 5:30 to 10pm. You can sometimes get served later on weekends. Nightclubs and bars are usually open daily until 2am, when they are legally bound to stop serving alcohol.

Car Rentals   For car rental information, see chapter 2.

Climate   See "When to Go" in chapter 2.

Convention Center   The Moscone Convention Center, 774 Howard St. (☎ 415/974-4000), between 3rd and 4th streets, was completed in 1981 and named for slain San Francisco mayor George Moscone. Part of a large revitalization project in the SoMa district, the center contains one of the world's largest column-free exhibition halls.

Dentist   In the event of a dental emergency, see your hotel concierge or contact the San Francisco Dental Society (☎ 415/421-1435) for 24-hour referral to a specialist. The San Francisco Dental Office, 132 The Embarcadero (☎ 415/777-5115), between Mission and Howard streets, offers emergency service and comprehensive dental care Monday and Friday from 8am to 4:30pm, Tuesday through Thursday from 10:30am to 7pm.

Doctor　Saint Francis Memorial Hospital, 900 Hyde St., between Bush and Pine streets on Nob Hill (☎ 415/353-6000), provides urgent-care service 24 hours; no appointment is necessary. The hospital also operates a physician-referral service (☎ 415/353-6566).

Driving Rules　See "Getting Around" earlier in this chapter.

Drugstores　There are Walgreens pharmacies all over town, including one at 135 Powell St. (☎ 415/391-4433). The store is open Monday through Saturday from 8am to midnight and on Sunday from 9am to 9pm, but the pharmacy has more limited hours; Monday through Friday they're open from 8am to 8pm, Saturday from 9am to 5pm, and Sunday from 10am to 6pm. The branch on Divisadero Street at Lombard (☎ 415/931-6415) has a 24-hour pharmacy. Merrill's Drug Center, 805 Market St. (☎ 415/781-1669), is open Monday through Friday from 7am to 10pm and on Saturday and Sunday from 7:30am to 10pm, but the pharmacy is only open Monday through Friday from 9am to 7pm and is closed on weekends. Both chains accept MasterCard and Visa.

Earthquakes　There will always be earthquakes in California, most of which you'll never notice. However, in case of a significant shaker, there are a few basic precautionary measures you should know. When you are inside a building, seek cover; do not run outside. Stand under a doorway or against a wall and stay away from windows. If you exit a building after a substantial quake, use stairwells, not elevators. If you are in your car, pull over to the side of the road and stop—but not until you are away from bridges, overpasses, telephone poles, and power lines. Stay in your car. If you're out walking, stay outside and away from trees, power lines, and the sides of buildings. If you're in an area with tall buildings, find a doorway in which to stand.

Emergencies　Dial 911 for police, ambulance, or the fire department; no coins are needed from a public phone. Emergency hotlines include the Poison Control Center (☎ 800/523-2222) and Rape Crisis (☎ 415/647-7273).

Information　See "Visitor Information" earlier in this chapter.

Liquor Laws   Liquor and grocery stores, as well as some drug-stores, can sell packaged alcoholic beverages between 6am and 2am. Most restaurants, nightclubs, and bars are licensed to serve alcoholic beverages during the same hours. The legal age for purchase and consumption is 21; proof of age is required.

Newspapers and Magazines   The city's two main dailies are the *San Francisco Chronicle* and the *San Francisco Examiner;* both are distributed throughout the city. The two papers combine for a massive Sunday edition that includes a pink "Datebook" section, an excellent preview of the week's upcoming events. The free weekly *San Francisco Bay Guardian,* a tabloid of news and listings, is indispensable for night life information; it's widely distributed through street-corner dispensers and at city cafes and restaurants.

Of the many free tourist-oriented publications, the most widely read are *Key* and *San Francisco Guide.* Both of these handbook-size weeklies contain maps and information on current events. They can be found in most hotels and in shops and restaurants in the major tourist areas.

Pharmacies   See "Drugstores" above.

Police   For emergencies, dial 911 from any phone; no coins are needed. For other matters, call 415/553-0123.

Post Office   There are dozens of post offices located all around the city. The closest office to Union Square is inside Macy's department store, 170 O'Farrell St. (☎ 415/956-3570). You can pick up mail addressed to you, and marked "General Delivery" (Poste Restante), at the Civic Center Post Office Box Unit, P.O. Box 429991, San Francisco, CA 94142-9991 (☎ 415/441 8329).

Safety   Few locals would recommend that you walk alone late at night in certain areas, particularly the Tenderloin, between Union Square and the Civic Center. Compared with similar areas in other cities, however, even this section of San Francisco is relatively tranquil. Other areas where you should be particularly alert are the Mission District, around 16th and Mission streets; the Fillmore area, around lower Haight Street; and the SoMa area south of Market Street. See "Safety" in chapter 2 for additional safety tips.

Taxes   An 8.5% sales tax is added at the register for all goods and services purchased in San Francisco. The city hotel tax is a whopping 12%. There is no airport tax.

Taxis   See "Getting Around" earlier in this chapter.

Television   In addition to the cable stations, available in most hotels, all the major networks and several independent stations are represented. They include: Channel 2, KTVU (FOX); Channel 4, KRON (NBC); Channel 5, KPIX (CBS); Channel 7, KGO (ABC); and Channel 9, KQED (PBS).

Time Zone   San Francisco is in the Pacific standard time zone, which is eight hours behind Greenwich Mean Time and three hours behind eastern standard time. To find out what time it is, call 415/767-8900.

Transit Information   The San Francisco Municipal Railway, better known as Muni, operates the city's cable cars, buses, and Metro streetcars. For custom information call Muni at 415/673-6864 during the week between 7am and 5pm and on the weekends between 9am and 5pm. At other times, recorded information is available.

Useful Telephone Numbers   Tourist information (☎ 415/391-2001); highway conditions (☎ 415/557-3755); KFOG Entertainment Line (☎ 415/777-1045); KMEL's Movie Phone Line (☎ 415/777-FILM); Grateful Dead Hotline (☎ 415/457-6388); Morrison Planetarium Sky Line (☎ 415/750-7141).

Weather   Call 415/936-1212 to find out when the next fog bank is rolling in.

4

Accommodations

*W*hether you want a room with a view or simply just a room, San Francisco is more than accommodating for its 11 million annual guests. Most of the city's 180 hotels are concentrated around Union Square, but there are also some smaller independent gems scattered around town. When reading over your options, keep in mind that prices listed are hotel rack rates (the published rates), and you should always ask for special discounts or, even better, vacation packages. Also, the prices listed below do not include state and city taxes, which total 14%. Other hidden extras include parking fees and hefty surcharges—up to $1 per local call—for telephone use.

The hotels listed below are classified first by area and then by price, using the following categories: **Very Expensive:** more than $175 per night; **Expensive:** $130 to $175 per night; **Moderate:** $80 to $130 per night; and **Inexpensive:** less than $80 per night. These categories reflect the price of an average double room during the high season, which runs approximately from April through September. Many hotels also offer rooms at rates above and below the price category that they have been assigned in this guidebook. Also note that we do not list single rates. However, some hotels, particularly more budget-oriented establishments, do offer lower rates for singles, so do inquire about these if you are traveling alone.

In general, hotel rates in San Francisco are rather inelastic; they don't vary much during the year because the city is so popular year-round. You should always ask about weekend discounts, corporate rates, and family plans; most larger hotels, and many smaller ones, offer them, but many establishments do not mention these discounts unless you make a specific inquiry. You will find nonsmoking rooms available in all of the larger hotels and many of the smaller hotels; establishments that are entirely nonsmoking are listed as such. Nowadays, the best advice for smokers is to confirm a smoking-permitted room in advance.

Most larger hotels will also be able to accommodate guests confined to wheelchairs or those who have other special needs. Ask when you make a reservation to ensure that your hotel of choice will be able to accommodate your needs, especially if you are interested in a bed and breakfast.

1 Union Square

VERY EXPENSIVE

Campton Place Hotel. 340 Stockton St. (between Post and Sutter sts.), San Francisco, CA 94108. ☎ **800/235-4300** or 415/781-5555. Fax 415/ 955-5536. 107 rms, 10 suites. A/C MINIBAR TV TEL. $220–$330 double; from $420 suite. Continental breakfast $12.50 extra. AE, CB, DC, MC, V. Parking $23. Cable car: Powell-Hyde and Powell-Mason lines (1 block west). Bus: 2, 3, 4, 30, or 45.

They don't miss a trick at this small, elegant luxury hotel. From the beautifully appointed guest rooms with extralarge beds and exquisite marble bathrooms to the bathrobes and top-notch toiletries, every necessity and whim is covered at Campton Place. The only downside: The rooms and hotel itself are cramped enough to make you wonder what you're forking over the big bucks for, but the superlative service almost makes up for it.

Dining/Entertainment: The Campton Place Restaurant, which serves three meals a day, is highly revered. The menu is

---

Reservations Services

Having reservations about your reservations? Then leave it up to the pros:

Bed and Breakfast California, P.O. Box 282910, San Francisco, CA 94128 (☎ **415/696-1690** or 800/872-4500; fax 415/ 696-1699), offers a selection of B&Bs ranging from $60 to $150 per night (two-night minimum). Accommodations range from simple rooms in private homes to luxurious, full-service carriage houses, houseboats, and Victorian homes.

San Francisco Hotel Reservation is a nifty Worldwide Web site that allows Internet users to make their reservations on-line. Plug in at **http://www.hotelres.com.**

San Francisco Reservations, 22 Second St., San Francisco, CA 94105 (☎ **800/667-1550** or 415/227-1500), arranges reservations for more than 200 of San Francisco's hotels and often offers discounted rates. Ask about their Events and Hotel Packages that include VIP or discount admissions to various San Francisco museums.

contemporary American, with dishes like stuffed, braised oxtail and saffron-steamed sea bass, priced from $19 to $30.

Services: 24-hour room service, concierge, evening turndown, laundry/valet, complimentary overnight shoe shine, morning newspaper. Business services such as typing, translating, and faxing available by request at the front desk.

Facilities: Access to nearby health club.

The Clift Hotel. 495 Geary St. (at Taylor St., two blocks west of Union Square), San Francisco, CA 94102. ☎ **800/437-8243** in the U.S. or 415/775-4700. Fax 415/441-4621. 326 rms, 31 suites. A/C MINIBAR TV TEL. $255–$400 double; from $405 suite. Continental breakfast $12.50 extra. AE, CB, DC, MC, V. Parking $23. Cable car: Powell-Hyde and Powell-Mason lines (2 blocks east). Bus: 2, 3, 4, 30, 38, or 45.

One of San Francisco's top luxury hotels, the Clift went through some shaky times in recent years as ownership changed hands, but everything seems to be back on track—enough so to win both Five-Star and Five-Diamond awards for the tenth year in a row. Located in the city's Theater District, two blocks from Union Square, the Clift's staff excels at pampering its guests and even manages to be cordial to the droves of tourists who wander slack jawed through the palatial lobby. The decor of the guest rooms leans toward old-fashioned, with high ceilings, elaborate moldings and woodwork, Georgian reproductions, and marble bathrooms with everything from hair dryers to plush terry-cloth robes. Thoughtful extras include padded hangers, individual climate controls, two-line telephones, and a scale in your dressing room. The windows also open—a nice touch for those guests who appreciate fresh air.

The Clift's "Young Travelers Program" provides traveling families with toys and games, diapers, bottles, children's books, and other amenities to help children and their parents feel at home. The hotel also accepts and pampers pets.

Dining/Entertainment: The French Room, open for breakfast, lunch, and dinner, specializes in seasonally appropriate California-French cuisine. The hotel's dramatic Redwood Room, which opened in 1933 and remains one of San Francisco's most opulent piano bars, has beautiful 22-foot-tall fluted redwood columns and is also famous for its Gustav Klimt murals. The lobby lounge serves cocktails daily and a traditional English tea Monday through Saturday.

Services: 24-hour room service, concierge, twice-daily maid service, overnight laundry and shoe polishing, one-hour pressing, evening turndown, complimentary in-room fax and computers.

Accommodations Near Union Square & Nob Hill

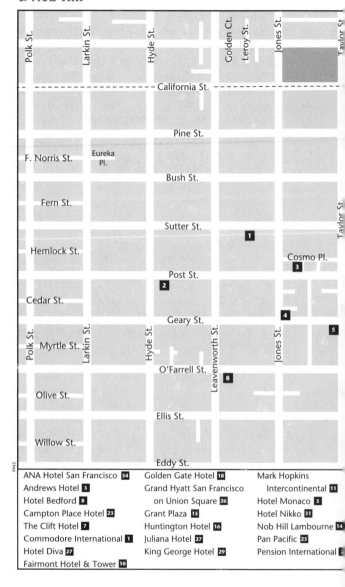

ANA Hotel San Francisco **34**	Golden Gate Hotel **18**	Mark Hopkins
Andrews Hotel **3**	Grand Hyatt San Francisco	Intercontinental **11**
Hotel Bedford **8**	on Union Square **26**	Hotel Monaco **5**
Campton Place Hotel **23**	Grant Plaza **15**	Hotel Nikko **31**
The Clift Hotel **7**	Huntington Hotel **16**	Nob Hill Lambourne **14**
Commodore International **1**	Juliana Hotel **27**	Pan Pacific **25**
Hotel Diva **27**	King George Hotel **29**	Pension International **2**
Fairmont Hotel & Tower **10**		

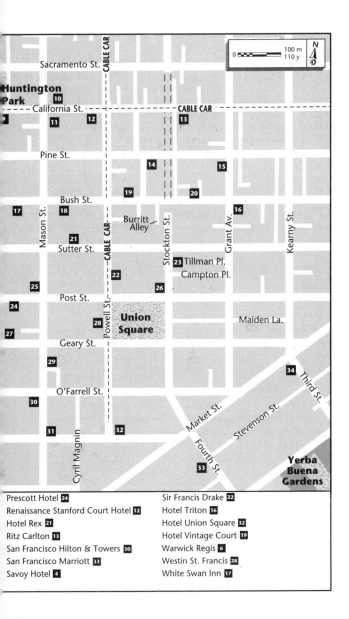

Sacramento St.

Huntington Park 10

California St. ----- CABLE CAR

Pine St.

Bush St.

Burritt Alley

Sutter St.

Tillman Pl.
Campton Pl.

Post St.

Union Square

Maiden La.

Geary St.

O'Farrell St.

Market St.

Stevenson St.

Third St.

Fourth St.

Yerba Buena Gardens

Prescott Hotel 24	Sir Francis Drake 22
Renaissance Stanford Court Hotel 12	Hotel Triton 16
Hotel Rex 21	Hotel Union Square 32
Ritz Carlton 13	Hotel Vintage Court 19
San Francisco Hilton & Towers 30	Warwick Regis 6
San Francisco Marriott 33	Westin St. Francis 28
Savoy Hotel 4	White Swan Inn 17

Facilities: 24-hour business center, gift shop, extensive fitness facility.

Grand Hyatt San Francisco on Union Square. 345 Stockton St. (between Post and Sutter sts.), San Francisco, CA 94108. ☎ **800/233-1234** or 415/398-1234. Fax 415/391-1780. 663 rms, 30 suites. A/C MINIBAR TV TEL. $250–$280 double (doesn't include breakfast); $195–$285 Regency room (including continental breakfast); from $350 suite. Continental breakfast $14.50 extra. AE, CB, DC, JCB, MC, V. Parking $24. Cable car: Powell-Hyde and Powell-Mason lines (2 blocks west). Bus: 2, 3, 4, 30, 38, or 45.

If the thought of a 10-second walk to Saks Fifth Avenue makes you drool and your credit cards start to sweat, this hotel is the place for you. Not only is the Grand Hyatt surrounded by all the downtown shopping, but it also boasts some of the best views in the area. The lobby is indeed *grand,* with Chinese artifacts and enormous ceramic vases, but sadly the well-kept rooms are little more than upscale basic with a corporate flare. They do have some elbow room and a small table and chairs, but the views from most of the 36 floors are truly spectacular. Accommodations include such amenities as TVs in the bathroom, first-run movies, and a telephone with computer-connection capability. Regency rooms are larger, and prices include continental breakfast and evening hors d'oeuvres. Three floors are also dedicated to Business Plan rooms, which contain private fax, telephone with computer hook-up, enhanced lighting, coffeemaker, iron and board, and hair dryer. They also include special services—24-hour access to compatible printer, photocopier, and office supplies, free local calls and credit card phone access, and daily newspaper. All for an additional $15.

Dining/Entertainment: The hotel's signature Plaza Restaurant has floor-to-ceiling windows overlooking Union Square. Breakfast, lunch, and dinner are served in a garden setting. Napper's Deli, an indoor/outdoor bistro, serves custom-cut sandwiches, seasonal salads, soups, and desserts; continental breakfasts are served here on weekends beginning at 8:30am. Club 36, on the 36th floor, serves cocktails with live jazz six nights a week and allows for a birds-eye view of downtown.

Services: Room service, concierge, free weekday morning town car service to the Financial District.

Facilities: Fitness center, tour desk, car-rental desk, fully equipped business center.

○ **Hotel Monaco.** 501 Geary St. (at Taylor St.), San Francisco, CA 94102. ☎ **800/214-4220** or 415/292-0100. Fax 292-0111. 177 rooms, 24 suites.

A/C MINIBAR TV TEL. From $170 double; from $295 suite. Call for discounted rates. AE, DC, DISC, JCB, MC, V. Parking $20. Bus: 2, 3, 4, 27, or 38.

This remodeled 1910 beaux arts building debuted in June 1995 and is the new diva of Union Square luxury hotels. For $24 million, the Kimpton Group did this place right—from the cozy main lobby with a two-story French inglenook fireplace to the guest rooms with canopy beds, Chinese-inspired armoires, bamboo writing desks, bold stripes, and vibrant color. Everything is brand-spanking new, in the best of taste, and as playful as it is serious. The decor, combined with the breathtaking neighboring restaurant, make this our favorite luxury hotel in the city. The only downside is that some rooms are too small.

Dining/Entertainment: The hotel's restaurant, the Grand Cafe, is the best room downtown. It is grand, in the true sense of the word, with sky-high ceilings, elaborate 1920s and 1930s style, and an amazing collection of local art. (See chapter 5, "Dining," for complete information.)

Services: Computer, complimentary wine hour nightly, concierge, overnight shoeshine, valet/laundry, two-line phones, secretarial services.

Facilities: Health club with steam, sauna, and massage; meeting and banquet facilities

Hotel Nikko. 222 Mason St. (at O'Farrell St.), San Francisco, CA 94102. ☎ **800/645-5687** or 415/394-1111. Fax 415/421-0455. 500 rms, 22 suites. A/C MINIBAR TV TEL. $225–$285 double; from $385 suite. AE, CB, DISC, JCB, MC, V. Parking $24. Cable car: Powell-Hyde and Powell-Mason lines. Bus: 2, 3, 4, 30, 38, or 45.

Part of Japan Airlines' international fleet of superluxury hotels, the 25-story Hotel Nikko combines the luxuries of both eastern and western cultures with heavenly results. Work out in the fitness center with your personal trainer; take a few laps in the glass-enclosed indoor swimming pool; rest in the Jacuzzi, Japanese sauna, or soaking tub; then top off the morning with a shiatsu massage before starting your day—what more could you ask for?

Ideally located near Union Square and the Theater District, the Nikko's penchant for pampering also carries on to the guest rooms, which feature top-of-the-line amenities such as two-line speaker phones with modem ports, blackout curtains, large windows with views of the city, and huge, marble bathrooms with separate tubs and showers. Suites include separate sitting areas, stereos, and entry halls (a Japanese tradition). Though the hotel's decor is a bit too staid for western tastes—simple furnishings and pearl gray tones predominate—the element of luxury ultimately prevails. Prices are steep, naturally, but the hotel's special "romance" packages ($129 per night with plenty of freebies) are perfect for special occasions.

Dining/Entertainment: The bistro-style Cafe 222 serves both California and Japanese cuisine for breakfast, lunch, and dinner. On the lobby level is a small sushi bar offering made-to-order sushi, as well as afternoon hors d'oeuvres and live music.

Services: 24-hour room service, twice-daily maid service, concierge, laundry/valet.

Facilities: Business center, swimming pool, fitness center, sauna, hot tub, shiatsu massage, tanning booth, gift and other shops.

Pan Pacific. 500 Post St. (at Mason St.), San Francisco, CA 94102. ☎ **415/771-8600.** Fax 415/398-0267. 300 rms, 29 suites. A/C MINIBAR TV TEL. $235–$335 double; from $375 suite. Continental breakfast $8 extra; American breakfast $14.25 extra. AE, DC, JCB, MC, V. Parking $24. Cable car: Powell Hyde and Powell Mason lines. Bus: 2, 3, 4, 30, 38, or 45.

If this were Hollywood, James Bond might hoodwink a villain here, magically drop down the skyrise's atrium, and disappear into the night. But all is quiet and intimate in the third-floor lobby, even though the skylight ceiling is another 18 floors up. The Pan Pacific is 21st century with Star Wars–like lighted corridors, artistically glitzy, enormous, and somehow romantic, all at the same time. The lobby's marble fountain with four dancing figures and its player piano set the mood for guests relaxing in front of the fireplace. The rooms are rather corporate, but in good taste, and immaculately clean and well stocked with all the luxurious extras, including lavish marble bathrooms with mini-TVs at the sink. Other amenities offered are in-room safes, three Touch-Tone phones, voice mail, and bathrobes. The hotel is also conveniently located close to Union Square.

Dining: The Pacific dining room serves breakfast, lunch, and dinner featuring California cuisine with Asian and French accents.

Services: 24-hour room service, concierge, laundry/valet, complimentary Rolls Royce transportation in the city.

Facilities: Business center.

✪ **Prescott Hotel.** 545 Post St. (between Mason and Taylor sts.), San Francisco, CA 94102. ☎ **800/283-7322** or 415/563-0303. Fax 415/ 563-6831. 167 rms, 35 suites. A/C MINIBAR TV TEL. $175 double; $235 Concierge level double (including breakfast and evening cocktail reception); from $265 suite. AE, CB, DC, MC, V. Parking $21. Cable car: Powell-Hyde and Powell-Mason lines (1 block east). Bus: 2, 3, 4, 30, 38, or 45.

The Prescott has always been one of our favorite hotels in San Francisco. The staff treats you like royalty, the rooms are beautiful and immaculate, the location—one block from Union Square—is perfect, and room service is provided by one of the best restaurants in the city: Postrio. (In fact, it's not unheard of for visitors to check into the Prescott just to get preferred seating.)

Dark tones of green, plum, and burgundy blend well with the cherry wood furnishings within each of the soundproofed rooms; the view, alas, isn't so pleasant. All bathrooms are supplied with terry-cloth robes and hair dryers, though only the suites have whirlpool bathtubs. "Club Level" guests are pampered with free continental breakfast, evening cocktails, and exercise bicycles or rowing machines brought up to your room on request (all for only $20 extra per night).

Dining/Entertainment: The hotel provides preferred seating for guests at Postrio Restaurant. Be sure to make reservations when you book your room (see chapter 5, "Dining," for complete information).

Services: Complimentary coffee and tea each morning, wine and hors d'oeuvres every evening in the living room, limousine service weekday mornings to the Financial District, concierge, twice-daily maid service, nightly turndown, same-day valet/laundry service, overnight shoe shine, room service from the Postrio.

Facilities: Access to off-premises health club, including swimming pool, free weights, and sauna.

San Francisco Hilton & Towers. 333 O'Farrell St. (between Mason and Taylor sts.), San Francisco, CA 94102. ☎ **800/445-8667** or 415/771-1400. Fax 415/771-1607. 1,614 rms, 180 suites. A/C MINIBAR TV TEL. $215–$260 double; from $310 suite. Children stay free in parents' room. Continental breakfast $10 extra. AE, CB, DC, DISC, MC, V. Parking $24. Cable car: Powell-Hyde and Powell-Mason lines (1 block east). Bus: 2, 3, 4, 30, 38, or 45.

Complete with bustling conventioneers, anxious smokers, and a line to register that resembles airport check-in, the Hilton's lobby is so enormous and busy it feels more like a convention hall than a hotel. It's the Hilton's three connecting buildings (the original 19-story main building, a 46-story tower topped by a panoramic restaurant, and a 23-story landmark with an additional 386 luxurious rooms and suites) that bring the swarms of visitors clamoring for a room. But even during quieter times, the sheer enormity of the place makes the Hilton somewhat overwhelming and its contents mysterious.

After you get past the sweeping grand lobby, jump on an elevator and wind through endless corridors to your room; you'll find the mystique ends with common, corporate accommodations. Some rooms' floor-to-ceiling views may be memorable, but the decor definitely is not. Unless you're staying in one of the more luxurious abodes, the feel and decor here is impersonal and plain—perfect for the conventioneers, but not for a romantic weekend.

Dining/Entertainment: Cityscape, on the 46th floor, serves classic California cuisine with a breathtaking 360° view; the retractable skylight exposes the night sky in all its grandeur. Kiki of Tokyo offers Japanese cuisine. The Mason Street Deli serves breakfast and lunch, and Intermezzo offers Italian-style food to eat in or to go. An elegant sidewalk cafe, The Café on the Square, provides a spot for watching the passing parade.

Services: Room service (6am to midnight), concierge, laundry, shoe shine.

Facilities: Swimming pool, health club, business center, car rental, tour desk, shopping arcade. Towers-level accommodations offer upgraded services, including separate registration lounge with complimentary breakfast, hors d'oeuvres, and daily newspaper.

San Francisco Marriott. 55 Fourth St. (between Market and Mission sts.), San Francisco, CA 94103. ☎ **800/228-9290** or 415/896-1600. Fax 415/442-0141. 1,366 rms, 134 suites. A/C MINIBAR TV TEL. $149–$189 standard double; $195–$265 concierge level double; from $350 suite. Continental breakfast $6.95 extra. AE, CB, DC, JCB, MC, V. Parking $24. Cable car: Powell-Hyde and Powell-Mason lines (3 blocks west). Muni Metro: All Market St. trams. All Market St. buses.

Some call it a masterpiece, others liken it to the world's biggest parking meter. Regardless, the Marriott is one of the largest buildings in the city, making it a popular stopover for convention-goers and those looking for a room with a view. Fortunately, the controversy does not extend to the rooms, so expect pleasant accommodations with large bathrooms and beds and exceptional city vistas. Rooms on the concierge level are more spacious and provide a lengthy list of complimentary services, including continental breakfast, afternoon snacks and beverages, evening hors d'oeuvres and canapés, and an open honor bar. Upon arrival, enter from Fourth Street, between Market and Mission, to avoid a long trek to the registration area.

Dining/Entertainment: Kinoko is a Japanese teppanyaki restaurant and sushi bar. Allie's American Grill, facing the hotel's central fountain, has a breakfast bar and two buffets that prepare made-to-order omelets; there is also a varied lunch and dinner menu. You can choose between the Atrium Lounge and the View Lounge, which has a truly panoramic view of the bay and Golden Gate Bridge (assuming there's no fog) as well as live entertainment.

Facilities: Indoor pool and health club, business center, tour desk, car-rental, and gift shop.

Westin St. Francis. 335 Powell St. (between Geary and Post sts.), San Francisco, CA 94102. ☎ **800/228-3000** or 415/397-7000. Fax 415/774-0124. 1,192 rms, 83 suites. A/C MINIBAR TV TEL. Main building: $185–$305 double; from $225 suite. Tower: $265–$305 double; from $375 suite. Extra person $30. Continental breakfast $12.50 extra. AE, DC, DISC, JCB, MC, V. Parking $24. Cable car: Powell-Hyde and Powell-Mason lines (direct stop). Bus: 2, 3, 4, 30, 45, or 76.

At the turn of the century Charles T. Crocker and a few of his wealthy buddies decided that San Francisco needed a world-class hotel, and up went the St. Francis. Since then, hoards of VIPs have hung their hats and hosiery here, including Emperor Hirohito, Queen Elizabeth II, Mother Teresa, King Juan Carlos of Spain, the Shah of Iran, and all the U.S. presidents since Taft. In 1972 the 32-story Tower was added, doubling the capacity and adding the requisite banquet and conference centers (as well Club Oz, the hotel's rooftop dance club). The older rooms of the main building vary in size and have more old-world charm than the newer tower rooms, but the Tower is remarkable for its great views of the city once you rise above the 18th floor.

Though too massive to offer the personal service you get at the smaller deluxe hotels on Nob Hill, few other hotels in San Francisco can match the majestic aura of the St. Francis. We know it sounds corny, but the St. Francis is so intertwined with the city's past that it truly *is* San Francisco: Stroll through the vast, ornate lobby and you can feel 100 years of history oozing from its hand-carved redwood paneling. Even if you stay elsewhere, it's worth a visit if only to partake in high tea at the Compass Rose, one of San Francisco's most enduring and enjoyable traditions.

Dining/Entertainment: Club Oz, a popular dance club with a hefty cover on weekend nights, is open nightly. The lobby-level Dewey's, a sports bar, offers a do-it-yourself luncheon buffet, and burgers and pizzas at night. Dutch Kitchen, also on the lower level, offers a basic breakfast menu. The Compass Rose is open daily for lunch and afternoon tea (3 to 5pm), with live music, dancing, champagne, cocktails, and caviar tasting in the evening.

Services: 24-hour room service, voice mail, baby-sitting referral, Westin Kids Club (great for families), laundry.

Facilities: Fitness center, business center, tour and car rental desks, barber/beauty salon, gift shop.

EXPENSIVE

✪ **Hotel Triton.** 342 Grant Ave. (at Bush St.), San Francisco, CA 94108. ☎ **800/433-6611** or 415/394-0500. Fax 415/394-0555. 140 rms, 7 suites. A/C MINIBAR TV TEL. $119–$179 double; $199–$279 suite. Continental breakfast $7.75 extra. AE, DC, DISC, MC, V. Parking $20. Cable car: Powell-Hyde and Powell-Mason lines (2 blocks west).

Executing a bold idea that was long overdue, hotelier magnate Bill Kimpton requisitioned a cadre of local artists and designers to "do their thing" to his latest acquisition, the Hotel Triton. The result was San Francisco's first three-star hotel to finally break the boring barrier. Described as vogue, chic, retro-futuristic, and even neo-Baroque, the Triton begs attention from the Daliesque lobby to the sumptuous designer suites à la Jerry Garcia, Wyland (the ocean artist), and Joe Boxer. Two dozen environmentally sensitive "EcoRooms"—biodegradable soaps, filtered water and air, all-natural linens—were also installed to please the tree-hugger in all of us. A mild caveat: Don't expect perfection; many of the rooms could use a little touching up here and there (stained curtains, chipped furniture), and service isn't as snappy as it could be. If you can live with this, and want to inject a little fun and style into your stay, then come join Dorothy and Toto for a trip far from Kansas.

Dining/Entertainment: Café de la Presse, a European-style newsstand and outdoor cafe, serves breakfast, lunch, and dinner. In the hotel lobby, complimentary coffee is served each morning and wine each evening.

Services: Room service, same-day laundry.

Facilities: Business center, exercise room.

Juliana Hotel. 590 Bush St. (at Stockton St.), San Francisco, CA 94108. ☎ **800/328-3880** or 415/392-2540. Fax 415/391-8447. 84 rms, 22 suites. A/C MINIBAR TV TEL. $135–$165 double; $169–$179 junior suite; $179–$189 executive suite. Special winter packages available. Continental breakfast $7.95 extra. AE, CB, DC, MC, V. Parking $16. Cable car: Powell-Hyde and Powell-Mason lines (1 block west). Bus: 2, 3, 4, 30, 38, or 45.

We love the lobby at this small, European-style hotel. With its rich, homey surroundings, English prints, and comfy couches facing a blazing fire, which is ensconced in brass and marble, it feels more like a rich friend's study than the entrance to a hotel. With the addition of daily papers hanging on a wooden rack, the Juliana has created a place that makes us want to kick up our feet and stay awhile. And with the complimentary coffee here by day and wine by night, there's no real reason to leave.

The rooms are light, spacious, and country-cute in a Laura Ashley kind of way, with floral drapes and bedspreads, white furnishings, and cozy, upholstered chairs. The bathroom, like the lobby, has homey touches like a large well-lit mirror, hair dryer, and a wicker basket holding soap and other house toiletries.

Services: Room service, laundry/valet, morning transport to the Financial District. Guests enjoy access to an off-premises health club.

Sir Francis Drake. 450 Powell St. (at Sutter St.), San Francisco, CA 94102. ☎ **800/227-5480** or 415/392-7755. Fax 415/677-9341. 412 rooms, 5 suites. A/C MINIBAR TV TEL. $149–$199 double; $185–$600 suite. AE, CB, DC, DISC, MC, V. Parking $23. Cable car: Powell-Hyde and Powell-Mason lines (direct stop). Bus: 2, 3, 4, 45, or 76.

It took a change of ownership and a multimillion-dollar restoration to save the Sir Francis Drake from becoming a Starbucks, but now this stately old queen is once again housing guests in grand fashion. Granted, this venerable septuagenarian is still showing signs of age (the owners admit there's still more work to be done), but the price of imperfection is certainly reflected in the room rate: a good $100 less per night than its Nob Hill cousins. The new Sir Francis Drake is a hotel for people who are willing to trade a chipped bathroom tile or oddly matched furniture for the opportunity to vacation in pseudo-grand fashion. Allow Tom Sweeny, the ever-ebullient (and legendary) Beefeater doorman, to handle your bags as you make your entrance into the elegant, captivating lobby. Sip cocktails at the superchic Starlight Lounge overlooking the city. Dine at Scala's Bistro, one the hottest new restaurants in the city. In short, live like the king or queen of Union Square without all the pomp, circumstance, and credit card bills.

Dining/Entertainment: Scala's Bistro at the lobby level serves excellent Italian cuisine in a stylish setting (see chapter 5, "Dining," for complete information). Café Expresso, a small Parisian-style corner cafe, does an equally commendable job serving coffees, pastries, and sandwiches daily. The Starlight Room on the 21st floor offers cocktails, entertainment, and dancing nightly with a panoramic view of the city.

Services: Room service, business services, valet, concierge.
Facilities: Exercise room, extensive meeting facilities.

Hotel Vintage Court. 650 Bush St. (between Powell and Stockton sts.), San Francisco, CA 94108. ☎ **800/654-1100** or 415/392-4666. Fax 415/433-4065. 106 rms, 1 suite. A/C MINIBAR TV TEL. $119–$159 double; $275

penthouse suite. AE, CB, DC, DISC, MC, V. Parking $16. Cable car: Powell-
Hyde and Powell-Mason lines (direct stop). Bus: 2, 3, 4, 30, 45, or 76.

Consistent personal service has prompted a loyal clientele at this
European-style hotel located two blocks north of Union Square.

The lobby, accented with dark wood, deep green, and rose, is
welcoming enough to actually spend a little time in, especially when
the nightly complimentary California wines are being poured.

But the varietals don't stop at ground level. Each tidy room, renovated in 1995, is named after a winery and mimics a wine country
excursion with its floral bedspreads, matching drapes, and trellised
wall-to-wall loop carpeting. Opus One, the deluxe, two-room
penthouse suite, includes an original 1912 stained-glass skylight, a
wood-burning fireplace, a whirlpool tub, a complete entertainment
center, and panoramic views of the city.

The hotel's dining room, Masa's, serving traditional French
fare, is one of the top restaurants in San Francisco (see chapter 5,
"Dining," for complete information). Services include free morning
transportation to the Financial District, tour desk, and car-rental
service. There is also access to an off-premises health club. Breakfast
available in dining room.

○ **White Swan Inn.** 845 Bush St. (between Taylor and Mason sts.), San
Francisco, CA 94108. ☎ **415/775-1755.** Fax 415/775-5717. 23 rms,
3 suites. MINIBAR TV TEL. $145–$160 double; $195 romance suites; $250
two-room suite. Extra person $15. Rates include full breakfast. AE, MC, V.
Parking $19. Cable car: California St. line (1 block north). Bus: 1, 2, 3, 4,
27, or 45.

From the moment you are buzzed in to this well-secured inn, you'll
know you're not in a generic bed and breakfast. More than 50 teddy
bears grace the lobby, and if that doesn't cure homesickness, complimentary homemade cookies, tea, and coffee will. The romanti-
cally homey rooms are warm and cozy—the perfect place to snuggle
up with a good book. They're also quite big, with hardwood
entryways, rich, dark wood furniture; working fireplaces; and an
assortment of books tucked in nooks (in case you forgot one).
The decor is English elegance at its best, if not to excess, with floral prints almost everywhere. Wine and hors d'oeuvres are served
every evening. The Romance suites are not much better than regular rooms, just a little bigger with the addition of chocolates and
champagne. Its location—2¹/₂ blocks from Union Square—makes
this 1900s building a charming and serene choice with service and
style to satisfy the most discriminating traveler. All guests enjoy
access to an off-premises health club.

Dining/Entertainment: Each morning a generous breakfast is served in a common room just off a tiny garden. Afternoon tea is also served, with hors d'oeuvres, sherry, wine, and home-baked pastries. You can have your sherry in front of the fireplace while you browse through the books in the library. Note that there's no smoking.

Services: Concierge, laundry, evening turndown, morning newspaper, overnight shoe shine.

MODERATE

Andrews Hotel. 624 Post St. (between Jones and Taylor sts.), San Francisco, CA 94109. ☎ **800/926-3739** or 415/563-6877. Fax 415/928-6919. 43 rms, 5 suites. MINIBAR TV TEL. $86–$109 double; $119 petite suite. Rates include continental breakfast and evening wine. AE, DC, MC, V. Parking $15. Cable car: Powell-Hyde and Powell-Mason lines (3 blocks east). Bus: 2, 3, 4, 30, 38, or 45.

Two blocks west of Union Square, the Andrews was formerly a Turkish bath before its conversion in 1981. As is fitting with Euro-style hotels, the rooms are small but well maintained and comfortable; white lace curtains and fresh flowers in each room add a light touch. Some rooms have shower only, and bathrooms in general tend to be tiny, but for the location—a few blocks from Union Square—and the price, the Andrews is a safe bet for an enjoyable stay in the city. An added bonus is the adjoining Fino Bar and Ristorante, which offers complimentary wine to its hotel guests in the evening.

Ⓢ **Hotel Bedford.** 761 Post St. (between Leavenworth and Jones sts.), San Francisco, CA 94109. ☎ **800/227-5642** or 415/673-6040. Fax 415/563-6739. 137 rms, 7 suites. MINIBAR TV TEL. $109–$129 double; from $175 suite. Continental breakfast $8.50 extra. AE, CB, DC, JCB, MC, V. Parking $18. Cable car: Powell-Hyde and Powell-Mason lines (4 blocks east). Bus: 2, 3, 4, or 27.

For the price and location (three blocks from Union Square) the Bedford offers a darn good deal. You won't be paying for lavish furniture, but you will find clean, large, sunny rooms, not to mention an incredibly enthusiastic, attentive, and professional staff. Each accommodation is well furnished with king, queen, or two double beds, VCR, writing desk, and armchair. Many rooms have priceless views of the city.

The hotel's Wedgewood Lounge is a small, beautiful mahogany bar opposite the registration desk. Canvas Café, an enormous eatery located behind the lobby, is under separate management. Services include room service (for breakfast only), valet parking, and complimentary wine in the lobby each evening from 5 to 6pm. There's a video library, and free morning limousine service to the Financial District.

✪ **Commodore International.** 825 Sutter St. (at Jones St.), San Francisco, CA 94109. ☎ **800/338-6848** or 415/923-6800. Fax 415/923-6804. 113 rms. TV TEL. $69–$89 double or twin. AE, DC, MC, V. Parking $12. Bus: 2, 3, 4, 27, or 76.

If you're looking to pump a little fun and fantasy into your vacation, this is the place. Before its new owners revamped the aging Commodore from top to bottom, it—well, okay, it sucked. Then along came San Francisco hotelier Chip Conley who, pumped with his success in transforming the Phoenix Hotel into a rocker's retreat, instantly recognized this dilapidated eyesore's potential, added it to his collection, then let his hip-hop decor designers do their magic. The result? One groovy hotel. Stealing the show is the Red Room, a Big Apple–style bar and lounge that reflects no other spectrum but ruby red (you gotta see this one). The stylish lobby comes in a close second, followed by the adjoining Titanic Café, a cute little diner serving buckwheat griddlecakes and dragon fire salads. Appealing to the masses, Chip left the first four floors as standard no-frills rooms, though quite clean and comfortable while, converting the top two floors in Neo-Deco overtones (well worth the extra $10 per night).

✪ **Hotel Diva.** 440 Geary St. (between Mason and Taylor sts.), San Francisco, CA 94102. ☎ **800/553-1900** or 415/885-0200. Fax 415/346-6613. 98 rms, 12 suites. A/C TV TEL. $119 double; $139 junior suite, $300 villa suite. Rates include continental breakfast. AE, DC, DISC, JCB, MC, V. Parking $17. Bus: 38 or 38L.

Appropriately named, the Diva is the prima donna of San Francisco's modern hotels and one of our favorites. A showbiz darling when it opened in 1985, the Diva won "Best Hotel Design" by *Interiors Magazine* for its sleek, ultramodern interiors. A stunning profusion of curvaceous glass, marble, and steel mark the Euro-tech lobby, while the rooms, each spotless and neat, are softened with utterly fashionable "Italian Modern" furnishings. Nary a beat is missed with the toys and services either: VCRs (with discreet video vending machine), Nintendo, pay-per-view, valet parking, room service, complimentary room-delivered breakfast, and on-site fitness and business centers complete the package. Insider tip: Reserve one of the rooms ending in "09," which come with extralarge bathrooms with vanity mirrors and makeup tables.

King George Hotel. 334 Mason St. (between Geary and O'Farrell sts.), San Francisco, CA 94102. ☎ **800/288-6005** or 415/781-5050. Fax 415/391-6976. 138 rms, 2 suites. TV TEL. $125 double; $205 suite. Special-value packages available seasonally. Continental breakfast $5.75 extra. AE, CB, DC, DISC, JCB, MC, V. Parking $16.50. Cable car: Powell-Hyde and Powell-Mason lines (1 block west). Bus: 2, 3, 4, 30, 38, or 45.

Built in 1914 for the Panama-Pacific Exposition when rooms went for $1 per night, the King George has fared well over the years, continuing to draw a mostly European clientele. The location—surrounded by cable car lines, the theater district, Union Square, and dozens of restaurants—is superb, and the rooms are surprisingly quiet for such a busy location. Though the decor is a bit old fashioned, every room is meticulously neat and clean with full private baths and large beds. A big hit since it started a few years back is the hotel's English afternoon tea, served above the lobby Monday through Saturday from 3 to 6:30pm.

Services include 24-hour room service, concierge, laundry/valet, and business center.

Hotel Rex. 562 Sutter St. (between Powell and Mason sts.), San Francisco, CA 94102. ☎ **800/433-4434** or 415/433-4434. Fax 415/433-3695. 94 rms, 2 suites. MINIBAR TV TEL. $115–$160 double; $225 suite. AE, CB, DC, MC, V. Parking $14. Cable car: Powell-Hyde and Powell-Mason lines (1 block east). Bus: 2, 3, 4, 30, 38, or 45.

Joie De Vivre, the most creative hotel group in the city, recently acquired this historic building (formerly the Orchard Hotel), which is situated near several fine galleries, theaters, and restaurants. They've kept some of the hotel's imported furnishings, and it will remain a European boutique hotel, but they have given the lobby and rooms a half-million-dollar facelift, adding a decorative flare that makes their hotels among the most popular in town. The club-like lobby lounge is modeled after a 1920s library and is, like all their properties, cleverly stylish. Joie de Vivre is positioning the Rex as a hotel for the arts and literary community (not unlike the Algonquin Hotel in New York City), and in that spirit an antiquarian book store adjoins the lobby.

The renovated rooms, which are all above average in size, feature telephones with voice mail and data port and a new electronic key card system. If you have one of the rooms in the back, you'll look out over a shady, peaceful courtyard (that's something you won't get in New York City). Attention to the details makes Hotel Rex one of the better choices in this price range downtown.

Services: Room service, concierge, same-day laundry/dry cleaning, complimentary newspaper, and complimentary evening wine hour.

Facilities: Access to an off-premises health club across the street.

✪ **Savoy Hotel.** 580 Geary St. (between Taylor and Jones sts.), San Francisco, CA 94102. ☎ **800/227-4223** or 415/441-2700. Fax 415/441-2700. 70 rms, 13 suites. MINIBAR TV TEL. $115–$125 double; from $155 suite. Ask about package, government, senior, and corporate rates. Rates include continental breakfast. AE, CB, DC, DISC, MC, V. Parking $16. Bus: 2, 3, 4, 27, or 38.

Both travelers and *Travel and Leisure* agree that the Savoy is an excellent, and affordable, small hotel a few blocks off Union Square. The medium-size rooms are cozy French provincial, with 18th-century period furnishings, featherbeds, and goose-down pillows—plus modern conveniences such as remote-control color TVs and hair dryers. Other perks include triple sheets, turndown service, full-length mirrors, and two-line telephones. Guests also enjoy concierge service and overnight shoe-shine free of charge. Rates include complimentary late-afternoon sherry and tea and continental breakfast, served in the Brasserie Savoy, a seafood restaurant that brings even the locals downtown for dinner (see chapter 5, "Dining," for complete details).

Warwick Regis. 490 Geary St. (between Mason and Taylor sts.), San Francisco, CA 94102. ☎ **800/827-3447** or 415/928-7900. Fax 415/441-8788. 40 rms, 40 suites. A/C MINIBAR TV TEL. $110–$150 double. Rates include continental breakfast. AE, DC, DISC, MC, V. Parking $18. Cable car: Powell-Hyde and Powell Mason lines. Bus: 2, 3, 4, 27, 38.

Louis XVI may have been a rotten monarch, but he certainly had taste. Fashioned in the style of pre-Revolutionary France (ca. 18th century), the Warwick is awash with pristine French and English antiques, Italian marble, chandeliers, four-poster beds, hand-carved headboards, and the like. The result is an expensive-looking hotel that, for all its pleasantries and perks, is surprisingly affordable when compared to its Union Square contemporaries (singles are as low as $95). Honeymooners should splurge on the Fireplace rooms with canopy beds—ooh la la! Amenities include 24-hour room and concierge service, twice-daily maid service, complimentary shoeshine and newspaper, and valet parking. Adjoining the lobby is fashionable La Scene Café, the perfect place to start you day with a latte and end it with a nightcap.

INEXPENSIVE

Golden Gate Hotel. 775 Bush St. (between Powell and Mason sts.), San Francisco, CA 94108. ☎ **800/835-1118** or 415/392-3702. Fax 415/ 392-6202. 23 rms (14 with bath). TV. $65–$69 double without bath, $95–$109 double with bath. Rates include continental breakfast. AE, CB, DC, MC, V. Parking $12. Cable car: Powell-Hyde and Powell-Mason lines (1 block east). Bus: 2, 3, 4, 30, 38, or 45.

Among San Francisco's small hotels occupying historic turn-of-the-century buildings are some real gems, and the Golden Gate Hotel is one of them. It's two blocks north of Union Square and two blocks down (literally) from the crest of Nob Hill, with cable car stops at the corner for easy access to Fisherman's Wharf and Chinatown (the city's theaters and best restaurants are also within walking distance). But the best thing about the Golden Gate Hotel is that this is a family run establishment: John and Renate Kenaston are hospitable innkeepers who take obvious pleasure in making their guests comfortable. Each individually decorated room has handsome antique furnishings (plenty of wicker) from the early 1900s, quilted bedspreads, and fresh flowers (request a room with the claw-foot tub if you enjoy a good, hot soak). Most, but not all rooms have phones, and complimentary afternoon tea is served daily from 4 to 7pm.

Grant Plaza Hotel. 465 Grant Ave. (at the corner of Pine St.), San Francisco, CA 94108. ☎ **800/472-6899** or 415/434-3883. Fax 415/434-3886. 72 rms. TV TEL. $42–$65 double. MC, V. Parking $9.50. Cable car: Powell-Hyde and Powell-Mason lines (2 blocks west).

You won't find any free little bottles of shampoo here. What you will find are cheap accommodations and basic—and we mean *basic*—rooms right in the middle of Union Square/Chinatown action. The pattern-crazy lobby isn't easy on the eye, but it's mostly a thoroughfare anyway, so who could care? Many of the small rooms in this six-story building overlook Chinatown's main street. Corner rooms on higher floors are both larger and brighter. Expect little more than a soap dispenser in the small shower and bathroom. The Grant Plaza offers nothing more than decent value, but for 50 bucks, what do you expect? Note that no visitors are permitted in the rooms after 11pm and no breakfast is served.

2 Nob Hill

VERY EXPENSIVE

Fairmont Hotel & Tower. 950 Mason St. (at California St.), San Francisco, CA 94108. ☎ **800/527-4727** or 415/772-5000. Fax 415/772-5013.

538 rms, 62 suites. A/C MINIBAR TV TEL. Main building: $199–$299 double; from $620 suite. Tower: $239–$300 double; from $500 suite. Extra person $30. Continental breakfast $9.95 extra. AE, CB, DC, DISC, MC, V. Parking $25. Cable car: California St. line (direct stop).

The granddaddy of Nob Hill's elite cadre of ritzy hotels, the Fairmont wins top honors for the most awe-inspiring lobby in San Francisco. Even if you're not staying at the Fairmont, it's worth a side trip to gape at its massive, marble Corinthian columns, vaulted ceilings, velvet chairs, gilded mirrors, and spectacular wraparound staircase. Unfortunately, such ostentation doesn't carry over to the guest rooms, which are surprisingly ordinary (aside from the spectacular views from the top floors). In addition to the expected luxuries, guests will appreciate such details as goose-down pillows, electric shoe buffers, bath scales, large walk-in closets, and multiline phones with private voice mail.

Dining/Entertainment: Masons serves contemporary California cuisine, with live music Tuesday through Sunday. Bella Voce Ristorante features Italian American cuisine served by staff who occasionally pause for an aria or Broadway selection. The Crown offers deli lunches, dinner buffets, and Sunday brunch, with a panoramic view of the Bay Area. The Tonga Restaurant and Hurricane Bar offer Chinese and Polynesian specialties in a tropical ambience, as well as dancing and a generous happy hour. Afternoon tea is served daily in the hotel's lobby.

Services: 24-hour room service, twice-daily maid service, evening turndown, laundry/valet, 24-hour concierge, complimentary shoeshine, baby-sitting services, doctor on-call, complimentary morning limousine to the Financial District.

Facilities: Health club, business center, barbershop, beauty salon, pharmacy, shopping arcade.

Huntington Hotel. 1075 California St. (between Mason and Taylor sts.), San Francisco, CA 94108. ☎ **800/227-4683,** 800/652-1539 in California, or 415/474-5400. Fax 415/474-6227. 110 rms, 30 suites. MINIBAR TV TEL. $190–$240 double; from $290–$790 suite. Special packages available. Continental breakfast $9.95. AE, CB, DC, MC, V. Parking $19.50. Cable car: California St. line (direct stop). Bus: 1.

One of the kings of Nob Hill, the stately Huntington Hotel has long been a favorite retreat for Hollywood stars and political VIPs who desire privacy and security. Family owned since 1924—an extreme rarity among large hotels—the Huntington eschews pomp and circumstance; absolute privacy and unobtrusive service are its mainstay. Though the lobby, decorated in a grand 19th-century style, is rather petite, the guest rooms are quite large and feature Brunschwig and Fils fabrics and bed coverings, French-style furnishings, and views of the city. The lavish suites, so opulent as to be featured in *Architectural Digest*, are individually decorated with custommade and antique furnishings. Prices are steep, as you would expect, but special offers such as the Romance Package ($195 per couple, including free champagne, sherry, and limousine service) make the Huntington worth considering for a special occasion.

Dining/Entertainment: The Big Four restaurant offers expensive seasonal continental cuisine in of the city's most handsome dining rooms. Live piano music plays nightly in the lounge.

Services: Room service, concierge, complimentary limousine to the Financial District and Union Square, overnight shoe shine, laundry, evening turndown, complimentary morning newspaper, complimentary formal tea or sherry service upon arrival.

Facilities: Access to off-premises health club and spa.

Mark Hopkins Intercontinental. 1 Nob Hill (at California and Mason sts.), San Francisco, CA 94108. ☎ **800/327-0200** or 415/392-3434. Fax 415/421-3302. 390 rms, 28 suites. A/C MINIBAR TV TEL. $180–$230 double; from $375 suite. Continental breakfast $9.50 extra. AE, CB, DC, MC, V. Parking $23. Cable car: California St. line (direct stop). Bus: 1.

Built in 1926 on the spot where railroad millionaire Mark Hopkins's turreted mansion once stood, the 19-story Mark Hopkins gained global fame during World War II when it was considered de rigueur for Pacific-bound servicemen to toast their good-bye to the States in the Top of the Mark cocktail lounge. Nowadays the hotel caters mostly to convention-bound corporate executives who can afford the high rates. Each neoclassical room comes with all the fancy amenities you would expect from a world-class hotel, including custom furniture, plush fabrics, sumptuous baths, and extraordinary views of the city. (Tip: The even-numbered rooms on the higher floor overlook the Golden Gate.) A minor caveat with the hotel is that it has only three guest elevators, making a quick trip up to your room difficult during busy periods.

Dining/Entertainment: The plush and decidedly formal Nob Hill Restaurant offers international cuisine with a California flair nightly (as well as continental buffet breakfast each morning), while the Nob Hill Terrace, adjacent to the lobby, serves lunch, afternoon tea, cocktails, and dinner daily. The world renowned Top of the Mark lounge serves cocktails from 4pm to 1:30pm daily, Sunday brunch 10am to 2pm, and dancing to live music Wednesday through Saturday nights.

Services: 24-hour room service, concierge, evening turndown, overnight shoe shine, laundry, limousine, valet parking, and multi-lingual guest relations.

Facilities: Business center, health club, Executive Club floor, car-rental desk.

✪ **Ritz-Carlton.** 600 Stockton St. (between Pine and California sts.), San Francisco, CA 94108. ☎ **800/241-3333** or 415/296-7465. Fax 415/296-0288. 292 rms, 44 suites. A/C MINIBAR TV TEL. $275 double; $395 club-level double; from $575 suite. Weekend discounts and packages available. Continental breakfast $14.50 extra; breakfast buffet $18.50 extra; Sunday brunch $42. AE, CB, DC, DISC, MC, V. Parking $27. Cable car: Powell-Hyde and Powell-Mason lines (direct stop).

Ranked among the top hotels in the world by readers of *Conde Nast Traveler* (as well as *the* top hotel in the city), the Ritz-Carlton has been the benchmark of San Francisco's luxury hotels since it opened in 1991. A Nob Hill landmark, this former Metropolitan Insurance headquarters stood vacant for years until the Ritz-Carlton company acquired it and embarked on a massive four-year renovation. The interior was completely gutted and restored with fine furnishings, fabrics, and artworks, including a pair of Louis XVI French blue marble-covered urns with gilt mounts, and 19th-century Waterford candelabras. The rooms offer every possible amenity and service: Italian-marble bathrooms with double sinks, telephone, name-brand toiletries, plush terry bathrobes, and an in-room safe. The more expensive rooms take advantage of the hotel's location—the south slope of Nob Hill—and have good views of the city. Club rooms, located on the eighth and ninth floors, have a dedicated concierge, separate elevator-key access, and complimentary meals throughout the day.

Dining/Entertainment: The Ritz-Carlton Dining Room, voted among the nation's top restaurants by several magazines, serves dinner Monday through Saturday (see chapter 5, "Dining," for complete information). The Terrace Restaurant, less formal than the dining room, offers Mediterranean cuisine and outdoor dining in the courtyard. The lobby lounge offers afternoon tea and cocktails and sushi daily with low-key live entertainment from 3pm to 1am. Sunday brunch is easily one of the best in town.

Services: 24-hour room service, same-day valet, concierge, child care, complimentary morning newspaper, and shoeshine.

Facilities: Business center, an outstanding fitness center with pool, gift boutique, car-rental desk, VCR and video library.

Renaissance Stanford Court Hotel. 905 California St. (at Powell St.), San Francisco, CA 94108. ☎ **800/227-4736**, 800/622-0957 in California, or 415/989-3500. Fax 415/391-0513. 375 rms, 18 suites, A/C TV TEL. $205–$295 double; from $450 suite. Extra person 18 or over, $30. Continental breakfast $10.50 extra; American breakfast $16.50 extra. AE, CB, DC, DISC, MC, V. Parking $24. Cable car: Powell-Hyde and Powell-Mason lines (direct stop). Bus: 1.

The Stanford Court has maintained a long and discreet reputation as one of San Francisco's most exclusive, and expensive, hotels. Holding company with the Ritz, Fairmont, Mark Hopkins, and Huntington hotels atop Nob Hill, it was originally the mansion the Leland Stanford, whose legacy lives on in the many portraits and biographies that adorn the rooms. Frequented mostly by corporate executives, the rooms at first come across as austere and antiquated compared to most other top-dollar business hotels, but the quality and comfort of the furnishings are so superior that you're forced to admit there's simply no room for improvement. The Stanford Court also prides itself on its impeccable service; a nice touch is the complimentary tray of tea or coffee placed outside your door upon your request. The lobby, furnished in a 19th-century theme with Baccarat chandeliers, French antiques, and a gorgeous stained-glass dome, makes for a grand entrance, though the aroma of cigars emanating from the lounge tends to detract from the experience.

Many of the guest rooms have partially canopied beds, and all have writing desks, extremely comfortable beds, and oak armoires that conceal aging but adequate television sets. Bathrooms include mini-TV, telephone, heated towel racks, overhead heat lamps, and make-up mirrors.

Dining/Entertainment: Fournou's Ovens, the hotel's award-winning restaurant, features contemporary American cuisine in a romantic multilevel setting.

Services: Concierge, 24-hour room service, 24-hour laundry/valet, complimentary chauffeured car service to downtown destinations, complimentary morning newspaper and coffee or tea, evening turndown service, complimentary overnight shoeshine, baby-sitter on call.

Facilities: Fitness center; state-of-the-art business center.

EXPENSIVE

Nob Hill Lambourne. 725 Pine St. (between Powell and Stockton sts.), San Francisco, CA 94108. ☎ **800/274-8466** or 415/433-2287. 9 rms, 11 suites. A/C MINIBAR TV TEL. $155 double; $175–$250 suite. Rates include continental breakfast. AE, CB, DC, DISC, MC, V. Parking $20 valet. Cable car: California St. line (1 block north).

One of San Francisco's top "business-boutique" hotels, the Nob Hill Lambourne bills itself as an urban spa, offering on-site massages, facials, body scrubs, aromatherapy, waxing, manicures, pedicures, and yoga lessons to ease corporate-level stress. Even without this "hook," the Lambourne deserves a top-of-the-class rating. Sporting one of San Francisco's most stylish interiors, the hotel flaunts the comfort and quality of its contemporary French design. Top-quality, hand-sewn mattresses and goose-down comforters are complemented by a host of in-room accouterments that include fax machines, VCRs, stereos, kitchenettes, and coffeemakers. Bathrooms contain oversized tubs and hair dryers, as well as an "honor bar" of goodies like geranium and orange bath oil, herbal lip balm, and jasmine moisturizer, sold for $6 to $10 each. Suites include an additional sitting room, plus a choice of treadmill, Lifecycle, or rowing machine. On Friday and Saturday, all guests are invited to enjoy complimentary wine and hors d'oeuvres and a 15-minute neck and shoulder massage.

Services: Evening turndown, business services.

Facilities: Spa treatment room.

3　Financial District

VERY EXPENSIVE

ANA Hotel San Francisco. 50 Third St. (between Market and Mission sts.), San Francisco, CA 94103. ☎ **800/262-4683** or 415/974-6400. Fax 415/495-6152. 641 rms, 26 suites. A/C MINIBAR TV TEL. $220–$250 double; from $380 suite. Continental breakfast $8.75 extra. AE, DC, DISC, JCB, MC, V. Parking $23. Muni Metro: All Market St. trams. All Market St. buses.

The hotel's large number of rooms and fine location—just one block south of Market Street, and one block from the Moscone Convention Center—makes the ANA attractive to both groups and business travelers. Separate check-in facilities for conventioneers keep the main lobby clear and welcoming for independent guests.

Rooms have floor-to-ceiling windows and are well outfitted with three telephones (with voice mail and data port for computer modem connection). Corner suites look across the Bay Bridge and to Candlestick ("3COM") Park, and Executive Level rooms include continental breakfast and evening hors d'oeuvres.

Dining/Entertainment: Café Fifty-Three serves three meals daily, plus a special Sunday brunch and offers garden terrace seating. The adjacent lobby bar serves cocktails, wine, beer, and appetizers.

Services: Room service, concierge, twice-daily maid service, laundry/valet.

Facilities: Fitness center, business center, complimentary use of nearby tennis club, gift shop.

Hyatt Regency San Francisco. 5 Embarcadero Center, San Francisco, CA 94111. ☎ **800/233-1234** or 415/788-1234. Fax 415/398-2567. 805 rms, 45 suites. TV TEL. $205–$230 double; from $350 suite. Continental breakfast $6.95 extra. AE, CB, DC, MC, V. Parking $25. Muni Metro: All Market St. trams. All Market St. buses.

The Hyatt Regency, a convention favorite, rises from the edge of the Embarcadero Center at the foot of Market Street. The structure, with a 1970s, gray concrete, bunkerlike facade, is shaped like a vertical triangle, serrated with long rows of jutting balconies. The 17-floor atrium lobby, illuminated by museum-quality theater lighting, features flowing water and a simulated environment of California grasslands and wildflowers. The hotel was totally renovated in 1993.

Rooms are comfortably furnished. Each also has a voice-mail telephone and computer ports for modems. Some rooms have tea- and coffeemaking facilities, and private fax machines are available free upon request. Rooms with two double beds also include a sofa, easy chair, and cocktail table. The hotel's 16th and 17th floors house the Regency Club, with 102 larger guest rooms, private bar-lounges and games rooms, complimentary continental breakfast, after-dinner cordials, and private concierge.

Dining/Entertainment: The Eclipse Café serves three meals daily. The Thirteen-Views Bar seats about 200 and is open for morning coffee and evening cocktails. The Equinox, a revolving rooftop restaurant and bar, offers 360-degree city views.

Services: 24-hour room service, concierge, laundry, overnight shoeshine.

Facilities: Business center, access to off-premises health club, swimming pool, tennis courts.

✪ **Mandarin Oriental.** 222 Sansome St. (between Pine and California sts.), San Francisco, CA 94104. ☎ **800/622-0404** or 415/885-0999. Fax 415/433-0289. 154 rms, 4 suites. A/C MINIBAR TV TEL. $285–$330 double; from $405 junior suite. Continental breakfast $12.95 extra. AE, DC, JCB, MC, V. Parking $21. Muni Metro: Montgomery. All Market Street buses.

If we were seeking respite from researching this guide, we'd probably head straight here, jump into a Jacuzzi, and from 48 floors up, relax and admire the city we love most. We'd choose this hotel because all the rooms are located between the 38th and 48th floors of a downtown high-rise, which allows each of the large

Accommodations Around Town

 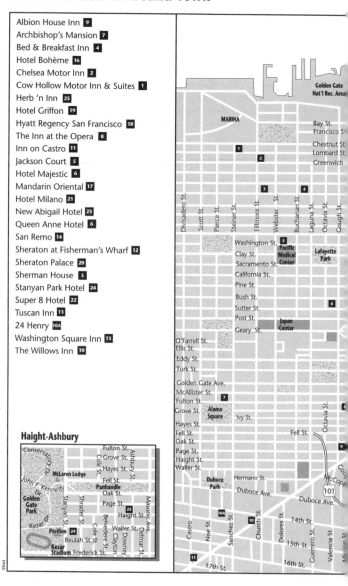
Haight-Ashbury

San Francisco
Bay

Municipal Pier
Pier 45   Pier 43 1/2
Pier 43   Pier 41
Pier 39
Pier 35
Aquatic
Park
Pier 33
Pier 31
Jefferson St.
Beach St.
North Point St. **12**
Bay St.
Francisco St. **14**
Pier 27

Chestnut St.
Lombard St.
Greenwich St.
Filbert St.
Union St.
Green St.
Vallejo St.
Broadway
Pacific Ave.
Jackson St.

Columbus Ave.

15

16

Tunnel

Embarcadero

Pier 23
Pier 19
Pier 17
Pier 15
Pier 9
Pier 7
Pier 5
Pier 3
Pier 1
Ferry Building
(World Trade Center)

Justin
Herman
Plaza

01

Van Ness Ave.
Polk St.
Larkin St.
Hyde St.
Leavenworth St.
Jones St.
Taylor St.
Mason St.
Powell St.
Stockton St.
Grant Ave.
Kearny St.
Montgomery St.
Sansome St.
Battery St.
Front St.
Davis St.
Drumm St.
Davis St.

17   **18**

19

San Francisco-
Oakland
Bay Bridge

80

Union
Square

20

Steuart St.
Spear St.
Main St.
Beale St.
Fremont St.
2nd St.
1st St.

Geary St. **22**
O'Farrell St.

Eddy St.

Market St.

21

4th St.

Moscone
Convention
Center

23

Market St.
Mission St.
Howard St.
Folsom St.
Harrison St.
Bryant St.
Brannan St.

5th St.

South Park

3rd St.

Delancey St.

9th St.
8th St.
10th St.
11th St.
12th St.

Townsend St.
King St.
Berry St.
Channel St.

4th St.
3rd St.

China Basin

Illinois St.

Van Ness Ave.
Folsom
Harrison
Alabama
Potrero Ave.

Division St.

Alameda St.

280

7th St.
6th St.

15th St.

0

54

53

accommodations extraordinary panoramic views of the bay and city. Not all rooms have tub-side views, but they do have luxurious marble bathrooms stocked with a natural loofah, a large selection of English toiletries, terry and cotton cloth robes, hair dryer, makeup mirror, and silk slippers. The rooms are less opulent, with a kind of reserved-contemporary decor of light colors, Asian accents, and handsome furnishings, including a spacious desk and sitting area. Since high rates make this mostly a business hotel, additional amenities include three two-line phones with fax hookups, as well as TVs with on-command video access to more than 80 movies.

Dining: Silks is a serene dining room that has won rave reviews melding California and Asian ingredients. See chapter 5, "Dining," for complete details.

Services: 24-hour room service, complimentary newspaper and shoeshine, concierge, laundry/valet.

Facilities: Business center, brand-new fitness center with cardio, Nautilus, and free weights.

Sheraton Palace Hotel. 2 New Montgomery St. (at Market St.), San Francisco, CA 94105. ☎ **800/325-3535** or 415/392-8600. Fax 415/543-0671. 517 rms, 33 suites. A/C MINIBARS TV TEL. $295–$355 double; from $650 suite. Additional person $25. Children under 18 sharing existing bedding stay free in parents' room. Weekend rates and packages available. Continental breakfast $13.50 extra; deluxe continental $15.75 extra. AE, DC, DISC, JCB, MC, V. Parking $20. Muni Metro: All Market St. trams. All Market St. buses.

The original 1875 Palace was one of the world's largest and most luxurious hotels, and every time you walk through the doors, you'll be reminded how incredibly majestic old luxury really is. The hotel was rebuilt after the 1906 quake and renovated in 1989, but the most spectacular attribute here is still the old regal lobby and the Garden Court, a San Francisco landmark that has been restored to its original 1909 grandeur. The Court is flanked by a double row of massive Italian-marble, Ionic columns and dangles 10 huge chandeliers. The real heart-stopper, however, is the 80,000-pane stained-glass ceiling. Regrettably, the rooms have that standardized, chain-hotel appearance. The on-site, fourth-floor health club features a skylight-covered lap pool, whirlpool, sauna, and exercise room.

Dining/Entertainment: The Garden Court serves American cuisine, afternoon tea Monday through Saturday, and drinks Monday through Saturday nights. On major holidays, the Court serves a $52 brunch worth indulging in. Maxfields's Restaurant, a traditional San Francisco grill, has turn-of-the-century charm and is open daily for lunch and dinner. Kyo-ya is an authentic Japanese restaurant with a separate street entrance. The Pied Piper Bar is named after the $2.5 million Maxfield Parrish mural that dominates the room.

Services: 24-hour room service, concierge, evening turndown, laundry/valet.

Facilities: Business service center, health club, lobby-level shops.

EXPENSIVE

✪ **Hotel Milano.** 55 Fifth St. (between Market and Mission sts.), San Francisco, CA 94103. ☎ **800/398-7555** or 415/543-8555. Fax 415/543-5843. 108 rms. A/C MINIBAR TV TEL. $129–$189 double; extra person $20. Continental breakfast $6 extra. AE, MC, V, AE, DC, JCB, MC, V. Parking $19. All Market St. buses.

Contemporary Italian design, simple and elegantly streamlined rooms, and a central location make Hotel Milano a popular choice for tourists and business people alike. The hotel also has a film production facility and private screening room to entice the film industry. But corporate travelers also resonate to the guest rooms, which feature everything a business executive could want, from fax/computer modem hookups to a Nintendo game system. Other features include in-room safe and soundproof windows. Some have spa tub, bidet, double lavatories, and television with VCR.

Dining: Just off the lobby is the renowned Chef Michel Richard's Bistro M serving breakfast, lunch, and dinner in an equally moderne setting.

Services: Room service, concierge, laundry/valet.

Facilities: Fitness center and spa with steam and sauna, business center.

4 Japan Center & Environs

EXPENSIVE

✪ **The Archbishop's Mansion.** 1000 Fulton St. (at Steiner St.), San Francisco, CA 94117. ☎ **800/543-5820** or 415/563-7872. 15 rms. TEL TV. $129–$385 double. Rates include continental breakfast. AE, MC, V. Free parking. Bus: 19, 31, or 38.

One thing is for certain: The Archbishop who built this 1904 belle epoque beauty was no Puritan. Drippingly romantic, the Archbishop's Mansion is one of the most opulent and fabulously adorned B&Bs you could possibly hope to stay in. The Don Giovanni suite—larger than most San Francisco houses—comes with a huge, angel-encrusted four-poster bed imported from a French castle, a palatial fireplace, elaborately embroidered linens, and a seven-head shower that you'll never want to leave. Slightly closer to earth is the Carmen suite, which has a deadly romantic combination of a claw-foot bathtub fronting a toasty, wood-burning fireplace. In the morning, breakfast is delivered to the guest rooms, and in the evenings complimentary wine is served in the elegant parlor.

Services: Laundry/valet, concierge, limousine service, complimentary morning newspaper.

✪ **Hotel Majestic.** 1500 Sutter St. (between Octavia and Gough sts.), San Francisco, CA 94109. ☎ **800/869-8966** or 415/441-1100. Fax 415/673-7331. 51 rms, 9 suites. TV TEL. $135–$170 double; from $260 suite. Group, government, corporate, and relocation rates available. Continental breakfast $8.50 extra. AE, DC, MC, V. Parking $14.

Tourists and business travelers adore The Majestic because it covers every professional need while retaining the ambience of a luxurious old-world hotel. It was built in 1902 and thankfully retains its original integrity—the lobby alone will sweep guests into another era with an overabundance of tapestries, tasseled brocades, Corinthian columns, and intricate, lavish detail.

Rooms are furnished with French and English antiques, the centerpiece of each being a large four-poster canopy bed; you'll also find custom-made, mirrored armoires and antique reproductions. Conveniences include a full-size, well-lit desk and clock-radio; extra bathroom amenities include bath robes. Some rooms also have fireplaces.

Dining/Entertainment: Café Majestic and Bar serves California and continental cuisine in a romantic setting and continues to intrigue a local clientele. Cocktails are offered.in the adjacent bar complete with French mahogany bar.

Services: Room service, laundry/valet, concierge, complimentary newspaper, and afternoon sherry.

MODERATE

✪ **Queen Anne Hotel.** 1590 Sutter St. (between Gough and Octavia sts.), San Francisco, CA 94109. ☎ **800/227-3970** or 415/441-2828. Fax 415/775-5212. 45 rms, 4 suites. TV TEL. $99–$150 double; $175 suite. Extra person $10. Rates include continental breakfast. AE, DC, MC, V. Parking $12. Bus: 2, 3, or 4.

The majestic 1890 Victorian, which was once a grooming school for upper-class young women, is today a stunning hotel. Restored in 1981 and renovated in 1995, the four-story building remains true to its heritage and emulates San Francisco's golden days. Walk under rich, red drapery to the immaculate and lavish "grand salon" lobby complete with English oak-paneling and period antiques. Rooms follow suit with antiques—armoires, marble-top dressers, and other Victorian pieces. Some have corner turret bay windows that look out on tree-lined streets, as well as separate parlor areas and wet bars; others have cozy reading nooks and fireplaces. All rooms have a telephone in the bathroom, a computer hook-up, and refrigerator. Guests can relax in the parlor, with fluted columns and an impressive floor-to-ceiling fireplace, or in the hotel library. There's a complimentary continental breakfast. Services include room service, concierge, morning newspaper, and complimentary afternoon tea and sherry. There's also access to an off-premises health club with a lap pool. If you're not partial to Union Square, this hotel comes highly recommended.

5 Civic Center

EXPENSIVE

✪ **The Inn at the Opera.** 333 Fulton St. (at Franklin St.), San Francisco, CA 94102. ☎ **800/325-2708** or 415/863-8400. Fax 415/861-0821. 30 rms, 18 suites. MINIBAR TV TEL. $125–$185 double; from $200 suite. Extra person $15. Rates include European buffet breakfast. AE, MC, V. Parking $19. Bus: 5, 21, 47, or 49.

Judging from its mild-mannered facade and offbeat location behind the Opera House, few would ever guess that The Inn at the Opera is one of San Francisco's, if not California's, finest small hotels. From the minute you walk in through the mullioned front door to a lobby decorated with silk and damask, upholstered antique chairs, hand-painted French screen, and a plush Oriental rug, you know you're about to be spoiled with sumptuousness. But don't take our word for it; Luciano Pavarotti, Placido Domingo, Mikhail Baryshnikov, and dozens of other stars of the stage throw their slumber parties here regularly, requisitioning the inn's luxurious restaurant and lounge, Act IV, along with a floor or two of rooms. Queen-size beds with huge stuffed pillows are standard in each pastel-hued guest room, along with elegant furnishings, wet bars, microwave ovens, refrigerators, and bouquets of fresh flowers. Baths include hair dryers, scales, terry-cloth robes, and French milled soaps. The larger rooms and suites are especially recommended for those who need elbow room; typical of small hotels, the least expensive "standard" rooms are short on space.

Dining/Entertainment: Act IV Restaurant, the hotel's fine dining room, provides an intimate setting for dinner, while the adjacent lounge with its leather chairs, glowing fire, and soft piano music is a favorite city meeting place (see chapter 5, "Dining," for complete information).

Services: 24-hour room service, concierge, laundry/valet, evening turndown, complimentary light pressing and overnight shoeshine, staff physician, complimentary limousine service to the Financial District, and morning newspaper.

Facilities: Business center.

MODERATE

Abigail Hotel. 246 McAllister St. (between Hyde and Larkin sts.), San Francisco, CA 94102. ☎ **800/243-6510** or 415/861-9728. Fax 415/861-5848. 59 rms, 1 suite. TV TEL. $84 double; $129 suite. Extra person $10. Rates include continental breakfast. AE, CB, DC, MC, V. Parking $12. Muni Metro: All Market St. trams. All Market St. buses.

The Abigail is one of San Francisco's rare sleeper hotels: Though it doesn't get much press, this is one the better medium-priced hotels in the city. Built in 1925 to house celebrities performing at the world renowned Fox Theater, what the Abigail lacks in luxury is more than made up in charm. The rooms, while on the small side, are clean, cute, and comfortably furnished with cozy antiques and down comforters. Morning coffee, pastries, and complimentary newspapers greet you in the beautiful faux-marble lobby designed by Shawn Hall, while lunch and dinner are served downstairs in the hot new 'organic' restaurant, the Millennium. Access to a nearby health club, as well as laundry and massage services, are available upon request.

6 Pacific Heights/Cow Hollow

VERY EXPENSIVE

✪ **Sherman House.** 2160 Green St. (between Webster and Fillmore sts.), San Francisco, CA 94123. ☎ **800/424-5777** or 415/563-3600. Fax 415/563-1882. 8 rms, 6 suites. TV TEL. $200–$400 double; from $600 suite. Continental breakfast $14 extra. AE, CB, DC, MC, V. Parking $16. Cable car: Powell-Hyde line. Bus: 22, 41, or 45.

How expensive is a night at the Sherman House? Put it this way: If you have to ask, you can't afford it. Built in 1876 by philanthropist/music publisher Leander Sherman, this magnificent Pacific Heights Victorian doubled as his home and playhouse for such guest stars as Enrico Caruso, Lillian Russell, and Victor Herbert. After years of neglect, it took four years and small fortune to restore the estate to its original splendor. Today the Sherman House sets the standard in San Francisco for privacy, personal service, and sumptuous furnishings. All rooms are individually decorated with authentic antiques in French Second Empire, Biedermeier, or English Jacobean style and contain queen-size canopy featherbeds along with ultra-rich tapestry fabrics and down comforters; all except one have fireplaces. Rooms also feature both TVs and stereos, and black granite bathrooms complete with bathrobes and whirlpool baths. The English-style Hyde Park room offers a fine Bay view from its cushioned window seat. The Jacobean-style Paderewski suite was formerly the Billiards room, and it retains the dark wainscoting and beamed ceiling. The least expensive room (number 203) is a twin furnished with English antiques but lacks a fireplace. The most expensive suite is the Thomas Church Garden suite, which consists of two rooms with one-and-a-half baths, and an adjoining sunken garden terrace with gazebo and pond.

Dining: The dining room has a very fine reputation, but because of a zoning dispute, it has recently lost its license to serve food to non-guests and is now open only to residents; this change may affect the standards. Currently, a fixed-price menu, without wine, is available for $70. Although the price is steep, the meal is quite elaborate. A limited à la carte menu is also available; main courses run from $27 to $30.

Services: Room service, butler who will discreetly unpack luggage, concierge, massage, personalized shopping, private chauffeuring.

Facilities: Business center.

EXPENSIVE

Jackson Court. 2198 Jackson St. (at Buchanan St.), San Francisco, CA 94115. ☎ **415/929-7670.** 10 rms. TV TEL. $122–$170 double. Rates include continental breakfast. AE, MC, V. Parking on street only.

The Jackson Court, a stately three-story brownstone Victorian mansion, is located in one of San Francisco's most exclusive neighborhoods, Pacific Heights. Its only fault—that it's far from the action—is also its blessing: If you crave a blissfully quiet vacation while swathed in elegant surroundings, this is the place. Each room is individually furnished with superior-quality antique furnishings; two have wood-burning fireplaces (de rigueur in the winter). The Blue Room, for example, features a brass and porcelain bed, Renaissance-style sofa, and inviting window seat, while the Garden Suite has handcrafted wood paneling and a large picture window looking out at the private garden patio. After breakfast, spend the day browsing the shops along nearby Union and Fillmore sts., then return in time for afternoon tea.

MODERATE

✪ **Bed & Breakfast Inn.** 4 Charlton Court (off Union St., between Buchanan and Laguna sts.), San Francisco, CA 94123. ☎ **415/921-9784.** 11 rms (4 with shared bath), 2 suites. $70–$90 double without bath, $115–$140 double with bath; $190–$275 suite. Rates include continental breakfast. No credit cards. Parking $10 a day at nearby garage. Bus: 41 or 45.

San Francisco's first bed-and-breakfast is composed of a trio of Victorian houses all gussied up in English country style, hidden in an cul-de-sac just off Union Street. While it doesn't have quite the casual ambience of neighboring Union Street Inn, the Bed and Breakfast Inn is loaded with charm. Each room is uniquely decorated with family antiques, original art, and a profusion of fresh flowers. The Garden Suite—highly recommended for families or groups of four—comes with a fully stocked kitchen, a living room with fireplace, two bedrooms, two bathrooms (one with a Jacuzzi tub), a study, and French doors leading out into the garden. Breakfast (freshly baked croissants; orange juice; and coffee, tea, or cocoa) is either brought to your room on a tray with flowers and a morning newspaper, or served in a sunny Victorian breakfast room with antique china.

Chelsea Motor Inn. 2095 Lombard St. (between Fillmore and Webster sts.), San Francisco, CA 94123. ☎ **415/563-5600.** Fax 415/346-9127. 60 rms. A/C TV TEL. $83–$95 double. AE, CB, DC, MC, V. Free parking. Bus: 22, 28, 30, or 76.

An establishment on the "motel strip" that stretches from the Golden Gate Bridge to Van Ness Avenue, the Chelsea Motor Inn is perfectly located for a stroll along Union Street. Expect generic, clean motel accommodations, with coffee makers in each room. No breakfast is offered.

INEXPENSIVE

Cow Hollow Motor Inn & Suites. 2190 Lombard St. (between Steiner and Fillmore sts.), at Steiner St., San Francisco, CA 94123. ☎ **415/921-5800.** Fax 415/922-8515. 117 rms, 12 suites. A/C TV TEL. $80 double, $7 extra per person; from $175 suite. Extra person $10. AE, DC, MC, V. Free parking. Bus: 28, 43, or 76.

If you're less interested in being downtown and more into playing in and around the beautiful bay-front Marina, check out this modest brick hotel smack in the middle of busy Lombard Street. There's no fancy theme here, but each room comes loaded with such amenities as cable TV, free local phone calls, free covered parking, and in-room coffeemakers. All the rooms were renovated in 1996, so you'll be sure to sleep on a nice firm mattress surrounded by clean, new carpeting and drapes.

7 Haight-Ashbury

MODERATE

Stanyan Park Hotel. 750 Stanyan St. (at Waller St.), San Francisco, CA 94117. ☎ **415/751-1000.** Fax 415/668-5454. 30 rms, 6 suites. TV TEL. $85–$105 double; from $135 suite. Rates include continental breakfast. Extra person $20. AE, CB, DC, DISC, MC, V. Parking $5. Muni Metro: N line. Bus: 7, 33, 71, or 73.

This small inn across from Golden Gate Park has operated as a hotel under a variety of names since 1904. Today it's a charming, three-story establishment decorated with antique furnishings, Victorian wallpaper, and pastel quilts, curtains, and carpets. Tub/shower baths come complete with massaging shower head, shampoos, and fancy soaps.

There are one- and two-bedroom suites. Each has a full kitchen, and formal dining and living rooms, and can sleep up to six comfortably; they're ideal for families. Complimentary tea and cookies are served each afternoon.

INEXPENSIVE

☺ **The Herb'n Inn.** 535 Ashbury St. (between Page and Haight sts.), San Francisco, CA 94117. ☎ **415/553-8542.** Fax 415/553-8541. 4 rms. TV (upon request). $60–$75 double, two-night minimum. MC, V. Parking with advance notice. Bus: 6, 7, 33, 43, 66, or 71.

For those of you who want to immerse yourself in the sights and sounds of San Francisco legendary Haight-Ashbury District without comprising on high-quality (and low-cost) accommodations, there's The Herb'n Inn. Run by sister/brother duo Pam and Bruce Brennan—who know the history and highlights of the Haight better than anyone—this modernized Victorian inn consists of four attractive guest rooms, a huge country-style kitchen, a sunny back garden, and the beginnings of Bruce's Psychedelic History Museum (a.k.a. the dining room). Top choice among the guest rooms is the Cilantro Room, which, besides being the largest, has the only private bath and a view of the garden—all for only $10 extra per night. The Tarragon Room has two small beds and private deck (optimal for smokers, who aren't allowed to fire up inside the house), while the large Coriander Room faces the near mythical intersection of Haight and Ashbury streets, where there's always *something* going on. A hearty full breakfast—waffles, crepes, popovers, potato pancakes—

is included, as well as office services (including fowarded e-mail), personal city tours à la Bruce, and plenty of free advice on how to spend you day in the city. Kids and lesbian/gay couples are also welcome.

8 North Beach/Fisherman's Wharf

EXPENSIVE

The Sheraton at Fisherman's Wharf. 2500 Mason St. (between Beach and North Point sts.), San Francisco, CA 94133. ☎ **800/325-3535** or 415/362-5500. Fax 415/956-5275. 517 rms, 7 suites. A/C TV TEL. $135–$200 double; from $375 suite. Extra person $20. Continental breakfast $7.95 extra. AE, CB, DC, DISC, MC, V. Parking $12. Cable car: Powell-Mason line (1 block east, two blocks south). Bus: 15, 32, or 42.

Built in the mid-1970s, this modern, three-story hotel isn't the most visually appealing of hotels (even their brochure doesn't show it from the outside), but it offers the reliable comforts of a Sheraton within San Francisco's most popular tourist area. In 1995 the hotel spent $4 million renovating the rooms and adding a Corporate Floor catering exclusively to business travelers.

Dining/Entertainment: Chanen's is a Victorian-style cafe serving breakfast, lunch, and dinner. Live jazz is played several nights a week along with cocktails and assorted appetizers.

Services: Room service, concierge, evening turndown.

Facilities: Outdoor heated swimming pool, access to nearby health club, business center, hair salon, car-rental desk, travel desk.

Tuscan Inn. 425 North Point St. (at Mason St.), San Francisco, CA 94133. ☎ **800/648-4626** or 415/561-1100. Fax 415/561-1199. 209 rms, 12 suites. A/C MINIBAR TV TEL. $165–$188 double; $208–$228 suite. Rates include evening fireside wine reception. AE, DC, DISC, MC, V. Parking $13. Cable car: Powell-Mason line. Bus: 42, 15, or 32.

The Tuscan Inn is, in our opinion, the best hotel at Fisherman's Wharf. Like an island of respectability in a sea of touristy schlock, the Tuscan exudes a level of style and comfort far beyond its neighboring competitors. Splurge on valet parking—cheaper than the wharf's outrageously priced garages—then saunter your way toward the plush lobby warmed by a grand fireplace. Even the rooms, each equipped with writing desks, armchairs, and handsome burgundy floral-print bedspreads, are a cut above. The only caveat is the lack of scenic views—a small price to pay for a good hotel in a great location.

Dining: The adjoining Cafe Pescatore, open for breakfast, lunch, and dinner, serves standard Italian fare in an airy, partial alfresco setting. (See chapter 5, "Dining" for complete information).

Services: Concierge, valet parking, room service, laundry service, voice mail.

MODERATE

✪ **Hotel Bohème.** 444 Columbus St. (between Vallejo and Green sts.), San Francisco, CA 94133. ☎ **415/433-9111.** Fax 415/362-6292. 15 rms. TV, TEL. $115 double. AE, DIS, DC, MC, V. Parking $20 at nearby public garage. Cable car: Powell-Mason line. Bus: 12, 15, 30, 41, 45, or 83.

Although located on the busiest strip in North Beach, this recently renovated hotel's style and demeanor is more reminiscent of a prestigious home in upscale Nob Hill. The rooms are small but hopelessly romantic, with gauze-draped canopies and walls artistically accented with lavender, sage green, black, and pumpkin. It's a few steps to some of the greatest cafes, restaurants, bars, and shops in the city, and Chinatown and Union Square are within walking distance.

Washington Square Inn. 1660 Stockton St. (between Filbert and Union sts.), San Francisco, CA 94133. ☎ **800/388-0220** or 415/981-4220. Fax 415/397-7242. 16 rms (5 with shared bath). TEL. $85–$95 with shared bath; $95–$165 with private bath; $180 with park view. Rates include continental breakfast. AE, DC, DISC, JCB, MC, V. Parking $17. Bus: 15, 30, 39, or 45.

Reminiscent of a traditional English inn right down to the cucumber sandwiches served during afternoon tea, this small, comely bed-and-breakfast is ideal for older couples who prefer a more quiet, subdued environment than the commotion of downtown San Francisco. It's located across from Washington Square in the North Beach District—a coffee-craver's haven—and within walking distance of Fisherman's Wharf and Chinatown. Each room is decorated in English floral fabrics with quality European furnishings and plenty of fresh flowers; a few rooms share baths. A continental breakfast is included, as are afternoon tea, wine, and hors d'oeuvres.

INEXPENSIVE

San Remo. 2237 Mason St. (at Chestnut St.), San Francisco, CA 94133. ☎ **800-352-REMO** or 415/776-8688. Fax 415/776-2811. 59 rms (none with bath), 1 suite. $55–$65 double; $85 suite. AE, DC, MC, V. Parking $8. Cable car: Powell-Mason line. Bus: 15, 22, or 30.

This is a small, European-style pension is one of the best budget hotels in San Francisco. Located in a quiet North Beach neighborhood and within walking distance of Fisherman's Wharf, the San

Remo originally served as a boardinghouse for dock workers displaced by the great fire of 1906. As a result, the rooms are small and bathrooms shared, but all is forgiven when it comes time to pay the bill. Rooms are decorated in a cozy country style with brass and iron beds, oak, maple, or pine armoires, and wicker furnishings; most have ceiling fans. The shared bathrooms, each one immaculately clean, feature claw-foot tubs and brass pull-chain toilets with oak tanks and brass fixtures. If the penthouse is available, book it: you won't find a more romantic place to stay in San Francisco for so little money.

9 South of Market

Hotel Griffon. 155 Steuart St. (between Mission and Howard sts.), San Francisco, CA 94105. ☎ **800/321-2201** or 415/495-2100. Fax 415/495-3522. 62 rms, 5 penthouse suites. A/C MINIBAR TV TEL. $165–$195 double; $275 penthouse suite. Rates include continental breakfast and newspaper. AE, DC, DISC, MC, V. Parking $15. All Market St. buses.

After dumping a cool $10 million on a complete rehab in 1989, the Hotel Griffon emerged as a top contender among San Francisco's small hotels. Ideally situated on San Francisco's historic waterfront and only steps from the heart of the Financial District, the Griffon is impeccably outfitted with contemporary features such as whitewashed brick walls, lofty ceilings, marble vanities, window seats, cherrywood furniture, and art deco–style lamps (really, this place is smooth). Be sure to request a Bay View room overlooking the Bay Bridge—it's well worth the extra $20—and inquire about the excellent weekend packages the hotel occasionally offers.

Dining/Entertainment: Rôti, which has evolved into a prime lunch spot for the nearby Financial District, occupies one side of the lobby, offering California-style food prepared on spit roasts and wood-burning ovens, and served from an open kitchen. The dining room and mezzanine contain rich wood accents and a view of the San Francisco Bay and Bay Bridge.

Services: Room service, laundry/valet, concierge.

Facilities: Access to nearby health club.

10 Gay & Lesbian Hotels

Most of the previously recommended hotels are undoubtedly "gay friendly," but San Francisco also has a number of hotels catering primarily to gay men and lesbians.

Inn on Castro. 321 Castro St., San Francisco, CA 94114 (at Market St.).
☎ 415/861-0321. 6 rms, two suites. TEL. $85–$120; suites $120. Rates
include full breakfast and evening brandy. AE, MC, V. Muni Metro: Castro St.

One of the better choices in the Castro a half block away from all
the action is this Edwardian-style inn decorated with contemporary
furnishings, original modern art, and fresh flowers throughout. Almost all rooms have private baths and direct-dial phones and color
TV available upon request. Most rooms share a small back patio,
and the suite has its own private outdoor sitting area.

24 Henry. 24 Henry St., San Francisco, CA 94114 (at Noe). ☎ **800/
900-5686** or 415/864-5686. Fax 415/864-0406. 5 rms (4 with bath),
5 suites. $75–$90 double; $95 suite, $25 extra person. Rates include continental breakfast. AE, MC, V. Muni Metro: J, F, K, L, M, or N. Bus: 8, 22,
or 37.

Its Castro location is not the only thing that makes 24 Henry a good
choice for gay travelers. The building, a 123-year-old Victorian on
a serene side street, is quite charming. The five guest rooms have
high ceilings, are adorned with period furniture and private phone
line with voice mail. Guests tired of tromping around the neighborhood can watch TV or read in the double parlor (where breakfast
is also served). The apartment suites sleep three comfortably and
include parlors, separate entrances, phones, and TVs; two have a full
kitchen. All rooms are nonsmoking.

The Willows Inn. 710 14th St. (between Church and Market sts.), San
Francisco, CA 94114. ☎ **415/431-4770.** Fax 415/431-5295. 10 rms
(none with bath), 1 suite. $86–$96 double; $105–$125 suite. Rates include
continental breakfast. AE, DISC, MC, V. Limited on street parking. Muni
Metro: Church Street Station (across the street). Bus: 8, 22, or 37.

Right in the heart of the gay Castro District, The Willows Inn em-
ploys a staff eager to greet and attend to visitors to San Francisco.
The inn's willow furnishings, antiques, and Laura Ashley prints add
a touch of romantic elegance. After a long and eventful day of
sightseeing and shopping, followed by a night of dancing and cruising, you will be tucked in with a "sherry and chocolate turndown."
The staff will appear the next morning with your personalized breakfast delivered with a freshly cut flower and the morning newspaper.
The place has simple elegance and quality and is eagerly sought out
by discriminating gay visitors to San Francisco. Extra amenities include direct-dial phones, alarm-clock radios, and kimono bathrobes.

5

Dining

*R*estaurants are to San Franciscans as bagels are to New Yorkers: indispensable. At last count, city residents had more than 3,300 reasons to avoid cooking at home, and actually spent more money on dining out than those of any other city in the nation.

As one of the world's cultural crossroads, San Francisco is blessed with a cornucopia of cuisines. Afghan, Cajun, Burmese, Jewish, Moroccan, Persian, Cambodian, Vegan—whatever you're in the mood for tonight, this town has got it covered. All you need is money, reservations, and an adventurous palate, because half the fun of visiting San Francisco is the rare opportunity to sample the flavors of the world in one fell swoop.

If you want a table at the expensive restaurants with the best reputations, you will probably need to book six to eight weeks ahead for weekends and several weeks ahead for a table during the week. And remember that it is against the law to smoke in any restaurant in San Francisco that has no bar; otherwise, smoking is allowed only in the bar area.

The restaurants below are divided first by area, then by price, using the following guide: **expensive,** more than $45 per person; **moderate,** $25 to $45 per person; **inexpensive,** less than $25 per person. These categories reflect the price of the majority of dinner menu items and include an appetizer, main course, coffee, dessert, tax, and tip.

1 Restaurants by Cuisine

AMERICAN

Boulevard (South of
   Market, *E*)
Cypress Club (North
   Beach, *E*)
Doidge's (Pacific Heights/
   Cow Hollow, *I*)

Fog City Diner (Around
   Town, *M*)
Hard Rock Café (Around
   Town, *I*)
Harris's (Pacific Heights/
   Cow Hollow, *E*)

Key to Abbreviations: *E*=Expensive; *I*=Inexpensive; *M*=Moderate; *VE*=Very Expensive

One Market (Financial District, *E*)

Patio Café (Gay Restaurants, *I*)

Planet Hollywood (Union Square, *I*)

Postrio (Union Square, *E*)

Sears Fine Foods (Union Square, *I*)

ASIAN/ITALIAN

Oritalia (Pacific Heights/ Cow Hollow, *M*)

CAJUN/CREOLE

The Elite Café (Pacific Heights/Cow Hollow, *M*)

CALIFORNIA

Act IV (Civic Center, *E*)

Bix (North Beach, *E*)

Café Flore (Gay Restaurants, *I*)

Hawthorn Lane (South of Market, *E*)

Moose's (North Beach, *E*)

"No Name" (Gay Restaurants, *I*)

Rumpus (Union Square, *M*)

Stars (Civic Center, *E*)

Val 21 (Mission District, *M*)

CALIFORNIA/ASIAN

Silks (Financial District, *E*)

CALIFORNIA/AUSTRIAN

Hyde Street Bistro (Around Town, *M*)

CALIFORNIA/FRENCH

Brasserie Savoy (Union Square, *M*)

Ritz-Carlton Dining Room (Around Town, *E*)

CALIFORNIA/ MEDITERRANEAN

Plumpjack Café (Pacific Heights/Cow Hollow, *M*)

CARIBBEAN

Cha Cha Cha (Haight-Ashbury, *I*)

CHINESE

Betelnut (Pacific Heights/ Cow Hollow, *M*)

Hong Kong Flower Lounge (Around Town, *I*)

House of Nanking (Chinatown, *I*)

Sam Wo (Chinatown, *I*)

Tommy Toy's (Financial District, *E*)

Yank Sing (South of Market, *M*)

CHINESE/DIM SUM

Hong Kong Flower Lounge (Around Town, *I*)

Yank Sing (South of Market, *M*)

CONTINENTAL

Carnelian Room (Financial District, *E*)

Grand Cafe (Union Square, *M*)

Lulu (South of Market, *M*)

Rubicon (Financial District, *E*)

FRENCH

Alain Rondelli (Around Town, *E*)

Charles Nob Hill (Around Town, *E*)

Fleur de Lys (Union Square, *E*)

Flying Saucer (Mission District, *M*)

Fringale Restaurant (South of Market, *M*)

La Folie (Pacific Heights/ Cow Hollow, *E*)

Masa's (Union Square, *E*)

FRENCH/ITALIAN

Bizou (South of Market, *M*)

Scala's Bistro (Union Square, *M*)

ITALIAN

Cafe Pescatore (Fisherman's Wharf, *M*)

Gira Polli (North Beach, *I*)

Il Fornaio (Around Town, *M*)

Kuleto's (Union Square, *M*)

L'Osteria del Forno (North Beach, *I*)

Mario's Bohemian Cigar Store (North Beach, *I*)

Pane e Vino (Pacific Heights/Cow Hollow, *M*)

Pasta Pomodoro (North Beach, *I*)

Puccini and Pinetti (Union Square, *M*)

Tommaso's (North Beach, *M*)

Zinzino (Pacific Heights/ Cow Hollow, *M*)

JAPANESE

Kabuto Sushi (Around Town, *M*)

Kyo-Ya (South of Market, *E*)

MEDITERRANEAN

Enrico's (North Beach, *M*)

42 Degrees (Around Town, *M*)

Zuñi Café (Civic Center, *M*)

MEDITERRANEAN/AMERICAN

Splendido (Financial District, *M*)

MEDITERRANEAN/ITALIAN

Little City Antipasta Bar (North Beach, *M*)

MEXICAN

Café Marimba (Pacific Heights/Cow Hollow, *M*)

La Canasta (Pacific Heights/ Cow Hollow, *I*)

Zona Rosa (Haight-Ashbury, *I*)

PERSIAN/MIDDLE EASTERN

Maykadeh (North Beach, *E*)

SEAFOOD

Alioto's (Fisherman's Wharf, *E*)

Aqua (Financial District, *E*)

Hayes Street Grill (Civic Center, *M*)

Sam's Grill and Seafood Restaurant (Financial District, *M*)

Swan Oyster Depot (Around Town, *I*)

Tadich Grill (Financial District, *M*)

SUSHI
Kabuto Sushi (Around
Town, *M*)
Kyo-Ya (South of Market, *E*)

THAI
Cha Am (South of
Market, *M*)

Manora's (South of
Market, *I*)

VEGETARIAN
Greens Restaurant,
Fort Mason (Pacific
Heights/Cow
Hollow, *M*)

2 Union Square
EXPENSIVE

✪ **Fleur de Lys.** 777 Sutter St. (at Jones St.). ☎ **415/673-7779.** Reservations recommended. Main courses $27–$35.50; five-course tasting menu $65; four-course vegetarian menu $50. AE, CB, DC, MC, V. Mon–Thurs 6–10pm, Fri–Sat 5:30–10:30pm. Bus: 2, 3, 4, 27, or 38. FRENCH.

Imagine a large version of Genie's (as in *I Dream of Genie)* live-in bottle; dark, cozy; with 700 yards of rich red floor-to-ceiling hand-painted fabric enclosing the room in lavish intimacy. Throw in dimly lit French candelabras, an extraordinary sculptural floral centerpiece, and about 20 tables filled with well-dressed diners. Welcome to one of the most renowned dining rooms in San Francisco. Fleur de Lys does everything seriously, from its foie gras starter to its petit fours after dinner. And with Chef Hubert Keller (who was President Clinton's first guest chef at the White House) in the kitchen, it's impossible to go wrong. You can order à la carte from the five-course tasting menu or from the four-course vegetarian menu. Start with the knockout blue potato chips with cauliflower purée and caviar. Try any of the "symphony" of appetizers, which include crispy sweetbreads with rock shrimp mousseline, citrus and peppercorn vinaigrette, and Beluga caviar with celery root blinis. Venture on to a main course, which might include herb-crusted salmon with mushrooms and spinach noodle pie or lamb loin with black truffles. Desserts are artistic creations and might feature chocolate-mousse mice or swans with meringue wings and raspberry coulis. A selection of 300 French and California wines makes this an all-around dining fantasy.

✪ **Masa's.** In the Hotel Vintage Court, 648 Bush St. (at Stockton St.). ☎ **415/ 989-7154.** Reservations required; accepted up to 21 days in advance. Main courses $30–$38.50; fixed-price dinner $68–$75. AE, CB, DC, DISC, MC, V. Tues–Sat 6–9:30pm. Closed first week in Jan and 4th week in July. Cable car: Powell-Mason and Powell-Hyde lines. Bus: 2, 3, 4, 30, or 45. FRENCH.

Dining Near Union Square & the Financial District

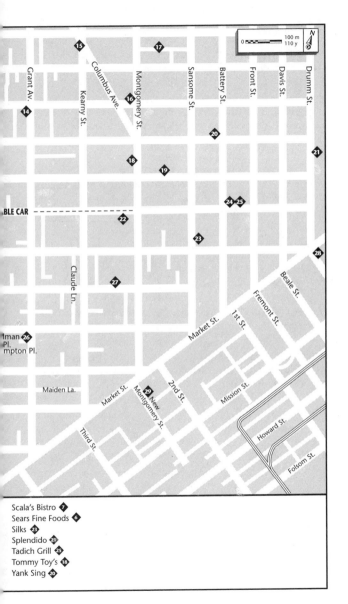

BLE CAR

Grant Av.

Columbus Ave.

Kearny St.

Montgomery St.

Sansome St.

Battery St.

Front St.

Davis St.

Drumm St.

Claude Ln.

Beale St.

Fremont St.

1st St.

Market St.

Maiden La.

Market St.

New Montgomery St.

2nd St.

Mission St.

Third St.

Howard St.

Folsom St.

0 ▬▬▬ 100 m
        110 y

N

Scala's Bistro **7**
Sears Fine Foods **6**
Silks **23**
Splendido **21**
Tadich Grill **25**
Tommy Toy's **18**
Yank Sing **20**

After the death of founder Masataha Kobayashi in 1984, local gourmets questioned the future of Masa's—but no more. Chef Julian Serrano's brilliant cuisine matched with a flawless wine list and exemplary (even unpretentious) service have solidified Masa's reputation as one of the country's great French outposts.

Either fixed price or à la carte, dinner is a memorable expense-be-damned experience from start to finish. If you wish, you can simply leave the decisions up to the kitchen. Serrano's passion for using only the highest quality ingredients accounts for the restaurant's four-star ranking—and budget-busting prices. A typical dinner may begin with the Sonoma foie gras in a Madeira truffle sauce, or poached lobster with potatoes, fried leek, and a truffle vinaigrette. Main entrées may include medallions of New Zealand fallow deer with zinfandel sauce and caramelized green apples, or the Atlantic black bass with a saffron sauce. Dessert, as you would imagine, is heavenly.

✪ **Postrio.** 545 Post St. (between Mason and Taylor sts.). ☎ **415/776-7825.** Reservations required. Main courses $6–$15 breakfast, $14–$15 lunch, $20–$26 dinner. AE, CB, DC, DISC, MC, V. Mon–Fri 7–10am, 11:30am–2pm, and 5:30–10:30pm; Sat–Sun 9am–2pm; bar daily 11:30am–2am. Cable car: Powell-Mason and Powell-Hyde lines. Bus: 2, 3, 4, or 38. AMERICAN.

They say the higher you climb, the longer it takes to fall, and that's certainly the case with Postrio. Ever since chefs Anne and David Gingrass left the kitchen to start their own enterprise, rumors have been flying that San Francisco's top restaurant isn't what it used to be (poor execution from the line tops the list). If its owners are crying, however, they're crying all the way to the bank, because it's a rare night when the kitchen doesn't perform to a full house.

Eating, however, is only half the reason one comes to Postrio. After squeezing through the perpetually swinging bar—which, in its own right, dishes out excellent tapas and pizzas from a wood-burning oven in the corner—guests are forced to make a grand entrance down the antebellum staircase to the cavernous dining room below (it's everyone's 15 seconds of fame, so make sure your fly is zipped). Pure Hollywood, for sure, but fun.

The menu, prepared by brothers Mitchell and Steven Rosenthal, combines Italian, Asian, French, and California styles with mixed results. When we last visited Postrio, the sautéed salmon, for example, was a bit overcooked, but the accompanying plum glaze, wasabi mashed potatoes, and miso vinaigrette were outstanding. Again with the grilled squab: It lacked flavor, but the accompaniment—a sweet potato foie gras spring roll—was pure genius.

The desserts, each artistically sculpted by pastry chef Janet Rikala, were the highlight of the evening. Despite the prime-time rush, service was friendly and infallible, as was the presentation.

MODERATE

✪ **Brasserie Savoy.** In the Savoy Hotel, 580 Geary St. (at Jones St.). ☎ **415/ 474-8686.** Reservations recommended. Main courses $11–$17. AE, DC, DISC, JCB, MC, V. Daily 6:30–11am and 5:30–10pm. Bus: 2, 3, 4, 27, or 38. CALIFORNIA/FRENCH.

If you're headed to the theater or are just looking for a good meal downtown, Brasserie Savoy is an excellent option. The atmosphere is French bistro, with a bright, busy dining room, black and white marble floors, and tables with beige and black leather, and woven chairs. The food is consistent, affordable, and delicious. Choices may include beef tenderloin with port sauce and green peppercorn butter, or duck breast with mille-feuille of potato and mushrooms served with a date purée and coffee sauce. On the lighter side, the crawfish risotto with red and green peppers, scallions, celery, and chive lemongrass butter is a perfect dish. Among the appetizers, the napoleon of braised rabbit with red onions, mushrooms, kalamata olives, and anise tuiles is a preferred choice, if it's offered, or any one of several freshly made salads. To finish, try the innovative crème brûlée.

Grand Cafe. 501 Geary St. (at Taylor St.). ☎ **415/292-0101.** Reservations accepted. Main courses $9.25–$16. AE, DC, MC, V. Daily 7am–3pm; Sun–Thurs 5–10pm, cafe menu until 1am; Fri–Sat 5–11pm, cafe menu until 2am. Bus: 2, 3, 4, 27, or 38. CONTINENTAL.

The Grand Cafe is hands down the most amazing room in the Union Square area. The cocktail area is swank and packed with a good-looking crowd, but walk back to the enormous but cozy dining area if you really want to be impressed. It's an architecturally restored, turn-of-the-century grand ballroom with 30-foot ceilings and an aura of old Europe interlaced with art nouveau and art deco. From every angle you'll see incredibly playful commissioned local art, which includes a towering bunny sculpture that you really must see for yourself. Though off to a shaky start in 1995, the fare is ambitious as well. Signature appetizers include a rich polenta soufflé served on a wild mushroom ragout with fonduta, and grilled eggplant napoleon. Move on to a main course, such as the lobster and shrimp ravioli in sorrel cream sauce or grilled Delmonico steak au poivre verte with pommes frites (steak with green pepper and french fries). The food, though not the absolute best in town, is very good, and the atmosphere and prices make it a worthwhile place to check out.

Kuleto's. 221 Powell St. (between Geary and O'Farrell sts., in the Villa Florence Hotel). ☎ **415/397-7720.** Reservations recommended. Breakfast $3–$8; main courses $8–$18. AE, CB, DC, DISC, MC, V. Mon–Fri 7–10:30am, Sat and Sun 8–10:30am; daily 11:30am–11pm. Cable car: Powell-Mason and Powell-Hyde lines. Muni Metro: Powell. Bus: 2, 3, 4, or 38. ITALIAN.

Story has it the owners of this popular downtown bistro were so delighted with the design of their new restaurant that they named it after the architect, Pat Kuleto. Whatever the reason, Kuleto's is truly a beautiful place filled with beautiful people who are here to see and be seen (don't come underdressed). The best plan of action is to skip the wait for a table, muscle a seat at the antipasto bar, and fill up on appetizers (which are often better than the entrées). For a main course, try the penne pasta drenched in a tangy lamb sausage marinara sauce, the clam linguini (generously overloaded with fresh clams), or any of the fresh fish specials grilled over hardwoods. If you don't arrive by 6pm, expect to wait—this place fills up mucha fasta.

Puccini & Pinetti. 129 Ellis St. (at Cyril Magnin). ☎ **415/392-5500.** Reservations recommended. Main courses $5–$13. AE, CB, DC, DISC, MC, V. Daily 11:30am–3:30pm, Sun–Thurs 5 –10pm, Fri–Sat 5–11pm. Bus: 27 or 38. Cable car: Powell-Mason line. ITALIAN.

It takes some *buco* bravado to open an Italian restaurant in San Francisco, but partners Bob Puccini and Steve Pinetti obviously did their homework, because this trendy little trattoria has been packed since the day it opened. The formula isn't exactly unique: good food at great prices. What really makes it work, though, is the upbeat, casual ambience, colorful decor, and live music Monday through Friday night—sort of like crashing a catered party.

The menu doesn't take any chances. Italian standbys—pastas, salads, wood-fired pizzas, grilled meats—dominate the menu. The grilled salmon with sautéed spinach has been well received, along with the stuffed, oven-roasted portobello mushroom antipasti and fresh-baked focaccia sandwiches. The creamy tiramisu makes for a proper finish.

✪ Rumpus. One Tillman Place (off Grant Ave., between Sutter and Post sts.). ☎ **415/421-2300.** Reservations recommended. Main courses $11.95–$16.95. AE, DC, MC, V. Mon–Sat 11:30am–2:30pm; Sun–Thurs 5:30–10pm; Fri–Sat 5:30–11pm. CALIFORNIA.

Tucked into a small cul-de-sac off Grant Avenue, you'll find Rumpus, a fantastic new restaurant serving well-prepared California fare at reasonable prices. The perfect place for a business lunch, shopping break, or dinner with friends, Rumpus is architecturally playful, colorful, and buzzing with conversation. Like most "in" restaurants in town, ahi tuna tartare is on the starters list. It is, however, wonderfully fresh, savory, and spiced with wasabi caviar. The pan-roasted chicken's crispy and flavorful crust is almost as delightful as the perfectly cooked chicken and mashed potatoes beneath it, and the quality cut of New York steak comes with a sweet-potato mash. If nothing else, make sure to stop in here for one of the best desserts we've ever had: the puddinglike chocolate brioche cake.

✪ **Scala's Bistro.** 432 Powell St. (at Sutter St.). ☎ **415/395-8555.** Reservations recommended. Breakfast $6–$9; lunch and dinner main courses $8–$17. AE, CB, DC, DISC, MC, V. Mon–Sun 6:30am–12am. Cable car: Powell-Hyde line. Bus: 2, 3, 4, 30, 45, or 76. FRENCH/ITALIAN.

We had heard so much hype about the new Scala's Bistro that we were sure it wouldn't live up to our expectations. Let's just say we were happily mistaken. Firmly entrenched at the base of the refurbished Sir Francis Drake Hotel, this latest venture by husband and wife team Giovanni (the host) and Donna (the chef) Scala is one of the best new restaurants in the city. The Parisian-bistro/old-world atmosphere blends just the right balance of elegance and informality, which means it's perfectly okay to have some fun here (and apparently most people do).

Drawing from her success at Bistro Don Giovanni in Napa, Donna has put together a fantastic array of Italian and French dishes that are priced surprisingly low. Start with the Earth and Surf calamari appetizer (better than anything I've sampled along the Mediterranean) or the grilled portobello mushrooms. The Golden Beet salad and Anchor Steam mussels are also good bets, as is the Cipolla Pazza: hot Italian sausage spaghetti served in a roasted onion. Generous portions of the moist, rich duck leg confit will satisfy hungry appetites, but if you can only order one thing, make it Scala's signature dish: the seared salmon. Resting on a bed of creamy buttermilk mashed potatoes and ensconced with a tomato, chive, and white wine sauce, it's one of the best salmon dishes I've ever tasted. Finish with the creamy Bostini cream pie, a dreamy combo of vanilla custard and orange chiffon cake with a warm chocolate glaze.

INEXPENSIVE

Planet Hollywood. 2 Stockton St. (at Market St.). ☎ **415/421-7827.** Reservations not accepted except for parties of 20 or more. $7.75–$18.95. AE, DC,

DISC, MC, V. Daily 11am–1am. Bus: 38 or any Market St. bus. Muni Metro: Any line. AMERICAN.

You won't find any locals here (or movie stars for that matter), but for some reason tourists can't help but flock to Planet Hollywood. Similar to the Hard Rock, this is a themed restaurant chain that, instead of music, exhibits movie memorabilia. Expect long lines to get in, plenty of fellow tourists, and an affordable menu featuring salads, sandwiches, pastas, burgers, pizzas, fajitas, and a few grilled meat items.

Sears Fine Foods. 439 Powell St. (between Post and Sutter sts.). ☎ **415/986-1160.** Reservations not accepted. Breakfast $3–$8; salads and soups $1.80–$8; main courses $5–$10. No credit cards. Wed–Sun 6:30am–3:30pm. Cable car: Powell-Mason, Powell-Hyde. Bus: 2, 3, 4, or 38. AMERICAN.

Sears would be the perfect place to breakfast on the way to work, but you can't always guarantee you'll get in the door before 9am. It's not just another pink-tabled diner run by motherly matrons, it's an institution, famous for its crispy, dark-brown waffles, light sourdough French toast, and Swedish dollar-sized pancakes. As the story goes, Sears was founded in 1938 by Ben Sears, a retired clown. It was his Swedish wife Hilbur, however, who was responsible for the legendary pancakes, which are still whipped up according to her family's secret recipe.

3 Financial District

EXPENSIVE

✪ **Aqua.** 252 California St. (between Battery and Front sts.). ☎ **415/956-9662.** Reservations recommended. Main courses $26–$32; six-course tasting menu $65; vegetarian tasting menu $45. AE, DC, MC, V. Mon–Fri 11:30am–2pm; Mon–Sat 5:30–10:30pm. All Market St. buses. SEAFOOD.

Without question, Aqua is San Francisco's finest seafood restaurant, light years beyond the genre of shrimp cocktails and lemon-butter sauce. Chef Michael Mina dazzles his customers with a bewildering juxtaposition of earth and sea. The salmon, for example, is first glazed in ginger, then spiced with sweet orange marmalade that contrasts perfectly with the sour reduction sauce of braised red cabbage. The Atlantic cod has a similar twist: lightly seared and fully flavored with a tangy cabernet reduction, then accompanied by a wonderful caramelized onion risotto. Mina's passion for exotic mushrooms pervades most dishes, for taste as well as for show (Mina is, to a fault, amazingly adept at the art of presentation). Desserts are equally impressive, particularly the spiced pumpkin brioche with cream cheese ice cream, and the chocolate tasting plate—a feast for the eyes as well as the palate. Steep prices prevent most people from making a regular appearance, but for special occasions or billable lunches, Aqua is highly recommended.

Carnelian Room. 555 California St. (at Montgomery St.). ☎ **415/433-7500.** Reservations recommended. Main courses $25–$55, $24.50 adult brunch, $12 children. AE, CB, DC, DISC, MC, V. Mon–Sun 6pm–10pm; Sun 10am–2:30pm Brunch. Cable car: California line. Bus: 1, 15, 9, or 42. CONTINENTAL.

By day, the Carnelian Room is the exclusive Banker's Club, accessible only to members or by invitation, but at night anyone with a big enough bankroll can dine among the clouds. Soaring 52 stories above San Francisco's Financial District on the top floor of the Bank of America building, the Carnelian Room is a definite contender for "Best View." Dark oak paneling, brass railings, and huge picture windows reek with romanticism, particularly if you're fortunate enough to get a window table. Though the menu is definitely upscale, it tends to cater to old-style banker's tastes; expensive meat dishes—New Yorks, tenderloins, rack of lamb, pork loin, veal—with rich, thick sauces dominate the menu. A wine cellar with some 36,000 bottles all but guarantees the proper vintage to accompany your meal.

One Market. 1 Market St. (at Steuart across from Justin Herman Plaza). ☎ **415/777-5577.** Reservations recommended. Main courses $18–$22. AE, DC, MC, V. Mon–Fri 11:30am–2pm, Sun 10am–2pm; Mon–Thurs 5:30–9:30pm, Fri 5:30–10pm, Sat 5–10pm, Sun 5–9pm. All Market St. buses. AMERICAN.

The enormous restaurant's decor, which is both cosmopolitan and folk-artsy, has been recently fine-tuned to complement renowned chef Bradley Ogden's farm fresh menu. Amidst tapestry, banquettes, mahogany, and slate floors, there's seating for 170 in main dining area. The bar, which features gold walls and sponge-painted mustard columns, displays a prominent colorful mural of a market scene. The menu changes frequently to reflect the freshest local ingredients and may start with Skookum and Fanny Bay oysters with homemade cocktail sauce and chili malt vinegar dressing and an array of oak-baked flatbread dishes. Main courses might include pan-roasted sea bass with smoked bacon, cabbage broth, and red wine onions or a Yankee pot roast with mashed red potatoes and root veggies. A corporate crowd convenes from 5 to 7pm weeknights for the $1 oysters and beer. The room picks up with live jazz Tuesday through Saturday and also during the Sunday brunch.

Rubicon. 558 Sacramento St. (between Sansome and Montgomery sts.).
☎ **415/434-4100.** Reservations recommended. Main courses $19–$24.
AE, MC, V. Mon–Fri 11:30am–2:30pm; Mon–Sat 5:30–10:30pm. Bus: 15 or 41.
CONTINENTAL.

Opened in 1994, Rubicon won instant publicity because of the fame
of its owners, film director Francis Ford Coppola and actor Robert
DeNiro. Named for Coppola's Napa Valley wine, Rubicon features
a contemporary and somewhat stiff dining room frequented by big-
business power-lunchers and an upscale, middle-aged crowd.

The menu changes frequently. Favorites among the 10 or so
appetizers include the ahi tuna carpaccio with radish vinaigrette,
sautéed foie gras with sautéed sunchokes and tamarind glaze, and
house-cured salmon with crisp potato chips and lemon vinaigrette.
About eight main courses are available that might include a sautéed
salmon with savoy cabbage, pearl onions, smoked bacon, and red
wine sauce; loin of lamb with potato and celery root galette and
chervil sauce; or Muscovy duck breast with braised turnips and tat
soi honey coriander sauce. Finish with the pecan date tart with
blood-orange sorbet or the bittersweet chocolate and peppermint
gâteau.

Silks. In the Mandarin Oriental Hotel, 222 Sansome St. (between Pine and California sts.). ☎ **415/885-0999.** Reservations recommended. 2-course meal
$32; 3 courses $39; 4 courses $47. AE, DC, MC, V. Mon–Fri 7–11:30am,
11:30am–2pm; nightly 6–9:30pm. Bus: 2, 38, or 42. CALIFORNIA/ASIAN.

Though the atmosphere is rather somber with burnt reds and golden
ambers; modern, free-form sculptures, and local artworks, it's still
regarded as one of the better dining rooms in the city. The menu
changes quarterly, melds California and Asian ingredients and styles,
and is offered in two, three, or four courses. If available, start with
the three-tuna tartare sampler with lime and caviar; the seared,
wrapped nori and crispy spring rolls; or the pan-seared striped bass
with roasted fennel ravioli, carrot and ginger consommé. Main
courses may include coriander-crusted tuna with soba noodles;
Asian-marinated lamb loin and spicy satay; and the signature grilled
yakitori quail with sweet potato purée, star anise, and foie gras
wontons. Follow with such desserts as banana cake with slices of
caramelized bananas and two kinds of ice cream.

Tommy Toy's. 655 Montgomery St. (at Columbus Ave. and Washington St.)
☎ **415/397-4888.** Main courses $16.95–$28.50. Fixed-price dinner $45.
AE, DC, JCB, MC, V. Mon–Fri 11:30am–2:30pm, daily 6–9:30pm. CHINESE.

Chinese food is to San Franciscans what pizza is to college students.
It's fast, delicious, and cheap. But Tommy Toy turned Chinese from

a take-out affair to a dress-up affair when he created an opulent, dark, and unmistakably Asian fine dining environment that cost a cool $1.5 million. The dining room, created after the 19th-century empress dowager's reading room, is accented with dimly lit candelabras and ancient paintings. Most evenings, the restaurant is crowded with tourists and some locals who come for the five-course fixed-price meal, which usually includes minced squab in lettuce leaves, lobster bisque soup served in a coconut and topped with puffed pastry, a whole lobster in black bean sauce, duck served with plum sauce, medallions of beef, and finally a light dessert of peach mousse. The à la carte menu flaunts vanilla prawns and other such delicacies. On the two occasions we've been here, once the food was very good, the next time it was just okay, and both times, the portions were substantial. Our only issue with Tommy Toy's is that if we were to throw down around $50 for a feast, we would do it at La Folie, Fleur de Lys, or Allain Rondelli where the food is remarkably special. But if you want romantic Chinese, this is as good as it gets.

MODERATE

Sam's Grill & Seafood Restaurant. 374 Bush St. (between Montgomery and Kearny sts.). ☎ **415/421-0594.** Reservations accepted for dinner and for 5 or more at lunch. Main courses $10–$20. AE, DC, MC, V. Mon–Fri 11am–9pm. Bus: 15, 45, or 76. SEAFOOD.

Power-lunching at Sam's is a San Francisco tradition, and they've been doing a brisk business with Financial District types for what seems like forever (they opened in 1867). The entrance, which holds a polished, small mahogany bar, opens onto a main dining room with high-backed booths. It's noisy at midday, but if privacy is your primary concern, choose one of the individually curtained booths that line the corridor to the left of the main dining room.

For lunch, consider the clam chowder, a charcoal-broiled filet of fish, and a dessert of French pancakes anisette. Shellfish, steak, and veal dishes round out the dinner menu.

Splendido. 4 Embarcadero Center (at Clay and Drum sts.). ☎ **415/ 986-3222.** Reservations accepted. Main courses $14–$23. AE, DC, DISC, MC, V. Mon–Fri 11:30am–2:30pm; daily 5:30–10pm. Bus: 15, 45, or 76. MEDITERRANEAN/AMERICAN.

Warm olive wood, flickering candles, rustic stone walls, hand-painted tiles, and hand-hewn beams create the illusion of an old Mediterranean getaway in the middle of metropolitan Embarcadero Four.

But it's not the decor alone that procures Kudos from *Gourmet* and other culinary magazines. The food is beautifully presented, lovingly prepared, and consistently delicious. Starters might include fish soup, crispy crab cakes, or ravioli with prosciutto, mascarpone, and shallots. Main courses include grilled swordfish served on a bed of sweet white corn and braised leeks or grilled loin of lamb with white-bean/garlic flan. Save some room for dessert—some say the tiramisu with chocolate pine-nut bark is the best in town. When the weather is pleasant, you can eat under a canopy on the outdoor patio, or choose the seating in front of the open kitchen. Be sure to glance in the exhibition bakery near entrance where you might see chefs rolling fresh pasta.

✪ **Tadich Grill.** 240 California St. (between Battery and Front sts.). ☎ **415/ 391-1849.** Reservations not accepted. Main courses $12–$18. MC, V. Mon–Fri 11am–10pm, Sat 11:30am–10pm. Muni Metro: All Market Street trams. All Market Street buses. SEAFOOD.

This famous, venerated California institution arrived with the gold rush in 1849 and claims to be the very first to broil seafood over mesquite charcoal, back in the early 1920s.

The original mahogany bar extends the entire length of the restaurant while no-nonsense white linen–draped tables are topped with big plates of sourdough bread. Power-lunchers get one of the seven enclosed, private booths.

For a light meal you might try one of the delicious seafood salads, such as shrimp or prawn Louis. Hot dishes include baked avocado with shrimp diablo, baked casserole of stuffed turbot with crab and shrimp à la Newburg, and charcoal-broiled petrale sole with butter sauce, a local favorite. Almost everyone gets a side order of big, tasty french fries.

4 Civic Center

EXPENSIVE

Act IV. In the Inn at the Opera, 333 Fulton St. (at Frankin St.). ☎ **415/ 553-8100.** Reservations recommended. Breakfast $5–$10; lunch courses $5–$12; main courses $19–$28. AE, MC, V. Mon–Sat 7–10am and 11:30am–2pm; Mon–Thurs 5:30–9:30pm, Fri–Sat 5:30–10:30pm. Bus: 5. CALIFORNIA

This small, intimate haven with its dark wood furnishings, Belgian tapestries, and elegant table settings is a popular venue for après-opera noshing. After a series of chef changes over the years, the management finally opted for a more traditional, substantial approach to its cuisine by hiring chef Kirke Byers, a long-time Californian with a penchant for sniffing out the finest local produce. Large portions of fresh, well-prepared meats and vegetables dominate each dish, such as the wonderful rack of lamb in a superb reduction sauce flavored with roasted garlic, carrots, turnips, and a potato gratin. The grilled Virginia striped bass with a tangy citrus vinaigrette and lemon aioli is another good choice. Perhaps the main reason people come here, though, is to listen to the live entertainment and for the chance encounter with the steady stream of celebrities who frequent the hotel.

✪ **Stars.** 150 Redwood Alley (between McAllister and Golden Gate off Van Ness). ☎ **415/861-7827.** Reservations required. Main courses $23–$28. AE, MC, V. Mon–Fri 11:30am–2pm; Mon–Tues 6–9:30pm, Wed–Sun 5:30–9:30pm. Bus: 19, 31, or 38. CALIFORNIA.

San Francisco's celebrity hot spot nonpareil, Stars is the brainchild of superstar chef Jeremiah Tower. The large, loud, and vibrant restaurant—swathed in glimmering hardwoods, brass, and mirrors—features the longest bar in the city, which does little to guarantee you'll find a free stool when the place is hopping. Critics complain the quality of the food is slipping (as prices increase), but it obviously doesn't deter local celebrities like Robin Williams and Mayor Willie Brown from making regular appearances.

Though the menu changes daily, among the half-dozen main courses you might find a braised veal ragout with egg noodles, cipollini onions, and wild mushrooms; medallion of pork loin with cabbage, leeks, and sauce hachee; or sea scallops with braised Belgian endive, lobster cream sauce, and tarragon. First courses exhibit the same approach. The crisp duck leg confit with white beans, mangos, and arugula; and the Belgian endive salad with white truffle oil, pistachio vinaigrette, and a toasted cheese sandwich are just two examples, along with an innovative minestrone of fish and shellfish chez Prunier. If you want to treat yourself extra well, order the house-cured sturgeon with mushrooms and deviled eggs or the foie gras with hazelnut toasts and watercress salad. Desserts are extraordinary, from the signature chocolate soufflé pastry layered with chocolate ganache and served with champagne sabayon, to the banana nut torte filled with praline and sliced bananas and frosted with white chocolate buttercream and a dark chocolate glaze, or any of the other offerings from tiramisu to Vermont maple cake.

MODERATE

✪ **Hayes Street Grill.** 320 Hayes St. (near Franklin St.). ☎ **415/863-5545.** Reservations recommended. Main courses $13.50–$18.25. AE, DC, MC, V.

Dining Around Town

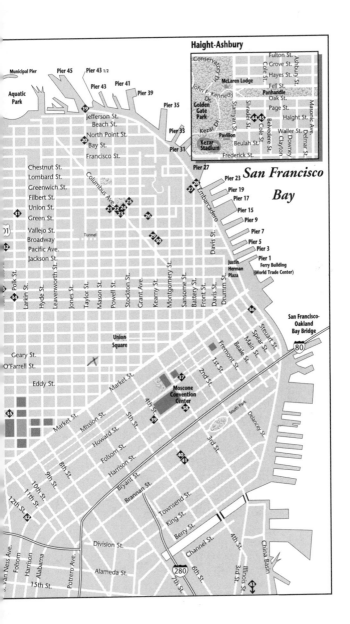

San Francisco Bay

Haight-Ashbury

Mon–Fri 11:30am–2pm and 5–8:30pm, Sat 6–10:30pm, Sun 5–8:30pm. Bus: 19, 31, or 38. SEAFOOD.

This small, no-nonsense seafood restaurant has built a solid reputation among San Francisco's picky epicureans for its impeccably fresh fish. Choices ranging from Hawaiian swordfish to Puget Sound salmon—cooked to perfection, naturally—are matched with your sauce of choice (Szechuan peanut, tomato salsa, herb shallot butter) and a side of their signature french fries. Fancier seafood specials are available too, such as bay scallops with chanterelle and shiitake mushrooms, as well as an impressive selection of garden-fresh salads and local grilled meats. Finish with the outstanding crème brûlée.

✪ **Zuñi Café.** 1658 Market St. (at Franklin St.). ☎ **415/552-2522.** Reservations recommended. Main courses $16–$22.50. AE, MC, V. Tues–Sat 7:30am–midnight, Sun 7:30am–11pm. Muni Metro: All Market St. trams. Bus: 6, 7, 71, or 75. MEDITERRANEAN.

Even factoring in the snotty wait staff, Zuñi Café is still one of our favorite places in the city to have lunch. Its expanse of windows and prime Market Street location guarantee good people-watching—a favorite San Francisco pastime—and chef Judy Rodgers's Mediterranean-influenced menu is wonderfully diverse and satisfying. For the full effect, sit at the bustling, copper-topped bar and peruse the foot-long oyster menu (half a dozen or so varieties on hand at all times); you can also sit in the stylish, exposed-brick dining room or on the outdoor patio. Though the changing menu always includes meat, such as New York steak with Belgian endive gratin, and fish, either grilled or braised in the kitchen's brick oven, the proven winners are Rodgers's brick oven–roasted chicken for two with Tuscan-style bread salad, the polenta appetizer with mascarpone, and the hamburger on grilled rosemary focaccia bread (a strong contender for the city's best burger). Whatever you decide, be sure to order a side of the shoestring potatoes.

5 Pacific Heights/Cow Hollow

EXPENSIVE

Harris's. 2100 Van Ness Ave. (at Pacific Ave.). ☎ **415/673-1888.** Reservations recommended. Main courses $18–$30. AE, CB, DC, DISC, JCB, MC, V. Mon–Fri 6–11pm, Sat–Sun 5–11pm. Bus: 38 or 45. AMERICAN.

Every big city has a great steak restaurant, and in San Francisco, it's Harris's. Proprietor Ann Lee Harris knows steaks; she grew up on a cattle ranch and married the owner of the largest feedlot in California. In 1976, the couple opened the Harris Ranch Restaurant on

Interstate 5 in central California, where they built a rock-solid reputation up and down the coast. The steaks, which can be seen hanging in a glass-windowed aging room, are cut thick—either New York–style or T-bone—and are served with a baked potato and seasonal vegetables.

Harris's also offers roast duckling, lamb chops, fresh fish, lobster, and venison, buffalo, and other types of game. Those who like brains rave about the restaurant's sautéed brains in brown butter.

Harris's wood-paneled dining room with curving banquettes is comfortably elegant.

✪ **La Folie.** 2316 Polk St. (between Green and Union sts.). ☎ **415/776-5577.** Reservations recommended. Main courses $22–$28. Five-course tasting menu $45. AE, DC, JCB, MC, V. Mon–Sat 5:30–10:30pm. Bus: 19, 41, 45, 47, 49, or 76. FRENCH.

For fantastic French food without attitude, La Folie is the place to feast. The minute you walk through the door, you'll know why this is many locals' favorite restaurant. The country-French decor is tasteful but not too serious, with whimsical chandeliers and a cloudy sky painted overhead. The staff is friendly, knowledgeable, and very accommodating; the food is outstanding. Unlike many renowned chefs, La Folie's Roland Passot is in the kitchen nightly, and it shows. Each of his California-influenced French creations is an architectural and culinary masterpiece. Best of all, they're served in a relaxed and comfortable environment. Start with an appetizer such as the roast quail and fois gras with salad, wild mushrooms, and roasted garlic—it's guaranteed to melt in your mouth. Main courses are not *petite* as in many French restaurants, and all are accompanied by flavorful and well-balanced sauces. Try the rôti of quail and squab stuffed with wild mushrooms and wrapped in crispy potato strings or the roast venison with vegetables, quince, and huckleberry sauce. Finish off with any of the delectable desserts.

MODERATE

Betelnut. 2030 Union St. (at Buchanan St.). ☎ **415/929-8855.** Reservations recommended. Main courses $9–$16. DC, MC, V. Sun–Thurs 11:30am–11pm, Fri–Sat 11:30am–midnight. Bus: 22, 41, or 45. CHINESE.

While San Francisco is teeming with Chinese restaurants, there are few that offer the posh, fashionable dining environment of this new restaurant on upscale Union Street. As the menu explains, the restaurant is themed after "Pejui Wu," a traditional Asian beer house offering local brews and savory dishes, but with the bamboo paneling, red Formica countertops, and low-hanging lamps, the place feels

less like an authentic harbor restaurant and more like a set out of
Madonna's movie *Shanghai Surprise*. Still, the atmosphere is pleasant, with dimly lit booths, ringside seating overlooking the bustling
stir-fry chefs, sidewalk tables (weather permitting), and body-to-
body flirting at the cramped but festive bar. Starters include sashimi
and tasty salt and pepper whole gulf prawns; main courses offer wok-
roasted clams with Thai basil and Singapore chili crab. While prices
seem reasonable, it's the incidentals such as white rice ($1.50 per
person) and tea ($3.50 per pot) that rack up the bill. Unfortunately,
the wait staff is often so inattentive it ruins the entire experience.
While the food is decent, it doesn't compare to many of the better
Chinese restaurants in the city. In fact, the only reason to choose this
restaurant over others is the atmosphere and their heavenly signature
dessert: a mouth-watering tapioca pudding with sweet red adzuki
beans.

Café Marimba. 2317 Chestnut St. (between Scott and Divisidero sts.).
☎ **415/776-1506.** Main courses $5–$13. AE, MC, V. Mon–Sun 11:30am–
12am. Bus: 30. MEXICAN.

As much as we hate to plug the yuppified Marina District, we have
to admit that we're completely addicted to Café Marimba's gilled
Yucatan-spiced snapper and grilled chicken tacos. Add just the right
amount of guacamole and pineapple salsa, and *acheewahwah* that's
good! The shrimp mojo de ajo is also a knockout (heck, even the
chips and guac are the best in town). For parties of three or more,
order the family style platter of grilled meats and vegetables and prepare to do battle. We're obviously not the only ones who fancy this
fun, festive cafe, so expect a long wait during peak hours (our MO
is to sneak seats at the bar and order there). But *hasta mañana* the
margaritas—*muy mal.*

The Elite Café. 2049 Fillmore St. (between Pine and California sts.). ☎ **415/
346-8668.** No reservations. Main courses $10.95–$21.95. AE, DC, DISC,
MC, V. Mon–Sat 5–11pm; Sun 10am–3pm and 5–10pm. Bus: 41 or 45. CAJUN/
CREOLE.

If the shellfish in the window doesn't get you in the door, the
festive atmosphere will. This place is always bustling with Pacific
Heights's beautiful people who come for fresh oysters, blackened
filet mignon with Cajun butter, redfish with crab and Creole cream
sauce, or any of the other well-spiced Cajun dishes. The high-backed
booths provide more intimate dining than the crowded tables and
bar. Brunch is good, too; all kinds of egg dishes—Benedict, sardou,
and many more—are offered along with bagels and lox.

✪ **Greens Restaurant.** Fort Mason. Building A, Fort Mason Center (enter Fort Mason opposite the Safeway at Buchanan and Marina sts.). ☎ **415/771-6222.** Reservations recommended 2 weeks in advance. Main courses $10–$13; fixed-priced dinner $38; brunch $7–$10. DISC, MC, V. Tues–Fri 11:30am–2pm, Sat 11:30am–2:30pm; Mon–Sat 8am–9pm and Sun 9am–2pm (bakery, Tues–Sat 9:30am–4:30pm, Sun 10am–3pm). Bus: 28 or 30. VEGETARIAN.

Knowledgeable locals swear by Greens, where executive chef Annie Somerville (author of *Fields of Greens*) cooks with the seasons, using produce from Green Gulch Farm and other local organic farms. Located in an old warehouse, with enormous windows overlooking the bridge and the bay, the restaurant is both a pioneer and a legend. A weeknight dinner might feature such appetizers as tomato, white-bean, and sorrel soup; or grilled asparagus with lemon, Parmesan cheese, and watercress and follow with such choices as spring vegetable risotto with asparagus, peas, shiitake and crimini mushrooms, and Parmesan cheese, or Sri Lankan curry made of new potatoes, cauliflower, carrots, peppers, and snap peas stewed with tomatoes, coconut milk, ginger, and Sri Lankan spices.

A special five-course dinner is served on Saturday. A recent example began with grilled asparagus, yellowfin potatoes, and peppers with blood-orange beurre blanc, followed by shiitake and crimini mushroom lasagna with leeks and mushroom port sauce. Desserts are equally adventuresome—try the chocolate pave with mint crème anglaise or the espresso ice cream with chocolate sauce. Lunch and brunch are somewhat simpler, but equally as inventive. An extensive wine list is available.

Like the restaurant, the adjacent bakery is also operated by the Zen Center. It sells homemade breads, sandwiches, soups, salads, and pastries to take home.

Oritalia. 1915 Fillmore St. (between Pine and Bush sts.). ☎ **415/346-1333.** Pasta $9–$14; main courses $15–$18.50. AE, MC, V. Mon–Sat 5–11pm; Sun 5–10pm. Bus: 41 or 45. ASIAN/ITALIAN.

If you can't decide between Italian and Asian food tonight, try both. Located on a busy section of Fillmore Street, Oritalia (derived from *Oriental* and *Italian*) has made its niche by blending the flavors of Italy, China, Korea, and Southeast Asia to create some truly unique dishes. Prince Edward mussels, for example, are mixed with Shao Xing wine and Chinese celery. Also popular are the Dungeness crab cakes with Tobiko caviar and a red pepper curry cream. Though full entrées are available, an assortment of the "Small Plates" makes for a more adventurous, family style dining experience. A charming, casual decor marked by papier-mâché paintings, hand-painted

pendant lamps, painted gourds, and textured walls by Japanese artist Yoshi Hayashi are the perfect complement to the multicultural
menu.

✪ **Pane e Vino.** 3011 Steiner St. (at Union St.). ☎ **415/346-2111.** Reservations recommended. Main courses $10–$18. MC, V. Mon–Sat 11:30am–
2:30pm; daily 5–10pm. Bus: 41 or 45. ITALIAN.

Pane e Vino is one of San Francisco's top and most authentic Italian restaurants, as well as our personal favorite. The food is consistently excellent (careful not to fill up on the outstanding breads
served upon seating), the prices reasonable, and the mostly Italian-
accented staff always smooth and efficient under pressure (you'll see).
The two small dining rooms, separated by an open kitchen that
emanates heavenly aromas, offer only limited seating, so expect a
wait even if you have reservations. A wide selection of appetizers is
offered, including a fine carpaccio, vitello tonnato (sliced roasted veal
and capers in a lemony tuna sauce), and the hugely popular chilled
artichoke stuffed with bread and tomatoes and served with a
vinaigrette. Our favorite, the antipasti of mixed grilled vegetables,
always spurs a fork fight. A similar broad selection of pastas is
available, including a flavorful pennette alla boscaiola with porcini
mushrooms and pancetta in a tomato cream sauce. Other specialties are grilled fish and meat dishes, including a chicken breast
marinated in lime juice and herbs. Top dessert picks are any of the
Italian ice creams, the crème caramel, and (but of course) the creamy
tiramisu.

✪ **PlumpJack Café.** 3127 Fillmore St. (between Filbert and Greenwich sts.).
☎ **415/563-4755.** Reservations recommended. Main courses $14–$20.
AE, MC, V. Mon–Fri 11:30am–2pm and 5:30–10:30pm, Sat 5:30–10:30pm. Bus:
41 or 45. CALIFORNIA/MEDITERRANEAN.

Wildly popular among San Francisco's style-setters, this small Cow
Hollow restaurant has quickly become the "in" place to dine. This
is partly due to the fact that it's run by one of the Getty clan (as in
J. Paul), but mostly because chef Maria Helm's food is just plain
good and the whimsical decor is a veritable work of art.

Though the menu changes weekly, you might find such appetizers as roasted portobello mushroom with vegetable stuffing,
reggiano, and cippolini onions, or a salad of watercress and Belgian
endive with kumquats, toasted pine nuts, shaved reggiano, and
champagne vinaigrette. Main dishes range from pasta (such as the
cavatappi with tiger prawns, green garlic, leeks, and roast tomato
sauce) to roast local halibut with grilled asparagus and blood-orange

chervil vinaigrette. Top it off with an apricot soufflé or the chocolate Kahlua torte. The extraordinarily extensive California wine
list—gleaned from the PlumpJack wine shop down the street—is
sold at next to retail, with many wines available by the glass.

✪ **Zinzino.** 2355 Chestnut St. (at Divisadero St.). ☎ **415/346-6623.** Reservations for 6 or more only. Main courses: $4–$9 brunch, $7:50–$9.50 lunch
and dinner. MC, V. Tues–Fri. 5:30–10pm, Sat–Sun 10am–4pm, 5:30–10pm.
Bus: 22 or 30. ITALIAN.

Usually we're under the impression that San Francisco needs other
cute Italian cafe like it needs a tsunami headed its way. Well, it may
not happen often, but we were wrong. Owner Ken Zankel and
Spago-sired chef Andrea Rappaport have combined forces to create
one of the city's top new Italian restaurants. Zinzino may look like
a tiny trattoria from the outside, but you could fit a small nuclear
sub in the space from the sun-drenched facade to the shaded back
patio of this former Laundromat.

Italian movie posters, magazines, and furnishings evoke memories of past vacations, but we rarely recall the food in Italy being this
good (and certainly not this cheap). Start off with the crispy calamari
with a choice of herbed aioli or tomato sauces (second only to Scala's
Earth and Turf), the roasted jumbo prawns wrapped in crisp
pancetta and bathed in a tangy balsamic reduction sauce, or the
peculiar-tasting shaved fennel and mint salad—or try them all.
Rappaport is giving Zuñi Café a run for its money with her version
of roasted half chicken, the most tender bird we've ever tasted ("It's
all the wood-fired oven," she admits); the accompanying goat cheese
salad and potato frisee were also superb. The perfect light lunch for
two is a half eggplant, half house-spiced Italian sausage pizza (a mere
$4.50 per person), savored with the requisite glass of Chianti at the
marble-topped wine bar. The huge focaccia sandwiches are also a big
hit with the handful of locals who are privy to this San Francisco
sleeper.

INEXPENSIVE

✪ **Doidge's.** 2217 Union St. (between Fillmore and Steiner sts.). ☎ **415/
921-2149.** Reservations accepted and essential on weekends. Breakfast
$5–$10; lunch $5–$8. MC, V. Mon–Fri 8am–1:45pm, Sat–Sun 8am–2:45pm.
Bus: 41 or 45. AMERICAN.

Doidge's is sweet, small, and always packed, serving up one of the
better breakfasts in San Francisco since 1971. Doidge's fame is based
on eggs Benedict; eggs Florentine runs a close second, prepared
with thinly sliced Motherlode ham. Invariably the menu includes a

gourmet omelet packed with luscious combinations, and to delight the kid in you, hot chocolate comes in your very own teapot. The six seats at the original mahogany counter are still the most coveted by locals.

S La Canasta. 2219 Filbert St. (at Fillmore St.). ☎ **415/921-3003.** Main courses $2.80–$6.15. No credit cards. Mon–Sat 11am–10pm. Bus: 22, 41, or 45. MEXICAN.

Unless you forge to the Mission District, burritos don't get much better (or bigger) than those served here at this tiny takeout establishment where you can stuff yourself with a huge chicken burrito for a mere $4.80. There are no seats here, though, so you'll just have to find another place to devour your grub; fortunately, the Marina Green is a short walk away and offers a million-dollar view no restaurant can boast. There is another location at 3006 Buchanan St. (at Union Street; ☎ 415/474-2627).

6 Haight-Ashbury

INEXPENSIVE

✪ Cha Cha Cha. 1801 Haight St. (at Schrader St.). ☎ **415/386-5758.** Reservations not accepted. Tapas $4–$7; main courses $9–$13. No credit cards. Mon–Sun 11:30am–4pm; Sun–Thurs 5–11pm, Fri–Sat 5–11:30pm. Muni Metro: N line. Bus: 6, 7, 66, 71, or 73. CARIBBEAN.

This is one of our all-time favorite places to come for dinner, but it's not for everybody. Cha Cha Cha is not a meal, it's an *experience*. Put your name on the mile-long list, crowd into the minuscule bar, and drink sangria while you wait (and fight not to spill when you get bumped by all the young, attractive patrons who are also waiting). When you do finally get seated (it usually takes at least an hour), you'll dine in a loud (and we mean *loud*) dining room with Santeria altars, banana trees, and plastic tropical tablecloths. The best thing to do is order from the tapas menu and share the dishes family style. The fried calamari, fried new potatoes, Cajun shrimp, and mussels in saffron broth are all bursting with flavor and are accompanied by rich, luscious sauces—but whatever you choose, you can't go wrong. This is the kind of place where you take friends in a partying mood, let your hair down, and make an evening of it. If you want all the flavor without the festivities, come during lunch.

S Zona Rosa. 1797 Haight St. (at Shrader St.). ☎ **415/668-7717.** Burritos $3.45–$4.83. No credit cards. Daily 11am–10:30pm. Muni Metro: N line. Bus: 6, 7, 66, 71, or 73. MEXICAN.

This is a great place to stop and get a cheap (and healthful) bite. The most popular items here are the burritos, which are made to order and include your choice of beans (refried, whole pinto, or black), meats, or vegetarian ingredients. You can sit on a stool at the window and watch all the Haight Street freaks strolling by, relax at one of five colorful interior tables, or take it to go and head to Golden Gate Park (it's just two blocks away). Zona Rosa is one of the best burrito stores around.

7 Fisherman's Wharf

EXPENSIVE

Alioto's. Fisherman's Wharf (at Taylor St.). ☎ **415/673-0183.** Reservations recommended. Main courses $7–$14 at lunch; dinner $10–$50. AE, CB, DC, DISC, MC, V. Mon–Sun 11am–11pm. Cable car: Powell-Hyde line. Bus: 30 or 42. SEAFOOD.

One of San Francisco's oldest restaurants, run by one of the city's most prominent families, the Aliotos, this Fisherman's Wharf landmark has a long-standing reputation for serving the Bay's best cioppino. The curbside crab stand, Oysteria Deli, and new Steam Kettle Bar are great for a quick, inexpensive dose of San Francisco's finest; for more formal and fancy selections, continue up the carpeted stairs to the multilevel, harbor-view dining room. Don't mess around with the menu: It's the Dungeness crab you're after. Cracked, caked, stuffed, or stewed, its impossible to get your fill, so bring plenty of money—particularly if you intend to order from Alioto's prodigious (and pricey) wine list. If you happen to be insane and don't care for cracked crab, the griddle-fried sand dabs and rex sole served with tartar sauce are also quite good.

MODERATE

Cafe Pescatore. 2455 Mason St. (at North Point St.). ☎ **415/561-1111.** Reservations recommended. Main courses $3.95–$7.95 breakfast, $10–$16 lunch or dinner. AE, DC, DISC, MC, V. Mon–Thurs 11:30am–10pm, Fri 11:30am–11pm; Sat–Sun 7am–3pm brunch, 3–5pm cafe menu; Sat 5–11pm, Sun 5–10pm. Cable Car: Powell-Mason line. Bus: 42, 15, or 39. ITALIAN.

Though San Francisco locals are a rarity at Cafe Pescatore, most agree that if they had to dine at Fisherman's Wharf, this cozy trattoria would be their first choice. Two walls of sliding glass doors offer pseudo-sidewalk seating when the weather's warm, although heavy vehicular traffic can detract from the alfresco experience. The general consensus is to order anything that's cooked in the open kitchen's wood-fired oven, such as the pizzas and roasts. A big hit with tourists is the calzone primavera—a pizza envelope sealed around artichokes, sweet yellow peppers, spinach, and goat cheese; the verde pizza (pesto-flavored prawns and spinach) and huge servings of roast chicken are also safe bets.

8   North Beach

EXPENSIVE

Bix. 56 Gold St. (between Sansome and Montgomery sts.). ☎ **415/433-6300.** Reservations recommended. Main courses $5–$12 lunch, $11–$25 dinner. AE, CB, DC, DISC, MC, V. Mon–Thurs 11:30am–11pm, Fri–Sat 11:30am–midnight, Sun 5–10pm. Bus: 15, 30, 41, or 45. CALIFORNIA.

If you feel like dressin' up and hittin' the town, this suave little back-alley bar and restaurant is a good place to start. Fashioned after a 1920s supper club, Bix is better known for its martinis than for its menu. Curving Honduran mahogany, massive silver columns, and art deco–style lighting set the stage for dancing to live music, though most locals settle for chatting with the friendly bartenders and noshing on appetizers. While the ultra-stylish setting tends to overshadow the food, Bix actually serves some pretty good grub. The lobster linguine with fresh prawns and mussels in a sun-dried tomato broth is the undisputed favorite, followed by the grilled filet mignon with mushrooms and chicken hash à la Bix. And for that special occasion, how can you say no to a round of $118 Beluga caviar on toast?

Cypress Club. 500 Jackson St. (between Montgomery St. and Columbus Ave.). ☎ **415/296-8555.** Reservations recommended. Main courses $23–$28. AE, CB, DC, MC, V. Sun–Thurs 5:30–10pm, Fri–Sat 5:30–11pm. Bus: 15 or 41. AMERICAN.

Combine Alladin's bedchamber, a handful of Far Side cartoons, and few hits of acid, and you still won't match the Daliesque decor of this pseudo supper club. It's not hard to find; just look for the tourists peering in the windows. Gilt banquettes, bulbous gilt columns, and udder-shaped light fixtures covered in billowing fabric create a lavish neo-Arabian atmosphere that, if you're in the neighborhood, is definitely worth a gander. Most of the regular clientele, dressed to blend, saunters around the bar. Those who wish to dine might start with foie gras, Dungeness crab rillette, or the sea scallops with curry, lemongrass, mango, and chervil. Main courses are equally extravagant, including the lobster with lemon emulsion and shaved black truffle; the maple-cured pork chop with pecan pancakes, collard greens, and grilled apple; or the wood-roasted chicken with wild mushrooms and rosemary soubise. Desserts are as creative as the decor.

Maykadeh. 470 Green St. (between Kearny St. and Grant Ave.). ☎ **415/ 362-8286.** Reservations recommended. Main courses $7.50–$16. MC, V. Mon– Fri 11:30am–2:30pm; Mon–Thurs 5–10:30pm, Fri 5–11pm, Sat noon–11pm, Sun noon–10:30pm. Bus: 15 or 41. PERSIAN/MIDDLE EASTERN.

If you're looking to add a little adventure to your evening dinner plans, this is the place. Surrounded by a sea of Italian bistros is one of San Francisco's best and most elegant Persian restaurants. The Middle East may no longer be the culinary capital of the world, but at Maykadeh you can still sample the exotic flavors that character- ize Persian cuisine. Of the dozen or so appetizers offered on the menu, some of the best are the eggplant with mint garlic sauce, the stuffed grape leaves, and the lamb tongue with lime juice, sour cream, and saffron (c'mon, live a little). About eight mesquite-grilled items are offered, including filet of lamb marinated in lime, home- made yogurt, saffron, and onions. House specialties include half a dozen vegetarian dishes, such as the eggplant braised with saffron, fresh tomato, and dried lime.

✪ **Moose's.** 1652 Stockton St. (between Filbert and Union sts.). ☎ **415/ 989-7800.** Reservations recommended. Main courses $8.50–$25. AE, CB, DC, MC, V. Mon–Thurs 11:30am–11pm; Fri–Sat 11:30am–midnight, Sun 10:30am– 11pm. Bus: 15, 30, 41, or 45. CALIFORNIA.

You'll see the big blue neon Moose out front long before you pass through the doors, and once inside you'll notice you're in the larg- est dining room in North Beach. This is where Nob Hill socialites and local politicians come to dine and be seen. But Moose's is not just an image. In fact, the dining room itself is rather sparse and unintimate, but the food, well, that's a different story. Everything that comes out of Moose's kitchen is way above par. The appetiz- ers are innovative, fresh, and well balanced (try Mediterranean fish soup with rouille and croutons that's cooked in the wood-fired oven), and the main courses (especially the meats) are perfectly pre- pared. The menu changes every few months and might include a grilled veal chop with potato galette and a variety of pasta, chicken, and fish dishes.

The bar, separated from the main dining room by a low, frosted- glass partition, remains busy long after the kitchen closes. Jazz featuring piano and bass is played there nightly.

MODERATE

Enrico's. 504 Broadway (at Kearny St.). ☎ **415/982-6223.** Reservations rec- ommended. Main courses $8–$13 lunch, $13–$19 dinner. AE, DISC, MC, V. Mon–Sun noon–11pm, Fri–Sat noon–2am; bar daily noon–2am. Bus: 12, 15, 30, or 83. MEDITERRANEAN.

Though it's taking its sweet time, North Beach's bawdy stretch of Broadway is on the road to rehabilitation. Helping things along is the newly refurbished version of Enrico's, a glitzy sidewalk restaurant and supper club that was once *the* place to hang out before Broadway took its seedy downward spiral. Families may want to skip this one, but anyone with an appreciation for live jazz (played nightly), late-night noshing, and weirdo-watching from the outdoor patio would be quite content spending an alfresco evening under the heat lamps. Chewy brick-oven pizza, zesty tapas, and even a good ole pepper-encrusted top sirloin with garlic mashed potatoes are hot items on the menu. The best part? No cover charge and killer burgers are served until 2am.

Little City Antipasta Bar. 673 Union St. (at Powell St.). ☎ **415/434-2900.** Reservations accepted only for parties of 6 or more. Main courses $13–$15. AE, MC, V. Daily 11:30am–midnight (bar 11:30am–2am). Cable car: Mason St. Bus: 15, 30, 41, or 45. MEDITERRANEAN/ITALIAN.

Like the name suggestions, this stylish, brick-walled beauty of a restaurant specializes in antipasto dishes—dozens of them. During the day it's mostly vacant, but come nightfall the place quickly fills with fashion-conscious swingers, who like to stroll in late and nosh on the baked brie and roasted garlic (served with plenty of bread). The Manila clams, prawns borracho (marinated in tequila, chiles, garlic, and lime), and grilled baby artichokes with a tomato-tarragon aioli are also good bets. The best pasta is tortellini covered with a sauce of Gorgonzola, roasted red bell peppers, and toasted walnuts. Other dishes (which change daily) might include five grilled pork chops with spicy apple chutney, or salmon baked in parchment with a Burmese marinade of onion and oyster sauce, turmeric, and jalapeños. The sacripantina (rum-soaked sponge cake layered with zabaglione) is a must.

Tommaso's. 1042 Kearny St. (at Broadway). ☎ **415/398-9696.** Reservations not accepted. Pasta and pizza $8–$17; main courses $10–$14. MC, V. Tues–Sat 5–10:30pm; Sun 4–9:30pm. Closed Dec 15–Jan 15. Bus: 15 or 41. ITALIAN.

From the street Tommaso's looks wholly unappealing; a drab, windowless brown facade sandwiched between sex shops. Then why are people always waiting in line to get in? Because everyone knows that Tommaso's bakes San Francisco's best pizza, and has for decades. The center of attention in the downstairs dining room is the chef, who continuously tosses huge hunks of garlic and mozzarella onto pizzas before sliding them into the oak-burning brick oven. Nineteen different toppings make pizza the dish of choice, even though

Italian classics such as veal marsala, chicken cacciatore, and a superb lasagna are also available (wonderful calzone, too). Half bottles of house wines are sold, as are homemade cannoli and good Italian coffee. If you can overlook the seedy surroundings, this fun, boisterous restaurant is great place to take the family.

INEXPENSIVE

Gira Polli. 659 Union St. (at Columbus Ave.). ☎ **415/434-4472.** Reservations recommended. Main courses $7.50–$12.50. AE, MC, V. Mon–Sun 4:30–9:30pm. Bus: 15, 30, 39, 41, or 45. ITALIAN.

I (Matthew) used to live three blocks from Gira Polli, and man-oh-man do I miss it. Whenever I'd rent a video, I'd drop by here for the Gira Polli Special: a foiled-lined bag filled with half a wood-fired chicken (scrumptious), Palermo potatoes (the best in the city), a fresh garden salad, perfectly cooked vegetables, and a soft roll—all for under $10. Next, I'd nab a bottle of good, cheap wine from the liquor store next door, take my goodies home, disconnect the phone, and love life for a while. (Tip: On sunny days, there's no better place in North Beach for a picnic lunch than Washington Square right across the street.)

✪ **L'Osteria del Forno.** 519 Columbus Ave. (between Green and Union sts.). ☎ **415/982-1124.** Sandwiches $4.50–$8; pizzas $10–$13; main courses $2.50–$7.95. No credit cards. Mon–Wed 11am–10pm, Fri–Sat 11am–10:30pm, Sun noon–10pm. Bus: 15 or 41. ITALIAN.

L'Osteria del Forno may only be slightly larger than a walk-in closet, but it's one of the top three Italian restaurants in North Beach. Peer in the window facing Columbus Avenue, and you'll probably see two Italian women with their hair up, sweating from the heat of their brick-lined oven that cranks out the best focaccia (and focaccia sandwiches) in the city. There's no pomp or circumstance involved: Locals come here strictly to eat. The menu features a variety of superb pizzas and fresh pastas, plus a few daily specials (pray for the roast pork braised in milk). Small baskets of warm focaccia bread keep you going till the entrées arrive, which should always be accompanied by a glass of house red.

Mario's Bohemian Cigar Store. 566 Columbus Ave. ☎ **415/362-0536.** Sandwiches $5–$6. No credit cards. Daily 10am–11pm. Closed Dec 24–Jan 1. Bus: 15, 30, 41, or 45. ITALIAN.

Across the street from Washington Square is one of North Beach's most popular neighborhood hangouts: Mario's. The century-old bar—small, well worn, and perpetually busy—is best known for its focaccia sandwiches, including meatball or eggplant. Wash it all down with an excellent cappuccino or a house Campari as you watch the tourists stroll by. And no, they don't sell cigars.

⊖ Pasta Pomodoro. 655 Union St. (at Columbus Ave.). ☎ **415/399-0300.** Main courses $3.95–$6.50. No checks or credit cards. Mon–Fri 11am–11pm, Sat noon–midnight, Sun noon–11pm. ITALIAN.

If you're looking for a good, cheap meal in North Beach, this place across from Washington Square can't be beat. There's usually a 20-minute wait for a table, but after you're seated you'll be surprised at how promptly you're served. Every dish is fresh and sizable, and best of all, they're a third of what you'll pay elsewhere. Winners include the spaghetti frutti di mare, with calamari, mussels, scallops, tomato, garlic and wine, or cavatappi pollo with roast chicken, sun-dried tomatoes, cream, mushrooms, and Parmesan—both are under $7. Avoid the cappellini Pomodoro or ask for extra sauce—it tends to be dry. Their second location, at 2027 Chestnut St. (at Fillmore) (☎ 415/474-3400), is equally good, but cramped and noisy.

9 Chinatown

INEXPENSIVE

✪ House of Nanking. 919 Kearny St. (at Columbus Ave.). ☎ **415/421-1429.** Reservations not accepted. Main courses $4.95–$7.95. No credit cards. Mon–Fri. 11am–10pm, Sat noon–10pm, Sun 4–10pm. Bus: 9, 12, 15, or 30. CHINESE.

To the unknowing passerby, the shoebox-sized House of Nanking has "greasy dive" written all over it. To its legion of fans, however, the wait—sometimes up to an hour—is worth what's on the plate. Located on the edge of Chinatown just off Columbus Avenue, this inconspicuous little diner is one of San Francisco's worst-kept secrets. When the line is reasonable, we drop by for a plate of pot stickers (*still* the best we've ever tasted) and chef/owner Peter Fang's signature shrimp-and-green-onion pancake served with peanut sauce. Trust the waiter when he recommends a special, or simply point to what looks good on someone else's table. Seating is tight, so prepare to be bumped around a bit, and don't expect good service; it's all part of the Nanking experience.

Sam Wo. 813 Washington St. (by Grant Ave.). ☎ **415/982-0596.** Reservations not accepted. Main courses $4–$5. No credit cards. Mon–Sat 11am–3am, Sun 12:30–9:30pm. Bus: 15, 30, 41, or 45. CHINESE.

Very handy for late-nighters, Sam's is a total dive that's well known and often packed. The restaurant's two pocket-size dining rooms are located on top of each other, on the second and third floors—take the stairs past the first-floor kitchen. You'll have to share a table, but this place is for mingling almost as much as for eating. The house specialty is jook (known as congee in its native Hong Kong)—a thick rice gruel flavored with fish, shrimp, chicken, beef, or pork; the best is Sampan, made with rice and seafood. Try sweet-and-sour pork rice, wonton soup with duck, or a roast-pork/rice-noodle roll. More traditional fried noodles and rice plates are available too. Chinese doughnuts sell for 50¢ each.

10 South of Market

EXPENSIVE

✪ **Boulevard.** 1 Mission St. (at Embarcadero and Steuart St.). ☎ **415/543-6084.** Reservations recommended. Main courses $17.75–$22. AE, DC, MC, V. Mon–Fri 11:30am–2pm; daily 5:30–10:30pm. Bus: 15, 30, 32, 42, or 45. AMERICAN.

Master restaurant designer Pat Kuleto and Chef Nancy Oaks have teamed up to create one of San Francisco most exciting new restaurants. Art nouveau interior-vaulted brick ceilings, floral-design banquettes, and fluid, tulip-shaped lamps set a dramatic scene for Oaks's equally impressive dishes. Start with the delicate, soft egg ravioli with spinach, ricotta, and shaved white truffles, then embark on such wonderful concoctions as wood-oven roasted sea bass on a bed of sun-dried tomato and roasted garlic mashed potatoes (she makes a mean cured pork loin, too). Vegetarian items, such as roasted portobello mushrooms layered with mashed sweet potatoes, are also offered. Three levels of formality—bar, open kitchen, and main dining room—keep things from getting too snobby. Though steep prices prevent most from making Boulevard a regular gig, you'd be hard pressed to find a better place for a special, fun-filled occasion.

✪ **Hawthorn Lane.** 22 Hawthorn Lane (at Howard St. between Second and Third sts.). ☎ **415/777-9779.** Reservations recommended. Jacket appropriate but not required. Main courses $9.50–$13 lunch, $19.50–$24 dinner. CB, D, DC, JCB, MC, V. Mon–Fri 11:30am–2pm, Sun–Thurs 5:30–10pm. BART: Montgomery station. Muni Metro: F, J, K, L, M, or N. Bus: 12, 30, 45, or 76. CALIFORNIA.

Ever since Anne and David Gingrass left Postrio, the food there has never quite recovered. Thankfully they're heading the kitchen at Hawthorn Lane, their new SoMa restaurant strategically located a block away from the Museum of Modern Art. Anne and David are a culinary team who prepare their menu based on the best and freshest ingredients available. Menus change with the seasons and reflect the Asian and European influences that made them famous under Wolfgang Puck. Step through the doors and you'll immediately notice this restaurant was planned by seasoned professionals. The bar area is comfortable and inviting, with both cocktail tables and bar seating; continue on to the dining room, where earthquake reinforcement beams divide the room in a way that is not only functional, but is also decorative and creates the illusion that each section is a more intimate environment. And the decor is just right: not too fancy or pretentious, but well-lit and decorated with bright artwork, fresh floral arrangements, and a leaf motif throughout. But where the Gingrass's expertise really shines is in the food. The bread basket that arrives at your table is overflowing with fresh-baked goods of all tastes and types. Each dish arrives beautifully presented without being too contrived, but usually with a whimsical accent, such as a leaf-shaped pastry or a bird made of a carrot sliver. Dishes are remarkably well balanced, and accompaniments are often more exciting than the main course itself. If it's on the menu, don't pass up the black cod appetizer served with a miso glaze and spinach rolls. The light, flaky seafood tempura with a vegetable salad is another show-stopper, as is the main course of quail glazed with maple and perched on the most delightful potato gratin. Desserts are as good to look at as they are to eat.

Kyo-Ya. In the Sheraton Palace Hotel, 2 New Montgomery St. (at Market St.). ☎ **415/546-5090.** Reservations recommended. Sushi $4–$8; main courses $20–$35; fixed-price menus $45–$65. AE, CB, DC, JCB, MC, V. Tues–Fri 11:30am–2pm and Mon–Sat 6–10pm. All Market St. trams. All Market St. buses. JAPANESE.

This restaurant offers an authentic Japanese experience, from the decor down to the service and most assuredly the food. Specialties feature the freshest sushi and sashimi, as well as grilled and nabemono dishes (kettle dishes cooked at the table). To start, try any of the appetizers and move on to the grilled butterfish with miso sauce. Complete dinners include kobachi, soup, rice, pickles, and dessert.

MODERATE

✪ **Bizou.** 598 Fourth St. (at Brannan St.). ☎ **415/543-2222.** Reservations recommended. Main courses $10.50–$17.50. AE, MC, V. Mon–Fri 11:30am–2:30pm; Mon–Thurs 5:30–10pm, Fri–Sat 5:30–10:30pm. Bus: 15, 30, 32, 42, or 45. FRENCH/ITALIAN.

Around town almost everyone sings Bizou's praises and with good reason: The restaurant's golden yellow walls and terra-cotta ceiling are warmly lit by antique light fixtures and art deco wall sconces, and provide an atmosphere perfect for a first date or an evening out with Mom. The wait staff is friendly and professional, and all the ingredients are fresh and in creative combinations. Our only complaint is that literally every dish is so rich and powerfully flavorful (including the salads), it's a bit of a sensory overload. The menu's starters include an Italian flatbread with caramelized onions, fresh herbs, and Parmesan cheese, pizzas, grilled calamari with a citrus salsa and salsa verde, and batter-fried green beans with dipping sauce. The main courses may include a sautéed sea bass with olive couscous, fennel, bay leaf, and dried orange peel or grilled veal tenderloin with sautéed spinach, and garlic mashed potatoes bathing in a buttery mustard sauce. All main course portions are substantial here, so don't overindulge on appetizers. And save a little room for dessert— the meringue covered in chocolate and topped with coffee ice cream and candied almonds is quite a treat. Too bad there are no cots in a back room here—after your meal, you'll need a nap.

Cha Am. 701 Folsom St. (at Third St.). ☎ **415/546-9711.** Reservations recommended for 3 or more. Main courses $5.95–$6.95 lunch, $6.95–$14.95 dinner. AE, MC, V, DC. Mon–Sat 11am–10pm, Sat–Sun 5–10pm, happy hour Mon–Fri 3–7pm. Bus: 9 or 15. THAI.

Cha Am is one of those sleeper restaurants you'd never find unless someone told you about it. Hidden behind the Moscone Center, this wonderful little Thai restaurant does a brisk lunch business when large conventions are in town (how conventioneers know about this place, we have no idea). A good opener is the Cha Am prawn appetizer: stuffed, grilled prawns layered with a spicy tamarind sauce. Other favorites are the mu yang (marinated sweet and sour pork chops) and pla sam rod (a whole striped bass that's deboned and deep fried until crispy, then topped with a spicy sweet-and-sour sauce)—a steal at $10.95. Service by the mostly Thai staff is efficient and friendly (be sure to ask them about the daily specials), and prices are surprisingly reasonable.

✪ **Fringale Restaurant.** 570 Fourth St. (between Brannen and Bryant sts.). ☎ **415/543-0573.** Reservations recommended. Main courses $9–$18; lunch $4–$12. AE, MC, V. Mon–Fri 11:30am–2:30pm; Mon–Sat 5:30–10:30pm. Bus: 30 or 45. FRENCH.

One of San Francisco's top restaurants, Fringale—French colloquial for "sudden urge to eat"—has enjoyed a week-long waiting list since the day chef/co-owner Gerald Hirigoyen first opened this small SoMa bistro. Sponged, eggshell-blue walls and other muted sand

and earth tones provide a serene dining environment, which is all but shattered when the 15-table room inevitably fills with Hirigoyen's fans. For starters, try the potato and goat cheese galette with black olives or the sheep's milk cheese and prosciutto tureen with figs and greens. Among the dozen or so main courses you might find a filet of tuna basquaise, pork tenderloin confit with onion and apple marmalade, or macaroni gratin with mushrooms. Desserts are worth savoring, too, particularly the hazelnut and roasted almond mousse cake or the signature crème brûlée with vanilla bean. The mostly French waiters provide uncharacteristically charming service, and prices are surprisingly reasonable.

✪ **Lulu.** 816 Folsom St. (at Fourth St.). ☎ **415/495-5775.** Reservations recommended. Main $7–$13 lunch courses $9–$17 dinner. AE, MC, V. Mon–Fri 7am–11pm, Sat–Sun 9am–10:30pm. Bus: 15, 30, 32, 42, or 45. CONTINENTAL.

It's hard not to love LuLu, even though there's always a long wait (reserve a table in advance or starve!), and it's one of the noisier rooms in town. The energy of the enormous, converted warehouse dining room is the thing: the expansive view of the sunken seating and open kitchen; the pizzas sliding in and out of the wood-fired oven; and the chefs communicating via headsets. It makes dining out an event. The main room seats 170, but even as you sit amidst a sea of stylish diners, the room somehow feels warm and convivial. And then there's the food, which is consistently delicious. Locals return again and again for the roasted mussels piled high on an iron skillet; the chopped salad with lemon, anchovies, and tomatoes; the pork loin with fennel, garlic, and olive oil; and any of the other wonderful dishes. Everything is served "family style" and is meant to be shared. Save room for dessert; opt for the gooey chocolate cake that oozes with chocolate to be scooped up with the side of melting ice cream. The adjoining cafe serves breakfast, and much of the menu remains at lunch, with the addition of gourmet sandwiches.

Yank Sing. 427 Battery St. (between Clay and Washington sts.). ☎ **415/781-1111.** Dim sum $2–$4.75 for 3 to 4 pieces. AE, DC, MC, V. Mon–Fri 11am–3pm. Cable car: California. Bus: 1 or 42. CHINESE.

Loosely translated as "a delight of the heart," Yank Sing does dim sum like no other restaurant we've visited. Poor quality of ingredients has always been the shortcoming of all but the most expensive Chinese restaurants, but Yank Sing manages to be both affordable *and* excellent. Confident, experienced servers take the nervousness out of novices—they're good at guessing your gastric threshold. Most dim sum dishes are dumplings, filled with tasty concoctions of pork, beef, fish, or vegetables. Congees (porridges), spareribs, stuffed crab claws, scallion pancakes, shrimp balls, pork buns, and other palate-pleasers complete the menu. Like most good dim sum meals, at Yank Sing you get to choose the small dishes from a cart that's continually wheeled around the dining room. Tip: Sit by the kitchen and you're guaranteed to get it while it's hot. A second location is at 49 Stevenson St. (off First St.) (☎ 415/ 541-4949).

INEXPENSIVE

Manora's. 1600 Folsom St. (at 12th St.). ☎ **415/861-6224.** Main courses $5.95–$10. MC, V. Mon–Fri 11:30am–2:30pm and 5–10pm; Sat 5–10:30pm; Sun 5–10pm. THAI.

Manora's cranks out some of the best Thai in town and is well worth a jaunt to its SoMa location. But this is no relaxed dining affair. It's perpetually packed (unless you come early), and you'll be seated sardine-like at one of the cramped but well-appointed tables. During the dinner rush, the noise level can make conversation almost impossible among larger parties, but the food is so darn good, you'll probably prefer to turn your head toward your plate and stuff your face. Start with a Thai iced tea or coffee and one of the tangy soups or the chicken satay, which comes with a decadent peanut sauce. Follow up with any of the wonderful dinner dishes—which should be shared—and a side of rice. There are enless options, including a vast array of vegetarian plates. Every remarkably flavorful dish arrives almost seconds after you order it, which is great if you're hungry, a bummer if you were planning a long, leisurely dinner. Come before seven or after nine if you don't want a loud, rushed meal.

11 Mission District

EXPENSIVE

✪ **Flying Saucer.** 1000 Guerrero St. (at 22nd St.). ☎ **415/641-9955.** Reservations recommended. Main courses $15–$24. No credit cards. Tues–Sun 5:30–9:30pm. FRENCH.

Outrageously yet artfully presented food is the hallmark of this Mission District fixture. Peering into the glassed-walled kitchen, diners can catch the kitchen staff leaning over plates, carefully standing a jumbo prawn on its head atop a baked column of potato polenta. Fish, beef, and fowl dishes are competently grilled, baked, or flamed before being surrounded by a flurry of sauces and garnishes. While the pricey food is certainly intense and flavorful, the overwhelming sensation at this bistro is visual. The party extends from the plate to the decor, where plastic flying saucers mingle with colorful murals and creative lighting. The menu changes frequently, and there are almost always specials. If you ask your waiter to bring you the chef's most flamboyant-*looking* offering, chances are you won't be disappointed. Reservations are essential, as is a blind eye to the sometimes infuriatingly snotty service.

MODERATE

Val 21. 995 Valencia St. (at 21st St.). ☎ **415/821-6622.** Reservations recommended. Main courses $8–$18. MC, V. Mon–Fri 5:30–10pm, Sat–Sun 10am–2pm and 5:30–10pm. Muni Metro: J line to 16th St. Station. CALIFORNIA.

Hip, eclectic decor, perpetually friendly service, and hefty portions of multiethnic fare have made Val 21 one of the Mission District's most popular restaurants. The menu changes frequently, although you might find such dishes as artichoke empanada, southwestern blackened chicken, or grilled salmon in a red curry sauce (plenty of vegetarian plates, too). Sometimes the menu gets a little too creative, sending mixed messages to your mouth, but the overall dining experience makes it worth the trip.

12 Around Town

EXPENSIVE

✪ **Alain Rondelli.** 126 Clement St. (between Second and Third aves.). ☎ **415/387-0408.** Reservations necessary Fri and Sat. Main courses $16–$19, tasting menu from $45. MC, V. Tues–Sun 5:30–10:30pm. Bus: 2 or 38. FRENCH.

French chef Rondelli does more than simply serve exquisite and innovative French food; he dishes up a gastronomic experience you're likely to dream about for years to come. You may order à la carte, but you'd be better off ordering from the 6-, 9-, 12-, or 20-course tasting menus (for the entire table only)—and to complete the experience, wine can be ordered by the half glass. One spoonful of the calamari—a "salad" of calamari, jalapeño, mint floating in a heavenly tomato water, and topped off with fresh carrot juice—and you'll be inclined to jump out of your chair and scream "*c'est magnifique!*" The house-made foie gras stuffed with black mission figs and served over warm brioche will melt you back into your seat, until you are again tempted to raise your fork for the crispy-skin salmon with quinoa pilaf and bell pepper, followed by the "Agneau" lamb, pot au Feu, oregano, lemon, and horseradish. Take a breather with poire and Roquefort (pear and Roquefort with champagne vinegar and black pepper gastric) before embarking on one of the sumptuous desserts. The grandest conjuration of all is that after such a didactic and tantalizing feast, you'll feel light as a feather, entirely satiated but not overly full, and you'll float out the front doors onto Clement Street as relaxed as if you just had a massage. If you're debating between dining here and La Folie, bear in mind that Rondelli's portions are smaller and the atmosphere is far more formal.

✪ **Charles Nob Hill.** 1250 Jones St. (at Clay St.). ☎ **415/771-5400.** Main courses $16–$26. AE, DC, MC, V. Daily 5:30–10pm. Cable car: California and Powell-Hyde lines. Bus: 1, 12, 27, 83. FRENCH.

We never knew beef could actually melt in your mouth until Aqua owner Charles Condy bought historic restaurant "Le Club" and introduced us to Aqua's executive chef Michael Mina's culinary magic (it really did melt!). The menu lists the "classically inspired light French fare," which is served in two divided dining rooms with velvet banquettes, fresh floral arrangements, and the loud buzz of the older socialite crowd. Start with a bowl of the soup of the day. When we dined here it was a spinach and roasted garlic soup with cumin-scented rock shrimp and crumbled bacon that was surprisingly beautiful, electric green, and overflowing with flavor. Scallop and black truffle pot pie is another must-try. And for the main course, you might choose the Poele (melt-in-your-mouth) of beef tenderloin with wild mushroom and potato torte, balsamic glazed onions, and foie gras, or a delicate seared red snapper with chive and preserved lemon juice, artichoke, and chanterelle ragout. Although the room itself is romantic, the atmosphere and noise level are too convivial for real intimacy. But it sure is fun to watch everyone else. Wrap up the evening with the outstanding pear and Roquefort tart. Lunch hours were in the works when this book went to press, so call for details. And no matter what, don't drive here unless you valet it; you may spend over an hour looking for parking.

✪ **Ritz-Carlton Dining Room.** 600 Stockton St. (at California St.). ☎ **415/296-7465.** Reservations recommended. Fixed-price menu $37–$57. AE, DC, DISC, MC, V. Mon–Sat 6am–10pm. Cable car: Powell-Hyde and Powell-Mason lines (direct stop). CALIFORNIA/FRENCH.

Never a hotel to do anything second best, when the Ritz-Carlton opened in 1991, it acquired one of the finest chefs in the country, Gary Danko, to help establish its dining room as one of the premier restaurants in San Francisco. And it worked.

The setting, as you would imagine, is regal and sumptuous: Crystal chandeliers, rich tapestries, elegant table settings, and live harp music reek of formality. The wait staff, trained to perfection by maître d' extraordinaire Nick Peyton, is equally impeccable. The star of this princely production, however, is Danko, winner of the 1995 James Beard Award—the Academy Award of the food world—for best chef in California. His penchant for seasonal Northern California produce combined with classic French techniques has drawn nothing but four-star reviews. Standout dishes include his pan-roasted squab stuffed with foie gras, leeks, and garlic confit, the warm grilled-quail salad with apricot-ginger chutney, and his legendary raspberry soufflé with fresh raspberry sauce. The menu, which changes monthly, offers a choice of three-, four-, or five-course dinners, the latter including wine paired with each course by Master Sommelier Emmanuel Kemiji for an additional $29. The dining room also features the country's only "rolling" cheese cart, laden with at least two dozen individually ripened cheeses.

MODERATE

Fog City Diner. 1300 Battery St. (at Lombard St.). ☎ **415/982-2000.** Reservations accepted. Main courses $11–$17. CB, DC, DISC, MC, V. Sun–Thurs 11:30am–11pm, Fri–Sat 11:30am–midnight. Bus: 42. AMERICAN.

Made famous by a Visa commercial, the restaurant looks like a genuine American metallic diner—but only from the outside. Inside, dark polished woods, inspired lighting, and a well-stocked raw bar tell you this is no hash-slinger.

Dressed-up dinner dishes include gourmet chili dogs, salads, sandwiches, burgers, pork chops, and pot roast. Fancier fish and meat meals include grilled catches of the day and thick-cut steaks. Lighter eaters can make a meal out of the long list of "small plates" that include sautéed mushrooms with garlic custard and seasoned walnuts; or quesadillas with chile peppers and almonds. The place is cute and the food is fine, but if your heart is set on coming here, do so at lunch—you'll be better off elsewhere if you want a special dinner.

✪ **42 Degrees.** 235 16th Street (at Illinois St., 1 block off Third St.). ☎ **415/777-5558.** Main courses $12.50–$18. Mon–Fri 11:30am–3pm; Wed–Sat 7–midnight. Reservations recommended. Bus: 22. MEDITERRANEAN.

Tucked behind the Esprit Outlet in the industrial area is the oh-so-chic jazz supper club 42 Degrees. A three-piece jazz trio sets the mood in the warehouselike, but velvet soft, two-story dining room. Sleek cocktailers hang out at the dark bar area, which specializes in scotches, cognacs, and a selection of small vintners' wines. The dining mezzanine has a men's smoking club feel with a great view of the Bay Bridge and the downstairs is all 1940s sophistication, from the red velvet curtains that frame 22-foot windows right down to the wait staff and clientele. There's also a dining patio that's a perfect spot for a sunny luncheon. Dishes are Mediterranean-influenced and the menu changes weekly, but usually includes house favorites such as hearts of romaine salad with Caesar dressing, marrow bones with toast, Atlantic salmon, and Niman-Schell meats. It's easier to book a table at lunch, but the time to come is for dinner when the chichi vibe is full-force.

Hyde Street Bistro. 1521 Hyde St. (between Pacific and Jackson sts.). ☎ **415/441-7778.** Reservations recommended. Main courses $12–$16. MC, V. Daily 5:30–10:30pm. Cable car: Powell-Mason and Powell-Hyde lines. CALIFORNIA/AUSTRIAN.

Small, intimate, and very European in style, the Hyde Street Bistro has been a neighborhood favorite for years. Ebullient chef/owner Albert Rainer combines his Austrian background with a California twist to create some truly captivating dishes such as strudel filled with a mélange of vegetables, and a roasted Sonoma chicken with a potato pancake and double blanched garlic. Of the many pasta dishes, Chef Rainer recommends ravioli with wild mushroom sauce, or penne with sausage, peppers, tomato, and eggplant. Save room for dessert; Ranier's brother Klaus works wonders with pastries. Parking in this neighborhood is ludicrous, so either splurge on valet or wear walking shoes.

Il Fornaio. Levi Plaza, 1265 Battery St. (bounded by Sansome, Battery, Union, and Greenwich sts.). ☎ **415/986-0100.** Prices $7.50–$18. AE, DC, MC, V. Mon–Thurs 7am–11pm; Fri–Sat 11:30am–midnight; Sun 9am–11pm. Bus: 12, 32, or 42. ITALIAN.

While we can't say Il Fornaio would be our choice if we could only eat at one spot for the rest of our lives, it's one of our favorite standbys, producing consistently good Italian fare at decent prices. Located in Levi Plaza a few minutes away from Pier 39, this trattoria has great atmosphere: It bustles, it's big, and though a little cramped, the decor is not overwhelming but smart Italian. By day it is buzzing with Financial District types and socialites, by night, with couples and gathering friends.

Stacks of fresh-baked Italian cookies behind glass greet you when you first walk through the door. If you don't have a reservation and can't wait to eat, pull up a stool at the marble-topped bar, where the view of the open kitchen and dining room is unobstructed. Better yet, on a sunny day, grab a patio table that looks onto Levi Plaza's fountain. The divided dining room, with high ceilings and enormous, Italian-style paintings, is also warm and convivial. The first of many delights is the basket of fresh-baked breads and breadsticks that arrive at your table accompanied by a dipping dish of olive oil. Complement them with any of the delicious salads or the daily soup (especially if it's carrot), then forge onward to any of the pastas, pizzas, or main courses. Our favorite is the rotisserie duck in balsamic vinegar, which Il Fornio somehow serves without all the fat you'd expect from duck and all the crispy skin you wish for. Desserts are decadent and wonderful. Try the tiramisu and a glass of rose grappa—a perfect way to end the meal. Breakfasts here are a treat as well.

Kabuto Sushi. 5116 Geary Blvd. (at 15th Ave.). ☎ **415/752-5652.** Sushi $3–$8; main courses $12–$20. AE, MC, V. Tues–Sat 5:30–11pm. Bus: 2, 28, or 38. JAPANESE.

For a town overflowing with seafood and pretentious taste buds, you'd think it'd be easier to find great sushi. But the truth is, finding an outstanding sushi restaurant in San Francisco is more challenging than spotting a parking space in Nob Hill. Still, chopsticking these fish-and-rice delicacies is one of the most joyous and adventurous ways to dine, and Kabuto is one of the best (and most expensive) places to do it. Chef Sachio Kojima, who presides over the small, ever-crowded sushi bar, constructs each dish with smooth, lightning-fast movements known only to master chefs. Last time we were here, we were lucky enough to sit next to some businessmen visiting from Japan who were ordering things we'd never seen before. We followed their lead and had perhaps the best sushi dinner to date. If you're big on wasabi, ask for the stronger stuff Kojima serves on request.

INEXPENSIVE

Hard Rock Café. 1699 Van Ness Ave. (at Sacramento St.). ☎ **415/885-1699.** Reservations sometimes accepted (depending on season). Main courses $5.50–$14. AE, MC, V. Sun–Thurs 11:30am–11pm, Fri–Sat 11:30am–midnight. Cable car: California. Bus: 1. AMERICAN.

Like its affiliated restaurants around the world, this loud, nostalgia-laden place offers big portions of decent food at moderate prices and plenty of blaring music to an almost exclusively tourist clientele. The real draw, of course, is the merchandise shop, which often has as long a line as the restaurant.

The cafe is decorated with gold records, historic front pages, and the usual "Save the Planet" clutter. The menu offers burgers, baby back ribs, grilled fish, chicken, salads, and sandwiches. Although it's nothing unique to San Francisco, the Hard Rock is a fine place to bring the kids and grab a bite.

✪ **Hong Kong Flower Lounge.** 5322 Geary Blvd. (between 17th and 18th aves.). ☎ **415/668-8998.** Most main dishes $5.95–$10.95; dim sum dishes $1.20–$3.20. Mon–Fri 11am–2:30pm, Sat–Sun 10am–2:30pm, daily 5–9:30pm. Bus: 1, 2, or 38. CHINESE/DIM SUM.

You know you're at a good Chinese restaurant when most people waiting for a table are Chinese. And if you come for dim sum, be prepared to stand in line because you're not the only one who's heard this is the best in town. The Hong Kong Flower Lounge has been one of our very favorite restaurants for years now. It's not the pink and green decor or the live fish swimming in the tank, or even the beautiful marble bathrooms; it's simply that every little dish that comes our way is so darn good. Don't pass up taro cake, salt-fried shrimp, shark-fin soup, and shrimp or beef crepes.

Swan Oyster Depot. 1517 Polk St. (between California and Sacramento sts.). ☎ **415/673-1101.** Reservations not accepted. Seafood cocktails $5–$8, clams and oysters on the half shell $6–$7.50 per half dozen. No credit cards. Mon–Sat 8am–5:30pm. Bus: 27. SEAFOOD.

Almost 85 years old and looking even older, Swan Oyster Depot is classic San Francisco. Opened in 1912, this tiny hole in the wall with the city's friendliest servers is little more than a narrow fish market that decided to slap down some stools. There are only 20 or so seats jammed cheek by jowl along a long marble bar. Most patrons come for a quick cup of chowder or a plate of half-shelled oysters that arrive chilling on crushed ice. The menu is limited to fresh crab, shrimp, oyster, and clam cocktails, Maine lobster, and Boston-style clam chowder. Fish is only available raw or smoked and to go. Beer and wine are available.

13 Gay-Friendly Restaurants

While you will see gay singles and couples at almost every restaurant in San Francisco, the following spots cater particularly to the gay set, but being gay is certainly not a requirement for enjoying them. Most are located in the Castro and all can be classified as inexpensive.

Café Flore. 2298 Market St. (at Noe St.). ☎ **415/621-8579.** Reservations not accepted. American breakfast $5.95; main courses $4.50–$7.50. No credit cards. Daily 7:30am–midnight. Muni Metro: F. Bus: 8. CALIFORNIA.

Sheathed with glass on three sides, and overlooking Market Street, Noe Street, and a verdant patio in back, Café Flore attracts young, bright, and articulate members of the gay (mostly male) community. Local wits refer to it as a place where body piercing is encouraged but not mandatory, although this kind of exhibitionism tends to be more prevalent in the evening than during the daytime.

Many of the menu items are composed of mostly organic ingredients, and include a succulent version of roasted (sometimes free-range) chicken, soups, pastas, and steaks. Café latte costs $2 a cup. Plan on hearing a lot of noise and possibly seeing a handsome young man sending not particularly furtive glances your way.

✪ "No Name." 2223 Market St. (between Sanchez and Noe sts.). ☎ **415/ 431-0692.** Reservations recommended. $12.95–$16.95. MC. V. Mon–Fri 11:30am–2:30pm, Sun 10am–2pm; Sun–Thurs 5:30–10pm, Fri–Sat 5:30–11pm. Muni Metro: F, L, K, or M. Bus: 8, 22, 24, or 37. CALIFORNIA.

It seems this new Castro area restaurant is already so popular, there's no big hurry to give it a name. Run by the owners of the infamous Cypress Club, the decor here is substantially less opulent than its counterpart, but the energy level is definitely more lively. Surrounded by hardwood floors, candles, streamlined modern light fixtures and loud music, festive gays and straights come here to cocktail on the heavy-handed specialty drinks and dine on grilled ahi tuna with pickled veggies and Canton noodles, or the ever popular roasted chicken with garlic mashed potatoes. This is currently *the* dining and schmoozing spot in the area.

Patio Café. 531 Castro St. (at 18th St.). ☎ **415/621-4640.** Reservations not accepted. Main courses $9.50–$12.50. AE, MC, V. Sun–Thurs 8am–10:30pm, Fri–Sat 8am–11pm. Bus: 24 or 33. AMERICAN.

Since the early 1970s, this Castro Street bar and restaurant had served as the rendezvous point for uncounted numbers of trysts, peccadilloes, and love affairs of all kinds that have blossomed within the premises. Originally established as The Baker's Café, it retains the original ovens that contributed to its early reputation, which are today purely decorative. Ringed with trellises and verdant plants, and set in the back yard of a cluster of shops, the patio features a glass roof (whose entertainment value derives from the heft and brawn of the staff, who climb skyward to manually crank it open during clement weather). Menu items include virtually any drink you can think of, and such dishes as Caesar salads, Chinese chicken salad (laced with fresh ginger), prime rib, roasted chicken, and grilled salmon with Cajun hollandaise sauce. The most popular drinks include a Melon Margarita ($3.75) and a Patio Mai-Tai ($4.75).

What to See & Do in San Francisco

S an Francisco's parks, museums, tours, and landmarks are favorite haunts for travelers the world over and offer an array of activities to suit every visitor. But it's not any particular activity or place that makes the city the most popular tourist destination in the world. It's San Francisco itself—its charm, its atmosphere, its perfect blend of big metropolis with small-town hospitality. No matter what you do while you're here—whether you spend all your time in central areas like Union Square or North Beach or explore the intricacies of outer neighborhoods—you're bound to collect a treasure of vacation memories that can only be found in this culturally rich, strikingly beautiful City by the Bay.

1 The Top Attractions

Alcatraz Island. Pier 41, near Fisherman's Wharf. ☎ **415/705-1045.** Admission (includes ferry trip and audio tour) $10 adults, $8.25 seniors 62 and older, $4.75 children 5–11. Winter daily 9:30am–2:45pm; summer daily 9:15am–4:15pm. Advance purchase advised. Ferries depart every half hour, at 15 and 45 minutes after the hour. Arrive at least 20 minutes before sailing time.

Visible from Fisherman's Wharf, Alcatraz Island (aka "The Rock") has seen a checkered history. It was discovered in 1775 by Juan Manuel Ayala, who named it after the many pelicans that nested on the island. From the 1850s to 1933, when the army vacated the island, it served as a military post protecting the Bay shoreline. In 1934, the buildings of the military outpost were converted into a maximum security prison. Given the sheer cliffs, treacherous tides and currents, and frigid temperatures of the waters, it was believed to be a totally escape-proof prison. Among the famous gangsters who were penned in cell blocks A through D were Al Capone, Robert Stroud, the so-called Birdman of Alcatraz (because he was an expert in ornithological diseases), Machine Gun Kelly, and Alvin Karpis. In 1963, after an apparent escape in which no bodies were recovered, the government closed the prison, and in 1972 it became part of the

Golden Gate National Recreation Area. The wildlife that was driven away during the military and prison years has begun to return—the black-crested night heron and other sea birds are nesting here again—and a new trail has been built that passes through the island's nature areas. Tours, including an audio tour of the prison block and a slide show, are given by the park's rangers, who entertain their guests with interesting anecdotes.

It's a popular excursion and space is limited, so purchase tickets as far in advance as possible. The tour is operated by **Red and White Fleet** (☎ **415/546-2700** or 800/229-2784 in California) and can be charged to a credit card (AE, MC, V; $2 per ticket service charge on phone orders). Tickets may also be purchased in advance from the Red and White Fleet ticket office on Pier 41.

Wear comfortable shoes and take a heavy sweater or windbreaker because even when the sun's out, it's cold. The National Parks Service also notes that there are a lot of steps to climb on the tour.

For those who want to get a closer look at Alcatraz without going ashore, two boat-tour operators offer short circumnavigations of the island. (See "Self-Guided & Organized Tours," below, for complete information.)

Cable Cars

Although they may not be San Francisco's most practical means of transportation, cable cars are certainly the best loved. Designated official historic landmarks by the National Parks Service in 1964, they clank up and down the city's steep hills like mobile museum pieces, tirelessly hauling thousands of tourists each day to nowhere in particular.

San Francisco's cable cars were invented in 1869 by London-born engineer Andrew Hallidie, who got the idea by way of serendipity. As the story goes, Hallidie was watching a team of overworked horses haul a heavily laden carriage up a steep San Francisco slope. As he watched, one horse slipped and the car rolled back, dragging the other tired beasts with it. At that moment Hallidie resolved that he would invent a mechanical contraption to replace such horses, and just four years later, in 1873, the first cable car made its maiden run from the top of Clay Street. Promptly ridiculed as "Hallidie's Folly," the cars were slow to gain acceptance. One early onlooker voiced the general opinion by exclaiming, "I don't believe it—the damned thing works!"

Even today, many visitors have difficulty believing that these vehicles, which have no engines, actually work. The cars, each weighing about six tons, are hauled along by a steel cable, enclosed under the street in a center rail. You can't see the cable unless you peer straight down into the crack, but you'll hear its characteristic clickity-clanking sound whenever you're nearby. The cars move when the gripper (*not* driver) pulls back a lever that closes a pincer-like "grip" on the cable. The speed of the car therefore is determined by the speed of the cable, which is a constant $9^1/_2$ miles per hour—never more, never less.

The two types of cable cars in use hold, respectively, a maximum of 90 and 100 passengers and the limits are rigidly enforced. The best views are had from the outer running boards, where you have to hold on tightly when taking curves. Everyone, it seems, prefers to ride on the running boards.

Often imitated but never duplicated, similar versions of Hallidie's cable cars have been used throughout the world, but all have been replaced by more efficient means of transportation. San Francisco planned to do so, too, but the proposal was met with so much opposition that the cable cars' perpetuation was actually written into the city charter in 1955. This mandate cannot be revoked without the approval of a majority of the city's voters—a distant and doubtful prospect.

San Francisco's three existing lines comprise the world's only surviving system of cable cars.

Coit Tower. Atop Telegraph Hill. ☎ **415/362-0808.** Admission (to the top of the tower) $3 adults, $2 seniors and students, $1 children 6–12. Daily 10am–6pm. Bus: 39 ("Coit").

In a city known for its great views and vantage points, Coit Tower is tops. Located atop Telegraph Hill, just east of North Beach, the round, stone tower offers panoramic views of the city and the Bay.

Completed in 1933, the tower is the legacy of Lillie Hitchcock Coit, a wealthy eccentric who left San Francisco a $125,000 bequest "for the purpose of adding beauty to the city I have always loved" and also as a memorial to its volunteer firemen. She had been saved from a fire as a child and thereafter held the city's firefighters in particularly high esteem.

Inside the base of the tower are the impressive murals titled *Life in California, 1934,* which were completed under the WPA during the New Deal. They were completed by more than 25 artists, many of whom had studied under Mexican muralist Diego Rivera.

The Exploratorium. 3601 Lyon St., in the Palace of Fine Arts (at Marina Blvd.). ☎ **415/563-7337** or 415/561-0360 for recorded information. Admission $9

Major San Francisco Sights

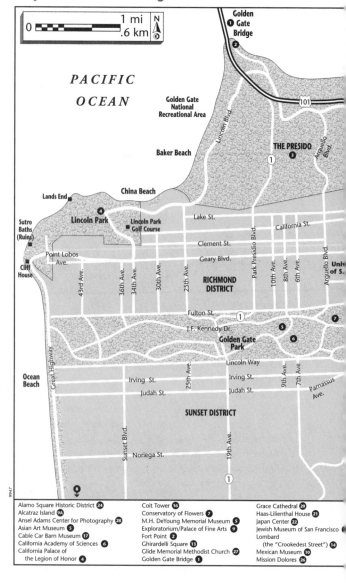

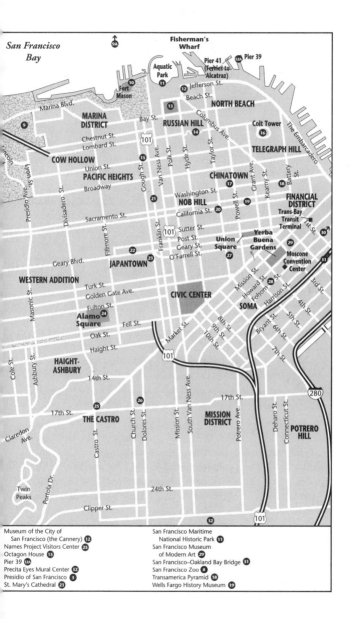

San Francisco Bay

Fisherman's Wharf

Pier 41 (Ferries to Alcatraz)

Pier 39

Aquatic Park

Fort Mason

Jefferson St.

Beach St.

NORTH BEACH

Marina Blvd.

MARINA DISTRICT

Bay St.

RUSSIAN HILL

Columbus Ave.

Coit Tower

TELEGRAPH HILL

Chestnut St.

Lombard St.

COW HOLLOW

Union St.

PACIFIC HEIGHTS

Broadway

Van Ness Ave.

Polk St.

Hyde St.

Taylor St.

Grant Ave.

Kearny St.

Battery St.

The Embarcadero

Presidio Ave.

Divisadero St.

Fillmore St.

Gough St.

Franklin St.

Washington St.

CHINATOWN

FINANCIAL DISTRICT

NOB HILL

California St.

Powell St.

Trans-Bay Transit Terminal

Sacramento St.

Sutter St.

Post St.

Geary St.

O'Farrell St.

Union Square

Yerba Buena Gardens

Geary Blvd.

JAPANTOWN

Moscone Convention Center

WESTERN ADDITION

Turk St.

Golden Gate Ave.

Fulton St.

Alamo Square

Fell St.

CIVIC CENTER

SOMA

Mission St.

Howard St.

Folsom St.

Harrison St.

Masonic St.

Oak St.

Haight St.

Market St.

8th St.

9th St.

10th St.

Bryant St.

5th St.

6th St.

7th St.

3rd St.

4th St.

Cole St.

Ashbury St.

HAIGHT-ASHBURY

14th St.

280

17th St.

Claredon Ave.

17th St.

THE CASTRO

Castro St.

Church St.

Dolores St.

Mission St.

South Van Ness Ave.

MISSION DISTRICT

Potrero Ave.

Deharo St.

Connecticut St.

POTRERO HILL

Twin Peaks

Portola Dr.

24th St.

Clipper St.

101

Museum of the City of San Francisco (the Cannery) 12

Names Project Visitors Center 25

Octagon House 15

Pier 39 12A

Precita Eyes Mural Center 32

Presidio of San Francisco 3

St. Mary's Cathedral 23

San Francisco Maritime National Historic Park 11

San Francisco Museum of Modern Art 29

San Francisco–Oakland Bay Bridge 31

San Francisco Zoo 8

Transamerica Pyramid 18

Wells Fargo History Museum 19

113

adults, $7 senior citizens, $5 children 6–17, $2.50 children 3–5, free for children under 3; free for everyone first Wed of each month. Summer (Memorial Day–Labor Day) and holidays, Mon–Tues and Thurs–Sun 10am–6pm, Wed 10am–9:30pm; the rest of the year Tues and Thurs–Sun 10am–5pm, Wed 10am–9:30pm. Closed Mon after Labor Day–Memorial Day (except holidays), Thanksgiving Day, and Christmas Day. Bus: 30 from Stockton St. to the Marina stop.

Scientific American magazine rates the Exploratorium as "the best science museum in the world," pretty heady stuff for this exciting hands-on science fair that contains more than 650 permanent exhibits that explore everything from giant bubble blowing to Einstein's Theory of Relativity. It's like a mad scientist's penny arcade, an educational funhouse and an experimental laboratory all rolled into one. Touch a tornado, shape a glowing electrical current, finger paint via computer, or take a sensory journey in total darkness in the Tactile Dome—you could spend all day here and still not see everything. Every exhibit at the Exploratorium is designed to be interactive, educational, safe, and, most importantly, fun. And don't think this is just for kids; parents inevitably end up being the most reluctant to leave. On the way out, be sure to stop in the wonderful gift store, which is chock-full of affordable brain candy.

The museum is located in the San Francisco's Marina District at the beautiful Palace of Fine Arts, the only building left standing from the Panama-Pacific Exposition of 1915, which celebrated the opening of the Panama Canal. The adjoining park and lagoon—the perfect place for an afternoon picnic—is home to ducks, swans, seagulls, and grouchy geese, so bring bread.

Golden Gate Bridge

The year 1996 marks the 60th birthday of what is possibly the most beautiful, and certainly the most photographed, bridge in the world. Often half veiled by the city's trademark rolling fog, San Francisco's Golden Gate spans tidal currents, ocean waves, and battering winds to connect the City by the Bay with the Redwood Empire to the north.

With its gracefully swung single span, spidery bracing cables, and sky-zooming twin towers, the bridge looks more like a work of abstract art than the practical engineering feat that it is, among the greatest of this century. Construction began in May 1937 and was completed at the then-colossal cost of $35 million. Contrary to pessimistic predictions, the bridge neither collapsed in a gale or earthquake nor proved to be a white elephant. A symbol of hope when the country was afflicted with widespread joblessness, the

Golden Gate single-handedly changed the Bay Area's economic life, encouraging the development of areas north of San Francisco.

The mile-long steel link, which reaches a height of 746 feet above the water, is an awesome bridge to cross. Traffic usually moves quickly, so crossing by car won't give you too much time to see the sights. If you drive ($3 toll, payable southbound) from the city, park in the lot at the foot of the bridge on the city side and make the crossing by foot. Back in your car, continue to Marin's Vista Point, at the bridge's northern end. Look back and you'll be rewarded with one of the greatest views of San Francisco.

Millions of pedestrians walk or bike across the bridge each year, gazing up at the tall red towers, out at the vistas of San Francisco and Marin County, and down into the stacks of ocean-going liners. You can walk out onto the span from either end, but be prepared: It's usually windy and cold, and the bridge vibrates. Still, walking even a short way is one of the best ways to experience the immense scale of the structure.

Bridge-bound Golden Gate Transit buses (☎ **415/332-6600**) depart every 30 to 60 minutes during the day for Marin County, starting from the Transbay Terminal at Mission and First streets and making convenient stops at Market and Seventh streets, at the Civic Center, and along Van Ness Avenue and Lombard Street.

Golden Gate National Recreation Area

San Francisco's Golden Gate National Recreation Area makes New York's Central Park look like a putting green. The largest urban park in the *world*, the GGNRA covers three counties along 28 miles of stunning, condo-free shoreline. Run by the National Parks Service, the Recreation Area wraps around the northern and western edge of the city, and just about all of it is open to the public with no access fees. The Muni bus system provides transportation to the more popular sites, including Aquatic Park, the Cliff House, Fort Mason, and Ocean Beach. For more information, contact the **National Park Service** (☎ **415/556-0560**).

Here is a brief rundown of the salient features of the park's peninsula section, starting at the northern section and moving westward around the coastline:

Aquatic Park, adjacent to the Hyde Street Pier, has a small swimming beach, although it's not that appealing (and darn cold). Far more entertaining is a visit to the ship-shaped museum across the lawn that's part of the San Francisco Maritime National Historical Park (see below for more information).

Golden Gate National Recreation Area

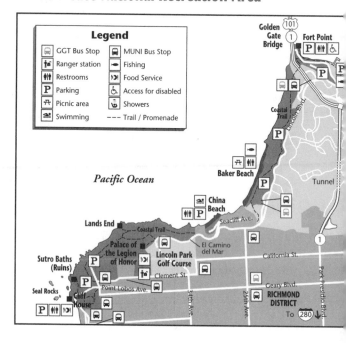

Fort Mason Center occupies an area from Bay Street to the shoreline and consists of several buildings and piers that were used during World War II. Today they are occupied by a variety of museums, theaters, and organizations as well as by **Greens** vegetarian restaurant, which affords views of the Golden Gate Bridge (see chapter 5, "Dining," for more information). For information about Fort Mason events call ☎ **415/441-5705.** The park headquarters is also at Fort Mason.

Farther west along the Bay at the northern end of Laguna Street is **Marina Green,** a favorite locals spot for kite-flying, jogging, and walking along the Promenade. The **St. Francis Yacht Club** is also located here.

From here begins the 3¹/₂-mile paved **Golden Gate Promenade,** San Francisco's best and most scenic biking, jogging, and walking path, which runs along the shore past **Crissy Field** (be sure to stop and watch the gonzo windsurfers) and ends at Fort Point under the Golden Gate Bridge.

Fort Point (☎ **415/556-1373**) was built in 1853 to protect the narrow entrance to the harbor. It was designed to house 500 soldiers

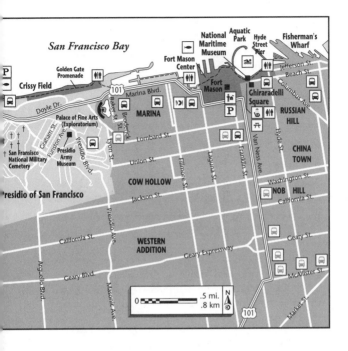

manning 126 muzzle-loading cannons. By 1900, the fort's soldiers and obsolete guns had been removed, but the formidable brick edifice still remains. Guided tours and cannon demonstrations are given at the site Wednesday through Sunday from 10am to 5pm.

Lincoln Boulevard sweeps around the western edge of the Bay to **Baker Beach,** where the waves roll ashore—a fine spot for sunbathing, walking, or fishing. Hikers can follow the Coastal Trail from Fort Point along this part of the coastline all the way to Land's End.

A short distance from Baker, **China Beach** is a small cove where swimming is permitted. Changing rooms, showers, a sundeck, and rest rooms are available.

A little farther around the coast appears **Lands End** looking out to Pyramid Rock. A lower and an upper trail provides a hiking opportunity amid windswept cypress and pine on the cliffs above the Pacific.

Still farther along the coast lies **Point Lobos,** the **Sutro Baths,** and the **Cliff House.** The latter has been serving refreshments to visitors since 1863 and providing views of Seal Rocks, home to a colony of sea lions and many marine birds. There's an information center here (open daily from 10am to 4:30pm; ☎ **415/556-8642**) as well as the incredible **Musée Mecanique,** an authentic old-fashioned arcade with 150 coin-operated amusement machines. Only traces of the Sutro Baths remain today to the northeast of the Cliff House. This swimming facility was a major summer attraction that could accommodate up to 24,000 people before it burned down in 1966.

A little farther inland at the western end of California Street is **Lincoln Park,** which contains a golf course and the Palace of the Legion of Honor.

The GGNRA also extends into Marin County, where it encompasses the **Marin Headlands, Muir Woods National Monument, Muir Beach** and **Stinson Beach,** and the **Olema Valley** behind the **Point Reyes National Seashore.**

Golden Gate Park

Everybody loves Golden Gate Park: people, dogs, birds, frogs, turtles, bison, and flowers. Literally everything feels unified here in San Francisco's enormous arboreal front yard. But this great city landmark wasn't always a favorite place to convene. It was conceived in the 1860s and 1870s but took its current shape in the 1880s and 1890s thanks to the skill and effort of John McClaren, a Scot who arrived in 1887 and began the landscaping of the park. Totaling 1,017 acres, the park is a narrow strip that stretches from the Pacific Coast inland. No one had thought about the challenge the sand dunes and wind would present to any landscape artist. McClaren, a clever lad, developed a new strain of grass called "sea bent," which he had planted to hold the sandy soil along the Firth of Forth, and he used this to anchor the soil here too. He also built the two windmills that stand on the western edge of the park to pump water for irrigation. Every year the ocean eroded the western fringe of the park, and he solved this problem too. It took him 40 years to build a natural wall, putting out bundles of sticks which were then covered with sand by the tides. Under his brilliant eye, the park took shape over the next 10 years.

For information on the park, head first to the **McClaren Lodge and Park Headquarters** (open Monday through Friday). There are several special gardens in the park, notably the Rhododendron Dell, the Rose Garden, the Strybing Arboretum, and at the western edge of the park, a springtime array of thousands of tulips and daffodils around the Dutch windmill.

Golden Gate Park

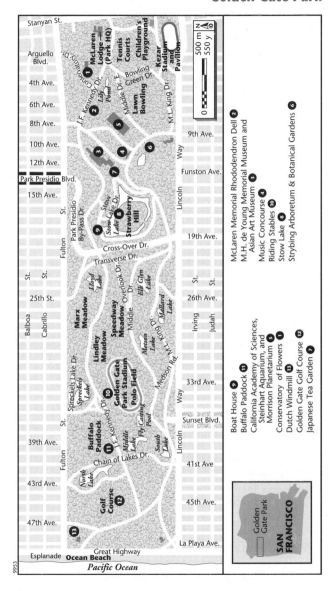

McLaren Memorial Rhododendron Dell ❷
M.H. de Young Memorial Museum and
Asian Art Museum ❸
Music Concourse ❹
Riding Stables ❿
Stow Lake ❽
Strybing Arboretum & Botanical Gardens ❻

Boat House ❾
Buffalo Paddock ⓫
California Academy of Sciences,
Steinhart Aquarium, and
Morrison Planetarium ❺
Conservatory of Flowers ❶
Dutch Windmill ⓭
Golden Gate Golf Course ⓬
Japanese Tea Garden ❼

In addition to the highlights below, the park contains several recreational facilities: tennis courts, baseball, soccer and polo fields, golf course, riding stables, fly-casting pools, and boat rentals at the Strawberry Hill boathouse. It is also the home of three major museums: the **M. H. de Young Memorial Museum,** the **Asian Art Museum,** and the **California Academy of Sciences** (see separate listings below). If you plan to visit all the park's attractions, consider buying the Culture Pass, which enables you to visit the three museums, the Japanese Tea Garden, and the Conservatory of Flowers for $10. Passes are available at each site and at the Visitor Information Center. For further information call ☎ **415/391-2000.** Enter the park at Kezar Drive, an extension of Fell Street. Bus: 16AX, BX, 5, 6, 7, 66, or 71.

CONSERVATORY OF FLOWERS (1878)   Built for the 1894 Midwinter Exposition, this striking assemblage of glass architecture contains a rotating display of plants and shrubs at all times of the year. The orchids in particular are spectacular. It's modeled on the famous glass house at Kew Gardens in London.

JAPANESE TEA GARDEN (1894)   McClaren hired the Hagiwara family to care for this garden developed for the 1894 Midwinter Exposition. It's a quiet place with cherry trees, shrubs, and bonsai crisscrossed by winding paths and high-arched bridges crossing over pools of water. Focal points and places for contemplation include the massive bronze Buddha that was cast in Japan in 1790 and donated by the Gump family, the Shinto wooden pagoda, and the Wishing Bridge, which reflected in the water looks as if it completes a circle. The garden is open daily from 9am to 6pm; the tea house (which invented the fortune cookie) serves from 10:30am to 5pm.

STRYBING ARBORETUM & BOTANICAL GARDENS   Six thousand plant species grow here—among them some very ancient plants in a special "primitive garden," rare species, and a grove of California redwoods. Docent tours are available during operating hours, which are Monday through Friday 8am to 4pm and Saturday and Sunday from 10am to 5pm.

STRAWBERRY HILL/STOW LAKE   Rent a paddle, row, or motor boat here and cruise around the circular lake as painters create still-lifes and joggers pass along the grassy shoreline. Ducks waddle around waiting to be fed, and turtles bathe on rocks and logs. Strawberry Hill, the 430-foot-high artificial island that lies at the center of Stow Lake, is a perfect picnic spot and boasts a bird's-eye view of San Francisco and the bay.

The Presidio

In October 1994, the Presidio was transferred from the U.S. Army to the National Park Service and became one of a handful of urban national parks that combines historical, architectural, and natural elements into one giant arboreal expanse. The 1,480-acre area incorporates a variety of terrain—coastal scrub, dunes, and prairie grasslands that shelter many rare plants and more than 150 species of birds, some of which nest here.

This military outpost has a 220-year history, stretching from its founding in September 1776 by the Spanish under José Joaquin Moraga to its closure in 1995. From 1822 to 1835 the property was in Mexican hands.

During the war with Mexico, American forces occupied the fort, and in 1848, when California became part of the Union, it was formally transferred to the United States. The Presidio expanded during the 1920s when Crissy Army Airfield (the first airfield on the West Coast) was established, but the major action was seen during World War II after the attack on Pearl Harbor. Soldiers dug foxholes along nearby beaches, and the Presidio became the headquarters for the Western Defense Command. Some 1.6 million men shipped out from nearby Fort Mason to fight in the Pacific and many returned to the hospital, whose capacity peaked one year at 72,000 patients. In the 1950s, the Presidio served as the headquarters for the Sixth U.S. Army and a missile defense post, but its role has slowly been reduced. In 1972, it was included in new legislation establishing the Golden Gate National Recreation Area; in 1989, the Pentagon decided to close the post and transfer it to the National Park Service.

Today, the area features more than 510 historic buildings, a scenic golf course, a national cemetery, and a variety of terrain and natural habitats. The National Park Service offers a variety of walking and biking tours around the Presidio; reservations are suggested. The **Presidio Museum,** located at the corner of Lincoln Boulevard and Funston Avenue (open 10am to 4pm Wednesday through Sunday), tells its story in dioramas, exhibitions, and photographs.

The **Visitor Information Center** is in Building 102 on the west side of Montgomery Street on the main parade ground (open daily from 10am to 5pm; ☎ **415/556-4323**). Take the 82X, 28, or 76 bus.

San Francisco Museum of Modern Art (MOMA). 151 Third St. (2 blocks south of Market St., across from Yerba Buena Gardens). ☎ **415/357-4000.** Admission $7 adults, $3.50 seniors and students 14–18, free for children 13 and under; half price for everyone Thurs 6–9pm, and free for everyone the first Tues of each month. Tues–Sun 11am–6pm (until 9pm Thursday). Closed Mon and holidays. Muni Metro: J, K, L, or M to Montgomery Station. Bus: 15, 30, or 45.

Swiss architect Mario Botta, in association with Hellmuth, Obata, and Kassabaum, designed the $62 million museum, which opened in SoMa in January 1995. The building is the most welcomed new development in years and has made SoMa one of the more popular areas to visit for tourists and residents alike. The museum's collection consists of more than 15,000 works, including close to 5,000 paintings and sculptures by artists such as Henri Matisse, Jackson Pollock, and Willem de Kooning. Other artists represented include Diego Rivera, Georgia O'Keeffe, Paul Klee, the Fauvists, and exceptional holdings of Richard Diebenkorn. MOMA was also one of the first to recognize photography as a major art form; its extensive collection includes more than 9,000 photographs by such notables as Ansel Adams, Alfred Steiglitz, Edward Weston, and Henri Cartier-Bresson. Docent-led tours are offered daily. Times are posted at the museum's admission desk. Phone for current details of upcoming special events.

The Caffé Museo, located on the right of the museum entrance sets a new precedent for museum food with flavorful and fresh soups, sandwiches, and salads that are as respectable as those served in many local restaurants.

No matter what, don't miss the MuseumStore, which carries a wonderful array of architectural gifts, books, and trinkets. It's one of the best stores in town.

2 More Attractions

CHURCHES & RELIGIOUS BUILDINGS

Some of San Francisco's churches and religious buildings are worth a special look. West of Union Square, you can see **Glide Memorial United Methodist Church,** at 330 Ellis St. There would be nothing special about this plain Tenderloin-area church if it weren't for its exhilarating pastor Cecil Williams. Williams's enthusiastic and uplifting preaching and singing with homeless and poor people of the neighborhood has attracted nationwide fame. In 1994, during the pastor's 30th anniversary celebration, singers Angela Bofill and Bobby McFerrin joined with comedian Robin Williams, author Maya Angelou, and talk-show queen Oprah Winfrey to honor him publicly. Reverend Williams's nondogmatic, fun Sunday services attract a diverse audience that crosses all socioeconomic boundaries. Services are held at 9 and 11am each Sunday. The closest Muni Metro stop is Powell, or you can take the no. 37 bus.

Grace Cathedral, located on Nob Hill on California Street, between Taylor and Jones streets, was begun in 1928 on the site of the Crocker mansion, but it was not completed until 1964. Although the cathedral, which was designed by architect Lewis P. Hobart, looks like it is made of stone, it is in fact constructed of reinforced concrete, beaten to achieve a stonelike effect. Among the more interesting features of the building are its stained-glass windows, particularly those by the French Loire studios, depicting such modern figures as Thurgood Marshall, Robert Frost, and Albert Einstein; the replicas of Ghiberti's bronze Doors of Paradise at the east end; the series of religious frescoes completed in the 1940s by Polish artist John de Rosen; and the 44-bell carillon.

Mission Dolores. 16th St. (at Dolores St.). ☎ **415/621-8203.** Admission $2 adults, $1 children 5–12. May–Oct daily 9am–4:30pm; Nov–Apr daily 9am–4pm; Good Fri 10am–noon. Closed Thanksgiving Day and Christmas Day. Muni Metro: J line to the corner of Church and 16th sts. Bus: 22.

San Francisco's oldest standing structure, the **Mission San Francisco de Assisi** (aka Mission Dolores) has withstood the test of time, as well as two major earthquakes, relatively intact. In 1776, at the behest of Franciscan Missionary Junípero Serra, Father Francisco Palou came to the Bay Area to found the sixth in a series of missions that dotted the California coastline. From these humble beginnings grew what was to become the city of San Francisco. The mission's small, simple chapel, built solidly by Native Americans who were converted to Christianity, is a curious mixture of native construction methods and Spanish-colonial style. A statue of Father Serra stands in the mission garden, although the portrait looks somewhat more contemplative, and less energetic, than he must have been in real life.

MUSEUMS

Ansel Adams Center for Photography. 250 Fourth St. ☎ **415/495-7000.** Admission $4 adults, $3 students, $2 seniors and children 12–17. Tues–Sun 11am–5pm; until 8pm the first Thurs of each month. Muni Metro: Powell. Bus: 30, 45, or 9X.

This popular SoMa museum features five separate galleries for changing exhibitions of contemporary and historical photography. One area is dedicated solely to displaying the works and exploring the legacy of Ansel Adams.

Asian Art Museum. In Golden Gate Park, near 10th Ave. and Fulton St. ☎ **415/668-7855** (recording); 415/752-2635 for the hearing impaired. Admission (including the M. H. de Young Memorial Museum and California Palace of the Legion of Honor) $6 adults, $4 seniors 65 and over, $3 youth 12–17, free for children 11 and under (fees may be higher for special exhibitions); reduced admission for everyone the first Wed (all day) of each month. Wed–Sun 10am–4:45pm. Bus: 5, 44, or 71.

Adjacent to the M. H. de Young Museum and the Japanese Tea Garden, this exhibition space, opened in 1966, can only display about 1,800 pieces from the museum's vast collection of 12,000. About half of the works on exhibit are in the ground-floor Chinese and Korean galleries and include world-class sculptures, paintings, bronzes, ceramics, jades, and decorative objects spanning 6,000 years of history. There is also a wide range of exhibits from more than 40 Asian countries—Pakistan, India, Tibet, Japan, Southeast Asia— including the world's oldest-known "dated" Chinese Buddha. The museum's free daily guided tours are highly informative and sincerely recommended. Call for times.

California Academy of Sciences. On the Music Concourse of Golden Gate Park. ☎ **415/221-5100** or 415/750-7145 for recorded information. Admission (aquarium and science exhibits) $7 adults, $4 students 12–17 and seniors 65 and over, $1.50 children 6–11, free for children under 6; free for everyone the first Wed of every month. Planetarium shows $2.50 adults, $1.25 children under 18 and seniors 65 and over. Labor Day–July 4 daily 10am–5pm; July 4–Labor Day daily 10am–7pm; first Wed of every month 10am–9pm. Muni Metro: N line to Golden Gate Park. Bus: 5, 71, or 44.

Clustered around the Music Concourse in Golden Gate Park are three outstanding world-class museums and exhibitions that are guaranteed to entertain every member of the family. The **Steinhart Aquarium,** for example, is the most diverse aquarium in the world, housing some 14,000 specimens, including amphibians, reptiles, marine mammals, penguins, and much more, in 189 displays. A huge hit with the youngsters is the California tide pool and a "hands-on" area where children can touch starfish and sea urchins. The living coral reef is the largest display of its kind in the country and the only one in the West. In the Fish Roundabout, visitors are surrounded by fast-swimming schools of fish kept in a 100,000-gallon tank. Seals and dolphins are fed every two hours, beginning at 10:30am; the penguins are fed at 11:30am and 4pm.

The **Morrison Planetarium** presents sky shows as well as laser light shows. Its sky shows offer guided tours through the universe projected onto a 65-foot domed ceiling. Approximately four major exhibits, with titles such as *Star Death: The Birth of Black Holes* and *The Universe Unveiled,* are presented each year. Related cosmos exhibits are located in the adjacent **Earth and Space Hall.** Sky shows are featured at 2pm on weekdays and hourly every weekend and holiday (☎ 415/750-7141 for more information). Laserium laser light shows are also presented in the Planetarium Thursday through Sunday nights (☎ 415/750-7138 for more information).

The **Natural History Museum** includes several halls displaying classic dioramas of fauna in their habitats. The **Wattis Hall of Human Cultures** traces the evolution of different human cultures and how they adapted to their natural environment; the "Wild California" exhibition in **Meyer Hall** includes a 14,000-gallon aquarium and seabird rookery, life-size battling elephant seals, and two larger-than-life views of microscopic life forms; in **McBean-Peterson Hall** visitors can walk through an exhibit tracing the course of $3^1/2$ billion years of evolution from the earliest life forms to the present day; in the **Hohfeld Earth and Space Hall** visitors can experience a simulation of two of San Francisco's biggest earthquakes, determine what their weight would be on other planets, see a real moon rock, and learn about the rotation of the planet at a replica of Foucault's Pendulum (the real one is in Paris).

Cable Car Barn Museum. Washington and Mason sts. ☎ **415/474-1887.** Free admission. Apr–Oct daily 10am–6pm; Nov–Mar daily 10am–5pm. Cable car: Both Powell St. lines stop by the museum.

If you've ever wondered how cable cars work, this nifty museum will explain (and demonstrate!) it all to you. Yes, this is a museum, but the Cable Car Barn is no stuffed shirt. It's the living powerhouse, repair shop, and storage place of the cable car system and is in full operation. Built for the Ferries and Cliff House Railway in 1887, the building underwent an $18 million reconstruction to restore its original gaslight-era look, install an amazing spectators' gallery, and add a museum of San Francisco transit history.

The exposed machinery, which pulls the cables under San Francisco's streets, looks like a Rube Goldberg invention. Stand in the mezzanine gallery and become mesmerized by the massive groaning and vibrating winches as they thread the cable that hauls the cars through a huge figure eight and back into the system via slack-absorbing tension wheels. For a better view, move to the lower-level viewing room where you can see the massive pulleys and gears operating underground.

Also on display here is one of the first grip cars developed by Andrew S. Hallidie, operated for the first time on Clay Street on August 2, 1873. Other displays include an antique grip car and trailer that operated on Pacific Avenue until 1929, and dozens of exact-scale models of cars used on the various city lines. There's also a shop where you can buy a variety of cable car gifts.

✪ **California Palace of the Legion of Honor.** In Lincoln Park (at 4th Ave. and Clement St.). ☎ **415/750-3600** or 415/863-3330 for recorded information. Admission (including the Asian Art Museum and M. H. de Young Memorial Museum) $6 adults, $4 seniors 65 and over, $3 youths 12–17, free for children 11 and under (fees may be higher for special exhibitions); free the second Wed of each month. Open Tues–Sun 10am–4:45pm; Open first Sat of the month until 8:45pm. Bus: 38 or 18.

Designed as a memorial to California's World War I casualties, the neoclassical structure is an exact replica of the Legion of Honor Palace in Paris, right down to the inscription "Honneur et Patrie" above the portal.

The Legion of Honor reopened in late 1995 after a two-year, $34.6 million renovation and seismic upgrading that was stalled by the discovery of almost 300 turn-of-the-century coffins. The exterior's grassy expanses, cliff-side paths, and incredible view of the Golden Gate make this an absolute must-visit attraction before you even get in the door. But the inside is equally impressive. The museum collection covers 4,000 years of art and includes paintings, sculpture, and decorative arts from Europe, as well as international tapestries, prints, and drawings. The chronological display of more than 800 years of European art includes one of the world's finest collections of Rodin sculpture.

M. H. de Young Memorial Museum. In Golden Gate Park (near 10th Ave. and Fulton St.). ☎ **415/750-3600** or 415/863-3330 for recorded information. Admission (including the Asian Art Museum and California Palace of the Legion of Honor) $6 adults, $4 seniors over 65, $3 youths 12–17, free for children 11 and under (fees may be higher for special exhibitions); reduced admission for everyone the first Wed of each month. Wed–Sun 10am–4:45pm (first Wed of the month until 8:45pm). Bus: 44.

One of the city's oldest museums, it's best known for its American art dating from colonial times to the 20th century, and includes paintings, sculptures, furniture, and decorative arts by Paul Revere, Winslow Homer, John Singer Sargent, and Georgia O'Keeffe. Special note should be taken of the American landscapes, as well as the fun trompe l'oeil and still-life works from the turn of the century.

Named after the late 19th-century publisher of the *San Francisco Chronicle,* the museum also possesses an important textile collection, with primary emphasis on rugs from central Asia and the Near East. Other collections on view include decorative art from Africa, Oceania, and the Americas. Major traveling exhibitions are equally eclectic, including everything from ancient rugs to great Dutch paintings. Call the museum to find out what's on. Tours are offered daily; call for times.

The museum's **Café de Young** is exceptional, serving daily specials that might include Peruvian stew, Chinese chicken salad, and Italian vegetables in tomato-basil sauce. In summer, visitors can dine in the garden, among bronze statuary. The cafe is open Wednesday through Sunday from 10am to 4pm.

Mexican Museum. Bldg. D, Fort Mason, Marina Blvd. (at Laguna St.). ☎ **415/441-0404.** Admission $3 adults; $2 children. Free first Wed of the month. Wed–Sun noon–5pm. Bus: 76 or 28.

The first museum in the nation dedicated to the work of Mexican and other Latino artists, the Mexican Museum maintains an impressive collection of art covering pre-Hispanic, colonial, folk, Mexican fine art, and Chicano/Mexican American art. Revolving art shows range from the art of New Mexican women to such subjects as Mexican surrealism. Note: The museum is expected to be relocated to the Yerba Buena Center area in 1998.

San Francisco Maritime National Historical Park. At the foot of Polk St. (near Fisherman's Wharf). ☎ **415/556-3002.** Admission (museum) free; (ships) $3 adults, $1 children 11–17, free for children under 11 and seniors over 62. Museum daily 10am–5pm; ships on Hyde St. Pier May 16–Sept 15 daily 10am–6pm, Sept 16–May 15 daily 9:30am–5pm. Closed Thanksgiving Day, Christmas Day, and New Year's Day. Cable car: Hyde St. line to the last stop. Bus: 19, 30, 32, 42, or 47.

Shaped like an art deco ship, the Maritime Museum is filled with sailing, whaling, and fishing lore. Remarkably good exhibits include intricate model craft, scrimshaw, and a collection of shipwreck photographs and historic marine scenes, including an 1851 snapshot of hundreds of abandoned ships, deserted en masse by crews dashing off to participate in the gold rush. The museum's walls are lined with beautifully carved, brightly painted wooden figureheads from old windjammers.

Two blocks east, at the Park's Hyde Street Pier, are several historic ships, now moored and open to the public.

At the pier's small-boat shop, visitors can follow the restoration progress of historic boats from the museum's collection. It's located behind the maritime bookstore on your right as you approach the ships.

Wells Fargo History Museum. 420 Montgomery St. (at California St.).
☎ **415/396-2619.** Admission free. Mon–Fri 9am–5pm. Closed bank holidays.
Muni Metro: Montgomery St. Bus: Any to Market St.

Wells Fargo, one of California's largest banks, got its start in the
Wild West. Its history museum, at the bank's head office, houses
hundreds of genuine relics from the company's whip and six-shooter
days, including pistols, photographs, early banking articles, posters,
and mining equipment.

Center for the Arts at Yerba Buena Gardens. 701 Mission St. ☎ **415/
978-2700.** Admission $4 adult, $2 seniors and students; free every first Thurs
of the month from 6–8pm. Tues–Sun 11am–6pm. Muni Metro: Powell or Montgomery. Bus: 30, 45, or 9X.

Cutting-edge computer art and multimedia shows are on view in the
high-tech galleries. The initial exhibition, "The Art of Star Wars,"
featured the special effects created by George Lucas for the film.

OTHER ATTRACTIONS

The Names Project AIDS Memorial Quilt Visitors Center. 2362-A
Market St. ☎ **415/863-1966.** Thurs–Tues noon–5pm, Wed noon–10pm.
Muni Metro: J, K, L, or M line to Castro St. Station; F line to Church and
Market sts.

The Names Project began in 1987 as a memorial for people who
have died from AIDS. The idea was to direct grief into positive action and help the world understand the devastating impact of AIDS.
Sewing machines and fabric were acquired, and the public was invited to make coffin-sized panels for a giant memorial quilt. More
than 31,000 individual panels now commemorate the lives of those
who have died of complications related to AIDS. Each has been
uniquely designed and sewn by the victims' friends, lovers, and
family members.

The AIDS Memorial Quilt, which would cover 12 football fields
if laid out end to end, was first displayed on the Capitol Mall in
Washington, D.C., during a 1987 national march on Washington
for lesbian and gay rights. Although sections of the quilt are often
on tour throughout the world, portions of the largest community art
project in the world are on display here. A sewing machine and
fabrics are also available here, free, for your use.

Lombard Street. Between Hyde and Leavenworth sts.

Known as the "crookedest street in the world," the whimsically
winding block of Lombard Street draws thousands of visitors each
year (much to the chagrin of neighborhood residents, most of whom
would prefer to block off the street to tourists). The angle of the

street is so steep that the road has to snake back and forth to make a descent possible. The brick-lined street zigzags around the residences' bright flower gardens that explode with color during warmer months. This short stretch of Lombard Street is one way, downhill, and fun to drive. Take the curves slowly and in low gear, and expect a wait during the weekend. Save your film for the bottom, where, if you're lucky, you can find a parking space and take a few snapshots of the silly spectacle. You can also walk the block, either up or down, via staircases (without curves) on either side of the street.

NEIGHBORHOODS

To really get to know San Francisco, break out of the downtown and Fisherman's wharf areas to explore the ethnically and culturally diverse neighborhoods. Walk the streets, browse the shops, grab a bite at a local restaurant—you'll find that San Francisco's beauty and charm is around every corner, not just at the popular tourist destinations.

Alamo Square Historic District

San Francisco's collection of Victorian houses, known as the "Painted Ladies," is one of the city's most famous assets. Most of the 14,000 extant structures date from the second half of the 19th century and are private residences. Spread throughout the city, many have been beautifully restored and ornately painted. The small area bordered by Divisadero Street on the west, Golden Gate Avenue on the north, Webster Street on the east, and Fell Street on the south—about 10 blocks west of the Civic Center—has one of the city's greatest concentrations of these Painted Ladies. One of the most famous views of San Francisco—seen on postcards and posters all around the city—depicts sharp-edged Financial District skyscrapers behind a row of Victorians. This fantastic juxtaposition can be seen from Alamo Square, in the center of this historic district, at Fulton and Steiner streets.

The Castro

Castro Street, between Market and 18th, is the center of the city's gay community anchored by the bookstore **A Different Light** and the many shops, restaurants, bars, and other institutions that cater to the community. Among the landmarks are **Harvey Milk Plaza, the Names Project Quilt,** and the **Castro Theatre,** a 1930s movie palace with Wurlitzer. The gay community began to move here in the late 1960s and early 1970s from the earlier gay neighborhood called Polk Gulch, which still has a number of gay-oriented bars and stores. Castro is one of the most lively streets in the city and the perfect place to shop for gifts and revel in how free-spirited this town is.

Chinatown

The first Chinese came to San Francisco in the early 1800s to work as servants. By 1851, there were 25,000 Chinese working in California, most of whom had settled in San Francisco's Chinatown. Fleeing famine and the Opium Wars, they had come seeking the promise of good fortune in the "Gold Mountain" of California, hoping to return with that prosperity to their families back in China. For the vast majority, the reality of life in California did not live up to the promise. First employed as workers in the gold mines during the gold rush, they were later used to build the railroads, working as little more than slaves and facing constant prejudice. Yet the community, segregated in the Chinatown ghetto, thrived. Growing prejudice led to the Chinese Exclusion Act of 1882, which halted all Chinese immigration for 10 years and limited it severely thereafter; the Chinese Exclusion Act was not repealed until 1943. The Chinese were also denied the opportunity to buy homes outside of the Chinatown ghetto until the 1950s.

Today San Francisco has the second largest community of Chinese in the United States (about 33☎ of the city's population is Chinese). More than 80,000 people live in Chinatown, but the majority of Chinese have moved out into newer areas like the Richmond and Sunset districts.

The gateway at Grant and Bush marks the entry to Chinatown. The **Chinese Historical Society of America,** at 650 Commercial St. (☎ **415/391-1188**), has a small but interesting collection relating to the Chinese in San Francisco. The heart of Chinatown is at Portsmouth Square where the Chinese practice tai chi in the morning and relax later in the day playing board games or just sitting quietly.

On Waverly Place, a street where the Chinese celebratory colors of red, yellow, and green are much in evidence, you'll find three temples, **Jeng Sen** at 146, **Tien Hou** at 125, and **Norras** at 109.

A block north of Grant, Stockton from 1000 to 1200, is the main shopping street of the community lined with grocers, fishmongers, tea sellers, herbalists, noodle parlors, and restaurants. Here, too, is the **Kon Chow Temple** at 855 above the Chinatown post office. Explore at your leisure.

Fisherman's Wharf & Vicinity

Few cities in America are as adept at wholesaling their historical sites as San Francisco, which has converted Fisherman's Wharf into one of the most popular tourist destinations in the world. Unless you come really early in the morning, you won't find any traces of the traditional waterfront life that once existed here; the only fishing going on around here is for tourists' dollars.

Originally called Meigg's Wharf, this bustling strip of waterfront got its present moniker from generations of fishers who used to base their boats here. Today, the bay has become so polluted with toxins that bright yellow placards warn against eating fish from these waters. A small fleet of fewer than 30 boats still operates from here, but basically Fisherman's Wharf has been converted into one long shopping mall stretching from Ghirardelli Square at the west end to Pier 39 at the east. Some people love it, others can't get far enough away from it, but most agree that Fisherman's Wharf, for better or for worse, has to be seen at least once in your life.

Ghirardelli Square, at 900 North Point, between Polk and Larkin streets (☎ **415/775-5500**), dates from 1864 when it served as a factory making Civil War uniforms, but it's best known as the former chocolate-and-spice factory of Domingo Ghirardelli. The factory has been converted into a 10-level mall containing 50-plus stores and 20 dining establishments. Scheduled street performers play regularly in the West Plaza. The stores generally stay open until 8 or 9pm in the summer and 6 or 7pm in the winter. Incidentally, the Ghirardelli Chocolate Company still makes chocolate, but it's located in a lower-rent district in the East Bay.

The Cannery, at 2801 Leavenworth St. (☎ **415/771-3112**), was built in 1894 as a fruit-canning plant and converted in the 1960s into a mall containing 50-plus shops and several restaurants and galleries, including **Jacks Cannery Bar** (☎ **415/931-6400**), which features 110 beers on tap (the most anywhere in the country). Vendors' stalls and sidewalk cafes are set up in the courtyard amid a grove of century-old olive trees, and on summer weekends street performers are out in force entertaining tourists. The **Museum of the City of San Francisco** (☎ **415/928-0289**), which traces the city's development with displays and artifacts, is on the third floor. The museum is free and is open Wednesday through Sunday from 10am to 4pm.

Pier 39, on the waterfront at Embarcadero and Beach Street (☎ **415/981-8030;** shops are open daily from 10:30am to 8:30pm), is a $4\frac{1}{2}$-acre, multilevel waterfront complex a few blocks

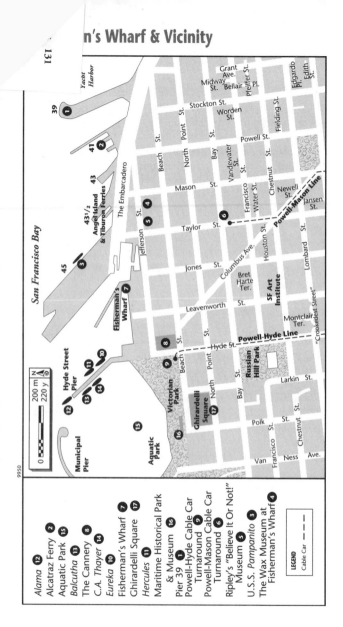

n's Wharf & Vicinity

131

San Francisco Bay

Yacht Harbor

Municipal Pier

Aquatic Park

Hyde Street Pier

Fisherman's Wharf

The Embarcadero

Victorian Park

Ghirardelli Square

Russian Hill Park

SF Art Institute

"Crookedst Street"

Powell-Hyde Line

Powell-Mason Line

Grant Ave.
Midway St. Bellair Pl.
Pfeiffer Pl.
Edgardo Pl. Edith St.
Stockton St.
Worden St.
Powell St.
Beach St.
North Point St.
Bay St.
Vandewater St.
Chestnut St.
Fielding St.
Newell St.
Jansen St.
Mason St.
Francisco St.
Water St.
Jefferson St.
Taylor St.
Houston St.
Columbus Ave.
Jones St.
Bret Harte Ter.
Leavenworth St.
Montclair Ter.
Hyde St.
Beach St.
North Point St.
Larkin St.
Bay St.
Polk St.
Francisco St.
Chestnut St.
Van Ness Ave.

39
1
41
2
43
43½ Angel Island & Tiburon Ferries
45
3
4
5
6
7
8
9
10
11
12
13
14
15
16
17

N
0   200 m
    220 y

9950

Alama **12**
Alcatraz Ferry **2**
Aquatic Park **15**
Balcutha **13**
The Cannery **8**
C.A. Thayer **14**
Eureka **10**
Fisherman's Wharf **7**
Ghirardelli Square **17**
Hercules **11**
Maritime Historical Park & Museum **16**
Pier 39 **1**
Powell-Hyde Cable Car Turnaround **9**
Powell-Mason Cable Car Turnaround **6**
Ripley's "Believe It Or Not!" Museum **5**
U.S.S. Pampanito **3**
The Wax Museum at Fisherman's Wharf **4**

LEGEND
Cable Car – – – –

132

east of Fisherman's Wharf. Constructed on an abandoned cargo pier, it is, ostensibly, a re-creation of a turn-of-the-century street scene, but don't expect a slice of old-time maritime life. This is the busiest mall of the lot and, according to the *London Observer,* the third most visited attraction in the *world* behind Disney World and Disneyland—with more than 100 stores, 10 bay-view restaurants, a two-tiered Venetian carousel, and a new big-screen Cinemax Theater showing the *Secret of San Francisco.*

The latest major addition to Fisherman's Wharf is Underwater World, a $38 million, 707,000 gallon marine attraction filled with sharks, stingrays, and more, all witnessed via a moving footpath that transports visitors through clear acrylic tunnels.

Accommodating a total of 350 boats, two marinas flank the pier and house the Blue and Gold bay sightseeing fleet. In recent years some 600 California sea lions have taken up residence on the adjacent floating docks. Until they abandon their new playground, which seems more and more unlikely, these playful, noisy creatures (some nights you can hear them all the way from Washington Square) create one of the best free attractions on the Wharf. Ongoing docent-led programs are offered at Pier 39 on weekends from 11am to 5pm that teach visitors about the range, habitat, and adaptability of the California sea lion.

Japantown/Japan Center

Today more than 12,000 citizens of Japanese descent live in San Francisco, or Soko, as it is often called by the Japanese who first emigrated here. Initially, they settled in Chinatown and also South of Market along Stevenson and Jessie streets from Fourth to Seventh. After the earthquake in 1906, SoMa became a light industrial and warehouse area and the largest Japanese concentration took root in the Western Addition between Van Ness Avenue and Fillmore Street, the site of today's Japantown. By 1940 it covered 30 blocks.

Japan Center is an Asian-oriented shopping mall occupying three square blocks bounded by Post, Geary, Laguna, and Fillmore streets. At its center stands the five-tiered Peace Pagoda, designed by world-famous Japanese architect Yoshiro Taniguchi "to convey the friendship and goodwill of the Japanese to the people of the United States." Surrounding the pagoda, in a network of arcades, squares, and bridges, are dozens of shops and showrooms featuring everything from TVs and tansu chests to pearls, bonsai (dwarf trees), and kimonos. When it opened in 1968, the complex seemed as modern as a jumbo jet. Today, the concrete structure seems less impressive, but it still holds some interesting surprises. The **Kabuki Hot Spring,** at 1750 Geary Blvd. (☎ **415/922-6002**), is the center's most famous tenant, an authentic traditional Japanese bathhouse with deep ceramic communal tubs, as well as private baths. The other delight is the **Ikenobo Ikebana Society,** in the Kintetsu Building, 1737 Post St. (☎ **415/567-1011**), which stocks everything you need to practice the art of flower arranging and also displays fine examples in its windows. The Japan Center also houses numerous restaurants, teahouses, shops, and the luxurious 14-story **Miyako Hotel.**

There is often live entertainment on summer weekends, including Japanese music and dance performances, tea ceremonies, flower-arranging demonstrations, martial-arts presentations, and other cultural events. The Japan Center is open Monday through Friday from 10am to 10pm, Saturday and Sunday from 9am to 10pm. It can be reached by the no. 2, 3, or 4 bus (exit on Buchanan and Sutter streets); or 22 or 38 (exit on the northeast corner of Geary Boulevard and Fillmore Street).

The Mission District

Once inhabited almost entirely by Irish immigrants, the Mission District is now the center of the city's Latino community, an oblong area stretching roughly from 14th to 30th streets between Potrero Avenue in the east and Dolores on the west. In the outer areas many of the city's finest Victorians still stand, though many seem strangely out of place in the mostly lower-income neighborhoods. The heart of the community lies along 24th Street between Van Ness and Potrero, where dozens of excellent ethnic restaurants, bakeries, bars, and specialty stores attract people from all over the city. Walking through the Mission District at night isn't a good idea, but it's usually quite safe during the day and highly recommended.

For an even better insight into the community, go to the **Precita Eyes Mural Arts Center** at 348 Precita Ave., at Folsom Street (☎ **415/285-2287**) and take one of the hour-long tours conducted on Saturday, which cost $4 for adults, $3 for seniors, and $1 for those under 18. You'll see 70 murals in an eight-block walk. Every year they also hold a Mural Awareness Week (usually the second week in May) when tours are given daily. Other signs of cultural life include a number of progressive theaters—Eureka, Theater Rhinoceros, and Theater Artaud, to name only a few.

At 16th and Dolores is the **Mission San Francisco de Assisi** (better known as **Mission Dolores**), which is the city's oldest surviving building (see the separate listing above) and the district's namesake.

Nob Hill

When the cable car was invented in 1873, this hill became the exclusive residential area of the city. The Big Four and the Comstock Bonanza kings built their mansions here, but they were all destroyed by the earthquake and fire in 1906. The only two surviving buildings were the Flood Mansion, which serves today as the Pacific Union Club, and the Fairmont, which was under construction when the earthquake struck. Today the burned-out sites of former mansions are occupied by the city's luxury hotels—the Mark Hopkins, the Stanford Court, the Fairmont, and the Huntington—as well as spectacular Grace Cathedral, which stands on the Crocker mansion site. It's worth a visit to Nob Hill if only to stroll around Huntington Park, attend a Sunday service at the Cathedral, or ooh and aah your way around the Fairmont's spectacular lobby.

North Beach

In the late 1800s, an enormous influx of Italian immigrants into North Beach firmly established this aromatic area as San Francisco's "Little Italy." Today, dozens of Italian restaurants and coffee houses continue to flourish in what is still the center of the city's Italian community. Walk down Columbus Avenue any given morning and you're bound to be bombarded with the wonderful aromas of roasting coffee and savory pasta sauces. Though there are some interesting shops and bookstores in the area, it's the dozens of eclectic little cafes, delis, bakeries, and coffee shops that give North Beach its Italian-Bohemian character.

South of Market (SoMa)

From Market Street to Townsend and the Embarcadero to Division Street, SoMa has become the city's newest cultural and multimedia center. The process started when alternative clubs began opening in the old warehouses in the area nearly a decade ago, followed by a wave of entrepreneurs seeking to start new businesses in what was once an extremely low-rent district comparing to the neighboring Financial District. Today, gentrification and high rents are well underway, spurned by a building boom that started with the Moscone Convention Center and continues today with the new **Center for the Arts at Yerba Buena Gardens** and the **San Francisco Museum of Modern Art,** all of which continue to be supplemented by other institutions, businesses, and museums that are moving into the area daily.

PARKS, GARDENS & ZOOS

In addition to Golden Gate Park and the Golden Gate National Recreation Area discussed in "The Top Attractions" section above, San Francisco boasts more than 2,000 additional acres of parkland, most of which is perfect for picnicking or throwing around a Frisbee.

One of our personal favorites is **Lincoln Park,** a 270-acre green on the northwestern side of the city at Clement Street and 34th Avenue. The **California Palace of the Legion of Honor** is here (see "Museums," above), as is a scenic 18-hole municipal golf course (see "Staying Active," below). But the best things about this park are the 200-foot cliffs that overlook the Golden Gate Bridge and San Francisco Bay. To get to the park, take bus no. 38 from Union Square to 33rd and Geary streets, then walk a few blocks to the park.

San Francisco Zoo & Children's Zoo. Sloat Blvd. and 45th Ave. ☎ **415/ 753-7080.** Admission (main zoo) $7 adults, $3.50 seniors and youths 12–15, $1.50 for children 3–11, and free for children 2 and under if accompanied by an adult; (children's zoo) $1, free for children under 3. Main zoo daily 10am–5pm; Children's zoo daily 11am–4pm. Muni Metro: L line from downtown Market St. to the end of the line.

Located between the Pacific Ocean and Lake Merced, in the southwest corner of the city, the San Francisco Zoo is among America's highest-rated animal parks. Begun in 1889 with a grizzly bear named Monarch donated by the *San Francisco Examiner,* the zoo now sprawls over 65 acres and is growing. It attracts up to a million visitors each year. Most of the 1,000-plus inhabitants are contained in landscaped enclosures guarded by concealed moats. The innovative Primate Discovery Center is particularly noteworthy for its many rare and endangered species.

Other highlights include Koala Crossing, which is linked to the new Australian WalkAbout exhibit that opened in 1995, housing kangaroos, emus, and walleroos; Gorilla World, one of the world's largest exhibits of these gentle giants; and Penguin Island, home to a large breeding colony of Magellanic penguins.

The Children's Zoo, adjacent to the main park, allows both kids and adults to get close to animals. The barnyard is alive with strokable domestic animals such as sheep, goats, ponies, and a llama. Also of interest is the Insect Zoo, which showcases a multitude of insect species, including the hissing cockroach walking sticks.

A free, informal walking tour of the zoo is available on weekends at 11am. The "Zebra Zephyr" train tour takes visitors on a 20-minute "safari" daily (in winter, only on weekends). The tour is $2.50 for adults, $1.50 for children 15 and under and seniors.

3 Especially for Kids

The following San Francisco attractions have major appeal to kids of all ages:

- Alcatraz Island *(p. 109)*
- Cable cars *(p. 110)*
- Cable Car Museum *(p. 125)*
- California Academy of Sciences, including Steinhart Aquarium *(p. 124)*
- The Exploratorium *(p. 111)*
- Golden Gate Bridge *(p. 114)*
- Golden Gate Park (including the Children's Playground, Bison Paddock, and Japanese Tea Garden) *(p. 118)*
- San Francisco Maritime National Historical Park and the historic ships anchored at Hyde Pier *(p. 127)*
- The San Francisco Zoo *(p. 136)*

In addition to the sights listed above, the following attractions are of particular interest to kids.

FAVORITES AT FISHERMAN'S WHARF

The following sights are all clustered on or near Fisherman's Wharf. To reach this area by cable car, take the Mason line to the last stop and walk to the wharf; by bus, take no. 30, 32, or 42. If you're arriving by car, park on adjacent streets or on the wharf between Taylor and Jones streets.

The Haunted Gold Mine. 113 Jefferson St. ☎ **415/202-0400.** Admission $5.95 adults, $4.95 seniors, $2.95 children 6–12, free for children under 6. Summer, Sun–Thurs 9am–11pm, Fri–Sat 9am–midnight; winter, Sun–Thurs 9am–10pm, Fri–Sat 9am–11pm.

Under the same ownership as the Wax Museum, the Haunted Gold Mine is a fun house complete with mazes, a hall of mirrors, spatial-disorientation tricks, wind tunnels, and animated ghouls. Even very young children will probably not find it too scary, and it's good old-fashioned carnival fun.

USS *Pampanito*. Pier 45, Fisherman's Wharf. ☎ **415/441-5819.** Admission $5 adults; $3 for seniors, students, and children 6–11; free for children under 6; $15 for a family. May–Oct daily 9am–9pm; Nov–Apr daily 9am–6pm.

This popular battle-scarred World War II fleet submarine saw plenty of action in the Pacific. It has been completely restored, and visitors are free to crawl around inside. An audio tour is available.

Ripley's Believe It or Not! Museum. 175 Jefferson St. ☎ **415/771-6188.** Admission $8 adults, $6.75 teens 13–17 and seniors over 60, $5 children 5–12, free for children under 5. June 15–Labor Day Sun–Thurs 9am–11pm and Fri–Sat 9am–midnight; the rest of the year Sun–Thurs 10am–10pm, Fri–Sat 10am–midnight.

This museum has been drawing curious spectators through its doors for 30 years. Inside, you will experience the extraordinary world of improbabilities: a one-third scale match-stick cable car, a human shrunken torso once owned by Ernest Hemingway, a dinosaur made from car bumpers, a walk through a kaleidoscope tunnel, and video displays and illusions. Robert LeRoy Ripley's infamous arsenal may lead you to ponder whether truth is in fact stranger than fiction.

Wax Museum. 145 Jefferson St. ☎ **415/202-0400.** Admission $9.95 adults, $7.95 for teens 13–17; $6.95 seniors over 60, $4.95 children 6–12, free for children under 6. Summer, Sun–Thurs 9am–11:pm, Fri–Sat 9am–midnight; the rest of the year, Sun–Thurs 9am–10pm, Fri–Sat 9am–midnight.

Conceived and executed in the Madame Tussaud mold, San Francisco's wax museum features more than 250 lifelike figures of the rich and famous. The "museum" donates the lion's share of its space to images of modern superstars like singer Michael Jackson and political figures like former president George Bush. Tableaux include "Royalty," "Great Humanitarians," "Wickedest Ladies," "World Religions," and "Feared Leaders," the last including Fidel Castro, Nikita Krushchev, Benito Mussolini, and Adolf Hitler. The Chamber of Horrors, which features Dracula, Frankenstein, and a werewolf, along with bloody victims hanging from meat hooks, is the stuff tourist traps are made of. It may also scare younger children.

4 Self-Guided & Organized Tours

The 49-Mile Scenic Drive

The self-guided, 49-mile drive is one easy way to orient yourself and to grasp the beauty of San Francisco and its extraordinary location. Beginning in the city, it follows a rough circle around the bay and passes virtually all the best-known sights from Chinatown to the Golden Gate Bridge, Ocean Beach, Seal Rocks, Golden Gate Park, and Twin Peaks. Originally designed for the benefit of visitors to San Francisco's 1939 and 1940 Golden Gate International Exposition, the route is marked with blue-and-white seagull signs. Although it makes an excellent half-day tour, this mini excursion can easily take longer if you decide, for example, to stop to walk across the Golden Gate Bridge or to have tea in Golden Gate Park's Japanese Tea Garden.

The San Francisco Visitor Information Center, at Powell and Market streets (see "Visitor Information" in chapter 3), distributes free route maps. Since a few of the Scenic Drive marker signs are missing, the map will come in handy. Try to avoid the downtown area during the weekday rush hours from 7 to 9am and 4 to 6pm.

Boat Tours

One of the best ways to look at San Francisco is from a boat bobbing on the bay. There are several cruises to choose from, many of which start from Fisherman's Wharf. There are two major companies.

Red and White Fleet, at Pier 41, Fisherman's Wharf (☎ **415/ 546-2700** or 800/229-2784 in California), is the city's largest boat tour operator, offering more than half a dozen itineraries on the bay. The fleet's primary ships are two-toned, double- and triple-deckers, capable of holding 150 to 500 passengers. You can't miss the observation tower ticket booths, at Pier 43^1/$_2$, located next to the Franciscan Restaurant.

The Golden Gate Bay Cruise is a 45-minute cruise by the Golden Gate Bridge, Angel Island, and Alcatraz Island. Tours cost $16 for adults, $12 for juniors 12 to 18 and seniors 62 and older, and $8 for children 5 to 11. Tour prices include audio narration in six languages: English, French, German, Japanese, Mandarin, and Spanish. They depart from Pier 41 and Pier 43^1/$_2$ several times daily. The Blue and Gold Fleet acquired this company in 1996 so details may vary. Call for departure schedules.

Blue and Gold Fleet, at Pier 39, Fisherman's Wharf (☎ **415/ 705-5444**), tours the bay year-round in a sleek, 400-passenger sightseeing boat, complete with food and beverage facilities. The fully narrated, 1^1/$_4$-hour cruise passes beneath the Golden Gate and Bay bridges, and comes within yards of Alcatraz Island. Frequent daily departures from Pier 39's West Marina begin at 10am during summer and 11am in winter. Tickets cost $15 for adults, $8 for juniors 5 to 17, and seniors over 62; children under 5 sail free.

Bus Tours

Gray Line, with offices in the Transbay Terminal, First and Mission streets, Pier 39, or Union Square (☎ **415/558-9400** or 800/ 826-0202), is San Francisco's largest bus tour operator. They offer several itineraries on a daily basis. There is a free pickup and return service between centrally located hotels and departure locations.

Reservations are required for most tours, which are available in several foreign languages including French, German, Spanish, Italian, Japanese, and Korean.

5 Staying Active

Half the fun in San Francisco takes place outdoors. If you're not in the mood to trek it, there are plenty of other things to do that will allow you to enjoy the surroundings.

BICYCLING

Two city-designated bike routes are maintained by the Parks and Recreations department. One winds $7^1/_2$ miles through Golden Gate Park to Lake Merced; the other traverses the city, starting in the south, and follows a route over the Golden Gate Bridge. These routes are not dedicated to bicyclists, and caution must be exercised. Helmets are recommended. A bike map is available from the San Francisco Visitor Information Center, at Powell and Mason streets (see "Visitor Information" in chapter 3), and from bicycle shops all around town.

Ocean Beach has a public walk and bikeway that stretches along five waterfront blocks of the Great Highway between Noriega and Santiago streets. It's an easy ride from Cliff House or Golden Gate Park.

Park Cyclery, at 1749 Waller St. (☎ **415/752-8383**), is one of two shops in the Haight Street/Stanyan Street area that rent bikes. Located next to Golden Gate Park, the cyclery rents mountain bikes exclusively, along with helmets, locks, and accessories. The charge is $5 per hour, $25 per day, and it's open Thursday through Tuesday from 10am to 6pm.

BOATING

At the **Golden Gate Park Boat House** (☎ **415/752-0347**) on Stow Lake, the park's largest body of water, you can rent a rowboat or pedal boat by the hour and steer over to Strawberry Hill, a large, round island in the middle of the lake, for lunch. There's usually a line on weekends. The boat house is open daily from June to September, from 9am to 4pm; the rest of the year, on Tuesday through Sunday, 9am to 4pm.

GOLF

San Francisco has a few beautiful golf courses. Unfortunately, the most lavish, including the course at the Presidio, are not open to the public. But if you're in town and are itching to put on your golf shoes and swing some clubs, there are two decent municipal golf courses.

Golden Gate Park Course. 47th Avenue and Fulton St. ☎ **415/751-8987.** Greens fees $10 per person Mon–Fri, $13 Sat–Sun. Daily 6am–dusk.

This small nine-hole course covers 1,357 yards and is par 27. All holes are par 3, tightly set, and well trapped with small greens. The course is a little weathered in spots, but it's a casual, fun, and inexpensive place to tee off local-style.

Lincoln Park Golf Course. 34th Avenue and Clement St. ☎ **415/ 221-9911.** Greens fees $23 per person Mon–Fri, $27 Sat–Sun. Daily 6:30am–dusk.

San Francisco's prettiest municipal course has terrific views and fairways lined with Monterey cypress trees. Its 18 holes encompass 5,081 yards, for a par 68, and the 17th hole has a glistening ocean view. This is the oldest course in the city and one of the oldest in the West.

HANDBALL

The city's best handball courts are in **Golden Gate Park,** opposite Seventh Avenue, south of Middle Drive East. Courts are available free, on a first-come, first-served basis.

RUNNING

The **Bay to Breakers Foot Race** is an annual 7^1/$_2$-kilometer run from downtown to Ocean Beach. Around 80,000 entrants gather—many dressed in wacky, innovative, and sometimes X-rated costumes for what's considered one of San Francisco's favored trademark events. The event is sponsored by the *San Francisco Examiner* and is held the Third Sunday of May ☎ 415/777-7770 for details.

The **San Francisco Marathon** is held annually in the middle of July. For further information, contact USA Track and Field (☎ **415/391-2123**).

SKATING (CONVENTIONAL & IN-LINE)

Although people skate in Golden Gate Park all week long, Sunday is best, when John F. Kennedy Drive, between Kezar Drive and Transverse Road, is closed to automobiles. A smooth "skate pad" is located on your right, just past the Conservatory. **Skates on Haight,** at 1818 Haight St. (☎ 415/752-8376), is the best place to rent either in-line or conventional skates, and is located only one block from the park. Protective wrist guards and knee pads are included free. The cost is $7 per hour for in-line Rollerblades, $6 per hour for "conventionals." Major credit card and ID deposit are required. The shop is open Monday and Wednesday to Friday from 11:30am to 6:30pm, and Saturday and Sunday from 10am to 6pm.

TENNIS

More than 100 courts throughout the city are maintained by the **San Francisco Recreation and Parks Department** (☎ 415/ 753-7001). All are available free, on a first-come, first-served basis. The exception are the 21 courts in Golden Gate Park; a $4 to $6 fee is charged for their use, and courts must be reserved in advance for weekend play. Call the number above on Wednesday from 7 to 9pm, or on Thursday and Friday from 9am to 5pm.

WALKING & HIKING

The **Golden Gate National Recreation Area** offers plenty of opportunities for walking and hiking. One pleasant walk, or bike ride, for that matter, is along the Golden Gate Promenade, from Aquatic Park to the Golden Gate Bridge. The $3^1/_2$-mile paved trail leads along the northern edge of the Presidio, out to Fort Point. You can also hike along the Coastal Trail all the way from near Fort Point to the Cliff House. The park service maintains several other trails in the city. For more information or to pick up a map of the Golden Gate National Recreation Area, stop by the park service headquarters at Fort Mason at the north end of Laguna Street (☎ 415/ 556-0560).

URBAN HIKES

Even if you're not intending to work off the extravagantly rich dinners you'll eat in San Francisco, you can't help but shed some calories as you explore the city's neighborhoods and sights. Real calf-burners include:

The **Filbert Street Steps,** between Sansome Street and Telegraph Hill. Scaling the sheer eastern face of Telegraph Hill, this 377-step climb wends its way through verdant flower gardens and charming 19th-century cottages. Napier Lane, a narrow wooden plank walkway, leads to Montgomery Street. Turn right, and follow the path to the end of the cul-de-sac where another stairway continues to Telegraph's panoramic summit.

The **Lyon Street Steps,** between Green Street and Broadway, were built in 1916. This historic stairway street contains four steep sets of stairs totaling 288 steps in all. Begin at Green Street and

Work It Out

While San Francisco has plenty to offer in the way of outdoor exercise and activities, there are plenty of indoor places to relieve stress, work up a sweat, or treat your body to a little TLC.

The **San Francisco Bay Club**, located at 150 Greenwich St., at Battery Street (☎ 415/433-2200), is one of the most exclusive and extensive gym-cum-spas in the Bay Area. Celebrities such as Tom Cruise, Cindy Crawford, and Hugh Grant have flexed a few muscles here when on location and regular members include the city's old and new elite. The club takes up almost a full block and offers three floors filled with health equipment, including two pools (one's heated); tennis, squash, racquetball and basketball courts; aerobics and yoga; free weights, cardiovascular, and Nautilus equipment; a sundeck; sauna, steam, and whirlpool; and a cafe. Although walk-in guests are not permitted, sign up for any of the luxurious spa treatments that you're extended full work-out privileges for the day. Services include massage, facials, manicures, and pedicures.

A more spiritual workout can be found at **The Mindful Body,** a center for movement, body, and personal inner work. It is located at 2876 California St., between Broderick and Divisadero (☎ 415/931-2639 for class schedules). After an intense yoga or stretch class, guided meditation, or massage, you'll be a new person.

Adventurers can hone their skills at **Mission Cliffs Rock Climbing Center** at 2295 Harrison, at 19th Street (☎ 415/550-0515). For $12 (plus $6 if you need rental equipment) you can climb 14,000 feet of terrain and 2,000 square feet of boulders. Lessons, which cost extra and include children's and outdoor programs, can be arranged. Once you're worn out, relax in the sauna.

If getting your heart rate up seems like a chore, take a less painful approach at the **Metronome**, which offers ballroom, swing, Latin, night club, and salsa dance classes for individuals and groups. Call for information on class times, package deals, and weekend dance parties (☎ 415/252-9000).

climb all the way up, past manicured hedges and flower gardens to an iron gate that opens into the Presidio. A block east, on Baker Street, another set of 369 steps descends to Green Street.

Though most drive to this spectacular vantage point, a more rejuvenating way to experience **Twin Peaks** is to walk up from the back roads of U.C. Medical Center (off Parnassus) or from either of the two roads that lead to the top (off Woodside or Clarendon avenues). Early morning is the best time to trek, when the city is quiet, the air is crisp, and the sightseers haven't crowded the parking lot. Keep an eye out for cars, since there's no real hiking trail and be sure to walk beyond the lot and up to the highest vantage point.

6 Spectator Sports

The Bay Area's sports scene includes several major professional franchises, including football, baseball, and basketball. Check the local newspapers' sports sections for daily listings of local events.

Baseball is represented by the **San Francisco Giants,** who play at 3 Com Park, Giants Drive and Gilman Avenue (☎ 415/467-8000), from April through October. The stadium is about 8 miles south of downtown. Tickets are usually available up until game time, but seats can be dreadfully far from the action. Tickets may be obtained through BASS Ticketmaster (☎ 510/762-2277). Special express bus service is available from Market Street on game days; call Muni (☎ 415/673-6864) for pickup points and schedule information. Bring a coat, as this 60,000-seat stadium is known for chilly winds.

The Bay Area's other team is the **Oakland Athletics,** who play at the Oakland Coliseum Complex, at the Hegenberger Road exit from I-880, in Oakland (☎ 510/430-8020). The 1989 world-champion A's play across the Bay. The stadium holds close to 50,000 spectators and is serviced by BART's Coliseum station. Tickets are available from the Coliseum Box Office or by phone through BASS Ticketmaster (☎ 510/762-2277).

Basketball is represented by the **Golden State Warriors,** who play at the Oakland Coliseum Complex, at the Hegenberger Road exit from I-880, in Oakland (☎ 510/638-6300). The NBA Warriors play basketball in the 15,025-seat Oakland Coliseum Arena. The season runs from November through April, and most games are played at 7:30pm. Tickets are available at the arena, and by phone through BASS Ticketmaster (☎ 510/762-2277).

The Bay Area once again has two professional **football** teams. The **San Francisco 49ers,** play at 3 Com Park, Giants Drive and Gilman Avenue (☎ 415/468-2249). Games are played on Sunday from August through December; kickoff is usually at 1pm. Tickets sell out early in the season, but are available at higher prices through ticket agents beforehand and from scalpers at the gate. Ask your hotel concierge or visit City Box Office, 141 Kearny St. (☎ 415/392-4400). Special express bus service is available from Market Street on game days; call Muni (☎ 415/673-6864) for pickup points and schedule information.

Also back in the Bay Area are the 49ers' arch enemy, the **Oakland Raiders.** Home games play at the Oakland Alameda County Coliseum, off the 880 Freeway (Nimitz) (☎ **800/949-2626** for ticket information).

7

Shopping

*L*ike its population, San Francisco's shopping is worldly and intimate. Every persuasion, style, era, and fetish is represented here, not in a big, tacky shopping mall, but rather in hundreds of quaint and dramatically different boutiques scattered throughout the city. Stores generally open at 10am and remain open until 6pm; many close on Sunday. Call ahead to ask about opening hours.

Sales tax in San Francisco is 8.5%.

1 Major Shopping Areas

Union Square and Environs   San Francisco's most congested and popular shopping mecca is centered around Union Square and enclosed by Bush, Taylor, Market, and Montgomery streets. Most of the big department stores and many high-end specialty shops are in this area. Be sure to venture to Grant Avenue, Post and Sutter streets, and Maiden Lane.

Chinatown   Chinatown is the antithesis of Union Square, with shops along Grant Avenue selling an eclectic variety of cheap goods, T-shirts, knockoffs, and other tourist-oriented trinkets. Most of the stores in Chinatown are open daily from 10am to 10pm.

Union Street   The Cow Hollow section of this trendy street, between Van Ness Avenue and Steiner Street, is the place for antiques, handcrafts, hip fashions, and deluxe glassware.

Fillmore Street   Some of the best shopping in town is packed into five blocks of Fillmore Street in Pacific Heights. From Jackson to Sutter streets, Fillmore is the perfect place to grab a bite and peruse the high-priced boutiques, craft shops, and incredible houseware stores.

Haight Street   The six blocks of upper Haight Street, between Central Avenue and Stanyan Street, are still the best place to shop for inexpensive, funky styles; antique and vintage clothing; Grateful Dead memorabilia; and kitsch. Along this street there's a healthy mix of boutiques, secondhand shops, and inexpensive restaurants.

Fisherman's Wharf and Environs The nonstop strip of waterfront malls that runs along Jefferson Street includes hundreds of shops, restaurants, and attractions. Ghirardelli Square, Pier 39, the Cannery, and the Anchorage are the major complexes.

2 Shopping A to Z

ART

The **San Francisco Gallery Guide,** a comprehensive, bimonthly publication listing the city's current shows, is available free by mail. Send a self-addressed stamped envelope to San Francisco Bay Area Gallery Guide, 1369 Fulton St., San Francisco, CA 94117 (☎ **415/921-1600**), or pick one up at the San Francisco Visitor Information Center. Most of the city's major art galleries are clustered downtown in the Union Square area, especially in the 400 and 500 blocks of Bush and Sutter.

BOOKS

Charlotte's Web. 2278 Union St. (between Steiner and Fillmore sts.). ☎ **415/441-4700.**

A first-rate children's bookstore, Charlotte's Web is notable for its particularly knowledgeable owner, who sells everything from cloth books for babies to histories and poetry for young adults. Nonliterary items include music cassettes, videos, posters, and cards.

City Lights Bookstore. 261 Columbus Ave. (at Broadway). ☎ **415/362-8193.**

Brooding literary types browse this famous bookstore owned by Lawrence Ferlinghetti, the renowned beat generation poet. The three-level bookshop prides itself on a comprehensive collection of art, poetry, and political paperbacks, as well as more mainstream books.

A Clean Well-Lighted Place. 601 Van Ness Ave. (between Turk St. and Golden Gate Ave.). ☎ **415/441-6670.**

Voted best bookstore by the *San Francisco Bay Guardian,* this independent has good new fiction and nonfiction sections and also specializes in music, art, mystery, and cookbooks.

McDonald's Bookshop. 48 Turk St. (at Market St.). ☎ **415/673-2235.**

San Francisco's biggest used-book shop claims to stock more than a million volumes, including out-of-print, esoteric, and hard-to-find books in all categories and languages.

Rand-McNally Map and Travel. 595 Market St. ☎ **415/777-3131.**

Hands down the best travel bookstore in the city, this corner shop features maps, atlases, and travel guides to all destinations, as well as educational games, toys, and globes.

Thomas Bros. Maps & Books. 550 Jackson St. (at Columbus Ave.). ☎ **415/ 981-7520** or 800/969-3072.

Thomas Bros. sells street, topographic, and hiking maps depicting San Francisco, California, and the world. A selection of travel-related books is also sold.

CHINA, SILVER & GLASS

Gump's. 135 Post St. (between Kearny St. and Grant Ave.). ☎ **415/ 982-1616.**

San Francisco's favored house-and-home store is located between Grant Avenue and Stockton Street. Founded almost a century ago, Gump's offers gifts and treasures ranging from Asian antiquities to contemporary art glass and exquisite jade and pearl jewelry. Many items are made specifically for the store. Gump's also has one of the most revered window displays each holiday season.

CRAFTS

The Canton Bazaar. 616 Grant Ave. (between Sacramento and California sts.). ☎ **415/362-5750.**

Amid a wide variety of handicrafts you'll find an excellent selection of rosewood and carved furniture, cloisonné enamelware, rose Canton chinaware, porcelain ware, carved jade, embroideries, jewelry, and antiques from mainland China.

The New Unique Company. 838 Grant Ave. (between Clay and Washington sts.). ☎ **415/981-2036.**

Primarily a calligraphy and watercolor supplies store, the shop also has a good assortment of books relating to these topics. In addition, there is a wide selection of carved stones for use as seals on letters and documents. The store will carve seals to order should you want a special design or group of initials.

Silkroute International. 3119 Fillmore St. (at Filbert St.). ☎ **415/ 563-4936.**

Owned and operated by an Afghan who offers fascinating wares, old and new, from his native country, the shop sells oriental and tribal rugs, kilims, dhurries, textiles, jewelry, clothing, pillows, arts, and antiques.

DEPARTMENT STORES

Three of the biggest in the city are **Macy's,** at the corner of Stockton and O'Farrell streets, on Union Square (☎ **415/397-3333**); **Neiman-Marcus,** at 150 Stockton Street, on Union Square (☎ **415/362-3900**); and **Nordstrom,** at 865 Market Street, in the San Francisco Shopping Centre, near the cable-car turnaround (☎ **415/243-8500**).

FASHIONS (MEN'S & WOMEN'S)

One by Two. 418 Hayes St. (at Gough St.). ☎ **415/252-1460.**

Hayes Valley features fashion comparable to New York's SoHo, though disappointing in comparison because there are so few shops. Still, if you're interested in the latest chic and wild trendy wear, browse local designer Al Abayan's boutique featuring urban sportswear with a modern twist. His style is young, clean, and colorful in thick, expensive fabrics. "In" wear doesn't come cheaply here, but you can bet you won't see everyone wearing your outfit in your hometown.

Three Bags Full. 2181 Union St. (at Fillmore). ☎ **415/567-5753.**

Snuggling up in a cozy sweater can be a fashionable event if you do your shopping at this pricey boutique, which carries the gamut in handmade and one-of-a-kind playful and extravagant knitwear. Other city locations are 500 Sutter St. and 3314 Sacramento St.

Wearever. 1420 Grant Ave. (between Union and Green sts.). ☎ **415/ 392-1248.**

Labels such as Double RL by Ralph Lauren, Mossimo, Calvin Klein, Miss Sixty, French Connection, and many others are featured at this small fashion boutique for both men and women. Also offered are silver rings made from antique American coins.

FASHIONS (MEN'S)

All American Boy. 463 Castro St. (between Market and 18th sts.). ☎ **415/ 861-0444.**

Long known for setting the mainstream style for gay men, All American Boy is the quintessential Castro clothing shop.

Citizen Clothing. 536 Castro St. (between 18th and 19th sts.). ☎ **415/ 558-9429.**

The Castro has some of America's best men's casual clothing stores, and this is one of them. Stylish (but not faddish) pants, tops, and accessories are sold here.

MAC. 5 Claude Lane (off Sutter St. between Grant Ave. and Kearny St.). ☎ **415/837-0615.**

The more classic than corporate man shops here for imported tailored suits in new and intriguing fabrics. Lines include London's Katherine Hamnette, Belgium's SO, Italy's Alberto Biani, New York's John Bartlett, and San Francisco's Lat Naylor. Their women's' store is located at 1543 Grant Ave. (between Filbert and Union streets) (☎ 415/837-1604).

FASHIONS (WOMEN'S)

Bella Donna. 539 Hayes St. (between Laguna and Octavia sts.). ☎ **415/861-7182.**

Another blessing to the small but growing Hayes Valley alternative shopping mecca is this expensive, but quality, boutique offering luxurious women's clothing, such as hand-knit sweaters, silky slip dresses, and fashionable knit hats. There's also a wonderful (albeit expensive) collection of vases and other household trinkets, as well as a small selection of remainder fabrics. Upstairs the wedding and bridal section focuses on the vintage look.

Métier. 50 Maiden Lane (at Grant Ave. and Kearny St.). ☎ **415/989-5395.**

Classic and sophisticated creations for women include European ready-to-wear lines and designers Peter Cohen, Harriet Selwyn, Alberto Biani, Victor Victoria, and local Lat Naylor, as well as a distinguished collection of Antique-style, high-end jewelry.

Solo Fashion. 1599 Haight St. (at Clayton St.). ☎ **415/621-0342.**

While strolling upper Haight, stop in here for a good selection of upbeat, contemporary, English-style street wear, along with a collection of dresses designed exclusively for this shop.

FASHIONS (CHILDREN'S)

Minis by Profili. 2042 Union St. (between Webster and Buchanan sts.). ☎ **415/567-9537.**

Christina Profili, a San Francisco native who used to design for Banana Republic, opened this children's clothing store selling her own creations. Every piece, from shirts to pants and dresses, is made from cotton or organic cotton. Every outfit perfectly coordinates with everything else in the store. Minis also offers educational and creative toys and storybooks with matching dolls.

FOOD

Golden Gate Fortune Cookies Co. 56 Ross Alley (between Washington and Jackson sts.). ☎ **415/781-3956.**

This tiny, touristy factory sells fortune cookies hot off the press. You can purchase them in small bags or in bulk, and if your order is large enough, you may even be able to negotiate your own message. Even if you're not buying, stop in to see how these sugary treats are made.

Joseph Schmidt Confections. 3489 16th St. (at Sanchez St.). ☎ **415/ 861-8682.**

Chocolate takes the shape of exquisite sculptural masterpieces—such as long-stemmed tulips and heart-shaped boxes—that are so beautiful, you'll be hesitant to bite the head off your adorable chocolate panda bear. But once you do, you'll know why this is the most popular chocolatier in town. Prices are also remarkably reasonable.

Pure T. 2238 Polk St. (between Vallejo and Green sts.). ☎ **415/441-7878.**

If you're asked to bring dessert to a dinner party or are simply aching for a treat, it'd be a sin to miss out on what we consider the best ice cream shop in the city. The freshly made, all natural ice creams here redefine "gourmet." They're light and delicate to the taste and flavored with, you guessed it, pure tea. Treat your tongue to a scoop of black currant or Thai tea and you'll be hooked.

GIFTS

Cost Plus Imports. 2552 Taylor St. (between North Point and Bay sts.). ☎ **415/928-6200.**

At the Fisherman's Wharf cable-car turntable, Cost Plus is a vast warehouse crammed to the rafters with Chinese baskets, Indian camel bells, Malaysian batik scarves, and innumerable other items from Algeria to Zanzibar. More than 20,000 items from 40 nations are purchased directly from their country of origin and packed into this well-priced warehouse. They also have a decent wine shop.

Distractions. 1552 Haight St. (between Ashbury and Clayton sts.). ☎ **415/ 252-8751.**

This is the best of the Haight St. shops selling pseudo-sixties memorabilia. You'll find retro hippie clothes, pipes, toys, and stickers liberally intermixed with tie-dyed Grateful Dead paraphernalia and lots of cool stuff to look at.

Off Your Dot. 2241 Market St. (between Sanchez and Noe sts.). ☎ **415/ 252-5642.**

Wonderfully attractive and artistic handmade gifts cover almost every inch of this Castro district store. There's everything from wall art to candles, picture frames, lamps, and glasswork here, and most of it is locally made; prices are the best in town.

PlaNetweavers Treasures Store. 1573 Haight St. (between Ashbury and Clayton sts.). ☎ **415/864-4415.**

There truly are real treasures here: a huge selection of unusual arts and collectibles including wind chimes, natural body products, jewelry, and crafts from around the world. Best of all, the store is committed to working with socially conscious vendors so you get an extra karma bonus when you shop here.

Quantity Postcards. 1441 Grant St. (at Green St.). ☎ **415/986-8866.**

You'll find the perfect postcard for literally everyone you know here, as well as some depictions of old San Francisco, movie stars, and Day-Glo posters featuring concert-poster artist Frank Kozik. Prices range from 15¢ to 75¢ per card, and even if you don't need any cards, you'll enjoy browsing the eclectic collection of mailables.

HOUSEWARES

Fillamento. 2185 Fillmore St. (at Sacramento St.). ☎ **415/931-2224.**

Fillamento's three floors are always packed with shoppers searching for the most classic, artistic, and refined housewares. Whether you're looking to set a good table or revamp your bedroom, you'll find it all here.

Victorian Interiors. 575 Hayes St. (at Laguna St.). ☎ **415/431-7191.**

Draped with an array of period floral wallpapers, this little store is the perfect place to shop for any Victorian fanatic. Along with traditional Victorian houseware such as wallpapers, moldings, drapery cornices and rods, tiles, fabrics, and carpets, you'll find a great collection of old pipes and knickknacks.

The Wok Shop. 718 Grant Ave. (at Clay St.). ☎ **415/989-3797.**

This shop has every conceivable implement for Chinese cooking, including woks, brushes, cleavers, circular chopping blocks, dishes, oyster knives, bamboo steamers, strainers—you name it. The shop also sells a wide range of kitchen utensils, baskets, handmade linens from China, and aprons.

Zinc Details. 1905 Fillmore St. (between Bush and Pine sts.). ☎ **415/776-2100.**

One of our favorite stores in the city, Zinc Details has received accolades from everyone from *Elle Decor Japan* to *Metropolitan Home* for its amazing collection of locally hand-crafted glass vases, pendant lights, ceramics, and furniture. Each piece is a true work of art created specifically for the store (except vintage items).

JEWELRY

The Magical Trinket. 524 Hayes St. (between Laguna and Octavia sts.). ☎ 415/626-0764.

Do-it-yourself jewelry makers beware. This store, brimming with beads, baubles, and bangles, will inspire you to make your own knickknacks and kick yourself for the prices you've been paying for costume jewelry in retail stores.

Old & New Estates. 2181A Union St. (at Fillmore St.). ☎ **415/346-7525.**

Buy yourself a bauble. Treat yourself to a trinket at this shop featuring top-of-the-line antique jewelry: pendants, diamond rings, necklaces, bracelets, and natural pearls.

Pearl Empire. 127 Geary St. (between Stockton St. and Grant Ave.). ☎ **415/362-0606.**

The Pearl Empire has been importing jewelry from all over the world since 1957. They are specialists in unusual pearls and jade, and offer restringing on the premises.

Union Street Goldsmith. 1909 Union St. (at Laguna St.). ☎ **415/776-8048.**

A showcase for Bay Area goldsmiths, this exquisite shop sells custom-designed jewelry in all karats. Many pieces emphasize colored stones in their settings.

MARKETS/PRODUCE

Farmers Market. Embarcadero, in front of the Ferry Building. ☎ **510/528-6987.**

Every Saturday from May to November, Northern California fruit, vegetable, bread, and dairy vendors join local restaurateurs in selling fresh delicious edibles. There's no better way to enjoy a bright San Francisco morning than strolling this gourmet street market and snacking your way through breakfast. You can also pick up locally made vinegars and oils—they make wonderful gifts.

RECORDS & CDS

Groove Merchant Records. 776 Haight St. (at Pierce and Steiner sts.). ☎ 415/252-5766.

Collectors of rare vinyl jazz, soul, funk and Latin must check out Groove Merchant, whose own record label was in the forefront of the Bay Area acid jazz movement and continues to reissue old and rare groove and contemporary artists.

Recycled Records. 1377 Haight St. (between Central and Masonic). ☎ **415/ 626-4075.**

Easily one of the best used-record stores in the city, this loud shop in the Haight has a good selection of promotional CDs and cases of used "classic" rock LPs. Sheet music, tour programs, and old *TV Guide*s are sold.

Rough Trade Records. 695 Third St. (at Townsend). ☎ **415/543-7091.**

Both mainstream and alternative (both new and used) CDs, tapes, and vinyl are sold in this well-stocked shop. Some local bands and hard-to-find international titles are available.

Streetlight Records. 3979 24th St. (between Noe and Sanchez sts.). ☎ **415/282-3550.**

Overstuffed with used music in all three formats, this place is best known for its records and excellent CD collection. Rock music is cheap here, and a money-back guarantee guards against defects. Their second location is at 2350 Market St. (between Castro and Noe streets) (☎ 415/282-8000).

SHOES

Birkenstock Natural Footwear. 1815 Polk St. (between Washington and Jackson sts.). ☎ **415/776-5225.**

This relaxed store is known for its California-style, form-fitting sandals. Other orthopedically correct shoes are also available, including Finn Comforts and traditional Danish clogs by Dansko.

Taming of the Shoe. 1736 Haight St. (at Cole St.). ☎ **415/221-4453.**

For both men and women, this contemporary shoe and boot shop is filled with the hippest names from America and Europe. It also sells many original styles under its own name, and vintage footwear from the 1950s, 1960s, and 1970s.

TOYS

The Chinatown Kite Shop. 717 Grant Ave. (between Clay and Sacramento sts.). ☎ **415/989-5182.**

This shop's astonishing assortment of flying objects includes attractive fish kites, wind socks in nylon or cotton, hand-painted Chinese paper kites, wood-and-paper biplanes, pentagonal kites, and do-it-yourself kite kits, all of which make great souvenirs or decorations. Computer-designed stunt kites have two or four control lines to manipulate loops and dives.

VINTAGE CLOTHING

Ⓢ **Aardvark's.** 1501 Haight St. (at Ashbury St.). ☎ **415/621-3141.**

One of San Francisco's largest second-hand clothing dealers, Aardvark's has seemingly endless racks of shirts, pants, dresses, skirts, and hats from the last 30 years.

Buffalo Exchange. 1555 Haight St. (between Clayton and Ashbury sts.). ☎ **415/431-7733.**

This large storefront on upper Haight Street is crammed with racks of antique and new fashions from the 1960s, 1970s, and 1990s. It stocks everything from suits and dresses to neckties, hats, handbags, and jewelry. Buffalo Exchange anticipates some of the hottest new street fashions. A second shop is located at 1800 Polk St. (at Washington Street) (☎ 415/346-5741).

La Rosa. 1711 Haight St. (at Cole). ☎ **415/668-3744.**

On a street packed with vintage clothing shops, this is one of the more upscale options, featuring a selection of high-quality, dry-cleaned second-hand goods. Formal suits and dresses are its specialty, but you'll also find sport coats, slacks, and shoes.

WINES

Wine Club San Francisco. 953 Harrison St. (between Fifth and Sixth sts.). ☎ **415/512-9086.**

The Wine Club is a discount warehouse that offers bargain prices on more than 1,200 domestic and foreign wines because they only mark up wholesale prices 6% to 12%. Bottles cost from $3.99 to $1,100.

8

San Francisco After Dark

*F*or up-to-date nightlife information, turn to the *San Francisco Weekly* and the *San Francisco Bay Guardian,* both of which contain comprehensive current listings. They are available free at bars and restaurants, and from street-corner boxes all around the city. *Where,* a free tourist monthly, also has information on programs and performance times; it's available in most of the city's finer hotels. The Sunday edition of the *San Francisco Examiner and Chronicle* also features a "Datebook" section, printed on pink paper, with information and listings on the week's upcoming events.

1 The Performing Arts

Tix Bay Area (☎ 415/433-7827) sells half-price tickets to theater, dance, and music performances on the day of the show only; tickets for Sunday and Monday events are sold on Saturday. They also sell advance, full-price tickets for most performances. A service charge, ranging from $1 to $3, is levied on each ticket. Only cash or traveler's checks are accepted for half-price tickets; Visa and MasterCard are accepted for full-price tickets. Tix is located on Stockton Street, between Post and Geary streets on the east side of Union Square (opposite Maiden Lane). It's open Tuesday through Thursday from 11am to 6pm, Friday and Saturday from 11am to 7pm.

Tickets to most theater and dance events can also be obtained through **City Box Office,** 153 Kearny St., Suite 402 (☎ 415/392-4400) and **BASS Ticketmaster** (☎ 510/762-2277). You can also try **Wherehouse** stores throughout the city. The most convenient location is at 30 Powell St.

CLASSICAL MUSIC

In addition to the San Francisco Symphony, there are a couple of important minor companies. Acclaimed by *The New York Times* as "the country's leading early music orchestra," the **Philharmonia Baroque Orchestra** (☎ 415/391-5252, box office 415/392-4400) performs usually in the Herbst Theatre from September to April.

Tickets cost $23 to $33. And the the **San Francisco Contemporary Music Players** (☎ **415/252-6235,** box office 415/978-ARTS), whose concerts are held at the Center for the Arts at Yerba Buena Gardens, feature modern chamber works by international artists. Tickets cost $14 for adults, $10 for seniors, and $6 for students.

San Francisco Symphony. Performing at Davies Symphony Hall, 201 Van Ness Ave. (at Grove St.). ☎ **415/864-6000** (box office). Tickets $10–$68.

Founded in 1911, the internationally respected San Francisco Symphony is now under the baton of Michael Tilson Thomas. The season runs from September to May. Summer symphony activities include a Composer Festival and a Summer Pops series.

OPERA

In addition to San Francisco's major opera company, you might also check out the amusing **Pocket Opera,** 333 Kearny St., Suite 703 (☎ **415/989-1855**). From mid-January through mid-June, this comic company stages farcical performances in English of well-known operas accompanied by a chamber orchestra. The staging is intimate and informal, without lavish costumes and sets. Performances are on Saturday or Sunday. Call for complete information and show times. Tickets cost $18 to $22.

San Francisco Opera. Performing at the Civic Auditorium and Orpheum Theater (the Opera House is currently closed for renovation). ☎ **415/864-3330** (box office). Tickets $25–$140.

The San Francisco Opera was the United States's first municipal opera, and is one of the city's cultural icons. It features celebrated stars, along with promising newcomers in traditional and avant-garde productions, all with English supertitles. The season starts in September and lasts just 14 weeks, with nightly performances (except on Mondays) and matinees on Sundays. Performances in January and February 1997 will be performed elsewhere, due to retrofitting of the Opera House. The fall of 1997 will be the 75th anniversary season, which will be held in the newly restored Opera House.

THEATER

The city's theater district is concentrated on a few blocks west of Union Square.

The city has a wide variety of offerings, many more than we have space to cover here—check the publications mentioned above to see what's currently in production. One good bet is **The Magic**

Theatre, Building D, Fort Mason Center, Marina Boulevard at Buchanan Street (☎ **415/441-8822**), a highly acclaimed company that presents the works of new playwrights and has nurtured the talents of such luminaries as Sam Shepard and Jon Robin Baitz. The season usually runs from September to July; performances are offered Wednesday through Sunday. Tickets cost $15 to $24 with discounts for students and seniors. **Theatre Rhinoceros,** 2926 16th St. (☎ **415/861-5079**), founded in 1977, was America's first (and still the foremost) theater ensemble devoted solely to works addressing gay and lesbian issues. The company presents five main stage shows and a dozen studio productions of new and classic works each year. The theater is located one block east of the 16th Street/Mission BART station.

✪ **American Conservatory Theater (A.C.T.).** Performing at the Geary Theater, 415 Geary St. (at Mason St.). ☎ **415/749-2228.** Tickets $13–$45.

The troupe is so venerated that A.C.T. has been compared to the superb British National Theatre, the Berliner Ensemble, and the Comédie Française. The season runs from October through May and features both classical and experimental works. The Geary sustained severe damage in the 1989 earthquake and has just reopened after an extensive renovation and seismic stabilization.

Lorraine Hansberry Theatre. Performing at 620 Sutter St. ☎ **415/474-8800.**

San Francisco's top African American theater group performs in a 300-seat theater off the lobby of the Sheehan Hotel, near Mason Street. Special adaptations from literature are performed along with contemporary dramas, classics, and world premieres. Phone for dates, programs, and ticket prices.

DANCE

In addition to the local companies, top traveling troupes like the Joffrey Ballet and American Ballet Theatre make regular appearances. Primary modern dance spaces include the **Theatre Artaud,** 450 Florida St., at 17th Street (☎ **415/621-7797**); the **Cowell Theater,** at Fort Mason Center, Marina Boulevard, at Buchanan Street (☎ **415/441-3400**); **Dancer's Group/Footwork,** 3221 22nd St., at Mission Street (☎ **415/824-5044**); and the **New Performance Gallery,** 3153 17th St., at Shotwell in the Mission District (☎ **415/863-9834**). Check the local papers for schedules or contact the theater box offices directly.

☼ **San Francisco Ballet.** For tickets and location information. ☎ **415/865-2000** or 415/703-9400. Tickets $10–$75.

The San Francisco Ballet is the oldest permanent ballet company in the United States and regarded as one of the country's finest. Under the artistic direction of Helgi Tomasson, the company performs an eclectic repertoire of full-length, neoclassical, and contemporary ballets. The season opens with performances of The Nutcracker in December and continues through May. While its regular theater, the War Memorial Opera House, is closed for renovations, the Ballet will perform in alternate theaters.

2 The Club & Music Scene

The hippest dance places are located South of Market Street (SoMa), in former warehouses, while most popular cafe culture is still centered in North Beach.

CABARET & COMEDY

Bay Area Theatresports (BATS). Bayfront Theater at the Fort Mason Center, Bldg. B, 3rd Floor. ☎ **415/824-8220.** Tickets $8.

This is an improvisational tournament, in which four-actor teams compete against each other, taking on improvisational challenges from the audience. Mondays only.

Beach Blanket Babylon. At Club Fugazi, 678 Green St. (between Powell St. and Columbus Ave.). ☎ **415/421-4222.** Tickets $18–$45.

A San Francisco tradition, Beach Blanket Babylon is a comedic musical send-up that is best known for its outrageous costumes and oversize headdresses. It's been playing almost 22 years now, and still almost every performance sells out. Those under 21 are welcome at Sunday matinees at 3pm when no alcohol is served; photo ID is required for evening performances. It's wise to write for tickets at least three weeks in advance, or obtain them through TIX.

Cobb's Comedy Club. In the Cannery at Fisherman's Wharf, 2801 Leavenworth St. (at Hyde St.). ☎ **415/928-4320.** Cover $5 Mon, $8–$15 Tues–Sun (plus a two-beverage minimum nightly).

Cobb's features national headliners. There is comedy every night, including a 13-comedian All-Pro Monday showcase (a three-hour marathon). Cobb's is open to those 18 and over, and occasionally to kids aged 16 and 17 if they are accompanied by an adult.

Finocchio's. 506 Broadway (at Kearny St.). ☎ **415/982-9388.** Cover $12–$15 (no drink minimum).

For more than 50 years this family run cabaret club has showcased the best female impersonators in a funny, *kitschy* show. Three different revues are presented nightly (usually Thursday through Saturday at 8:30, 10, and 11:30pm), and a single cover is good for the entire evening. Drinks begin at $2.75. Parking available next door at the Flying Dutchman.

Punch Line. 444 Battery St., plaza level (between Washington and Clay sts.). ☎ **415/397-4337** or 415/397-7573 for recorded information. Cover $5 Sun, $6–$15 Mon–Sat (plus a two-drink minimum nightly).

This is the largest comedy nightclub in the city. Three-person shows with top national and local talent are featured Tuesday through Saturday. Showcase night is Sunday, when 15 to 20 rising stars take the mike. There's an all-star showcase or a special event on Monday nights. Buy tickets in advance (if you don't want to wait in line).

ROCK & BLUES CLUBS

The Fillmore. 1805 Geary Blvd. (at Fillmore St.). ☎ **415/346-6000.** Tickets $16–$30.

Reopened after years of neglect, The Fillmore, made famous by promoter Bill Graham in the 1960s, is once again attracting big names. Check the local listings in magazines, or call the theater for information on upcoming events.

The Saloon. 1232 Grant Ave. (at Vallejo St.). ☎ **415/989-7666.** Cover $3–$5 Fri–Sat.

An authentic gold rush survivor, this North Beach dive is the oldest extant bar in the city. Popular with both bikers and daytime pinstripers, there's live blues nightly. Drinks run $3 to $5.

Slim's. 333 11th St. (at Folsom St.). ☎ **415/522-0333.** Cover $10–$20 (plus a two-drink minimum).

New Orleans–style Slim's is co-owned by musician Boz Scaggs, who sometimes takes the stage under the name "Presidio Slim." This glitzy restaurant/bar seats 300, serves California cuisine, and specializes in excellent American music—home-grown rock, jazz, blues, and alternative music—almost nightly.

JAZZ & LATIN CLUBS

Cesar's Latin Palace. 3140 Mission St. (at Army St.). ☎ **415/648-6611.** Cover $5–$8.

Live Latin bands perform to a very mixed crowd—ethnically, economically, and generationally. There's plenty of dancing and drinking in this high-energy club.

⭐ **Jazz at Pearl's.** 256 Columbus Ave. (at Broadway). ☎ **415/291-8255.** No cover, but there is a two-drink minimum.

This is one of the best venues for jazz in the city. Ribs and chicken are served with the sounds too. The live jams last until 2am nightly.

Mason Street Wine Bar. 342 Mason St. (at Geary St.). ☎ **415/391-3454.** No cover, except for special performances.

This contemporary bar offers live jazz nightly. Small cabaret tables with black club chairs face a small stage. More than 100 different wines are served from the half-moon–shaped bar. Glasses of wine begin at $4 each.

330 Ritch. 330 Ritch (between Third and Fourth sts. off Townsend). ☎ **415/541-9574.**

If you can find this place, you must be cool. It's located on a two-block alley in SoMa, and even locals have a hard time remembering how to get there. But once you do, expect happy hour cocktails (specials on a few select mixed drinks and draft brews), pool tables, and a hip, young crowd at play. Weekends, the place really livens up when live bands take center stage on Fridays, and the Latin lovers salsa all night to the spicy beat.

Masons and The New Orleans Room. In the Fairmont Hotel, 950 Mason St. (at California St.). ☎ 415/772-5259. Cover varies.

Cabaret reigns at Masons, while the adjoining New Orleans room features jazz. Call for information on featured entertainers.

CLUBS

The club scene is always changing. Most of the venues below are promoted as different clubs on various nights of the week, each with its own look, sound, and style. Discount passes and club announcements are often available at hip clothing stores and other shops along upper Haight Street.

Three Babes and a Bus (☎ 415/552-2582) runs regular nightclub trips on Friday and Saturday nights to the city's busiest clubs.

Club DV8. 540 Howard St. (between 1st and 2nd sts.). ☎ **415/777-1419** or 415/957-1730 for recorded information. Cover $5 Thurs, $10 Fri–Sat, $5 Sun (usually free before 10pm).

This SoMa club has been attracting the black-garb crowd longer than almost any other establishment. There are two DJs spinning music on separate dance floors, each perpetually packed with a lively 20-something crowd. The decor is an interesting mix of trompe l'oeil, pop art, candelabra, mirrors, and some extraordinary Daliesque props.

Club 1015. 1015 Folsom St. (at 6th St.). ☎ **415/431-0700.** Cover $10–$15.

Three levels and dance floors have made this a stylish stop along the nightclub circuit. Currently, **Dakota** (☎ **415/431-1200**) is held on Fridays from 10pm to 7am, featuring four different sounds: 1970s, progressive house, funk, and rare groove. Saturday is **gay night** (☎ **415/431-BOYS**). For other nights, call ahead.

Paradise Lounge. 1501 Folsom St. (at 11th St.). ☎ **415/861-6906.** Cover $3–$15.

Labyrinthine Paradise features three dance floors simultaneously vibrating to different beats. Smaller, auxiliary spaces include a pool room with a half dozen tables. Poetry readings are also given.

Sound Factory. 525 Harrison St. (at 1st St.). ☎ **415/543-1300.** Cover $10 (free before 10pm).

Herb Caen, who dubbed this the "mother of all discos," would never be found shaking it all night at this disco theme park. The maze of rooms and nonstop barrage of house, funk, lounge vibes, and club classics attracts swarms of young urbanites looking to rave it up until sometimes as late as 6am. Management tries to eliminate the riffraff by enforcing a dress code (no sneakers, hooded sweatshirts, or sports caps).

3 The Bar Scene

There are hundreds of bars throughout San Francisco, and although many are obscurely located and can't be classified by their neighborhood, the following is a general description of what you'll find and where.

- Chestnut and Union Street bars attract a postcollegiate crowd.
- Mission District haunts are frequented by young alternatives.
- Upper Haight caters to eclectic neighborhood cocktailers.
- Lower-Haight is skate/snowboarder grungy.
- Downtown pubs mix tourists with theater-goers and thirsty business people.
- North Beach serves all types.
- Castro caters to gay locals and tourists.
- South of Market (SoMa) offers an eclectic mix.

Here is a good cross-section of what the city has to offer.

Albion. 3139 16th St. (between Valencia and Guerrero sts.). ☎ **415/552-8558.**

This Mission District club is a grit-and-leather in-crowd place packed with artistic types and various SoMa hipsters. Live music plays Sunday between 5 and 8pm and ranges from ragtime and blues to jazz and swing.

Edinburgh Castle. 950 Geary St. (between Polk and Larkin sts.). ☎ **415/ 885-4074.**

Since 1958 this legendary Scottish pub has been known for unusual British ales on tap and the best selection of single-malt scotches in the city. It's decorated with Royal Air Force mementos, horse brasses, steel helmets, and an authentic Ballantine caber used in the annual Scottish games. Avoid Saturday nights unless you like bagpipes. Fish and chips are always available.

✪ **Harry Denton's.** 161 Steuart St. (between Mission and Howard sts.). ☎ **415/882-1333.** Cover charge after 9pm: $3 Wed; $5 Thurs; $10 Fri–Sat (free other times).

Early evening it's filled with working "suits" and secretaries on the prowl. But when the stately restaurant with mahogany bar, red velvet furnishings, and chandeliers clears away dining utensils and turns up the music, a glitzy crowd pulls up to valet with their boogie shoes on. The front lounge features R&B or jazz performers while there's disco and pop dancing in the back room.

Johnny Love's. 1500 Broadway. ☎ **415/931-6053.** Cover Fri–Sat $9, $5 Wed–Thurs. Free before 9pm.

The city's quintessential singles spot and one of the best bars in town to dance to live music. There's a small dance floor and live music several nights a week; when it's jumping, this joint is a real scene. Love's serves decent food, too, but your money's best spent on drinks.

Julie's Supper Club. 1123 Folsom St. (at 7th St.). ☎ **415/861-0707.** Cover charge after 9pm; $5 Fri–Sat (unless a full meal is ordered).

Crowded and lively, it offers an array of appetizers and live music on Friday and Saturday nights.

Perry's. 1944 Union St. (at Laguna St.). ☎ **415/922-9022.**

If you read *Tales of the City,* you already know that this bar and restaurant has a colorful history as a pick-up place for Pacific Heights and Marina singles. Though the times are not as wild, locals still come to casually check out the happenings at the dark mahogany bar.

Persian Aub Zam Zam. 1633 Haight St. (at Clayton St.). ☎ **415/861-2545.**

Step through the forbidding metal doors and you'll feel as if you're in *Casablanca.* And although it's full of character, regulars come here for the acerbic owner/bartender, Bruno, who kicks almost everyone else out. Order a Finlandia vodka martini and you'll be allowed to stay. Sit at the bar; the tables are "closed."

The Redwood Room. In the Clift Hotel, 495 Geary St. ☎ **415/775-4700.**

A true art deco beauty, this ground-floor lounge is one of San Francisco's most comfortable and nostalgic piano bars. Its gorgeous redwood interior was completely built from a single 2,000-year-old tree. It's further enhanced by the large, brilliantly colored Gustav Klimt murals.

BREWPUBS

Gordon-Biersch Brewery. 2 Harrison St. (on the Embarcadero). ☎ **415/243-8246.**

Gordon-Biersch Brewery is San Francisco's largest brew-restaurant, serving decent food and tasty brew. There are always several beers to choose from, ranging from light to dark.

San Francisco Brewing Company. 155 Columbus Ave. (at Pacific St.). ☎ **415/434-3344.**

Surprisingly low key for an ale house, this cozy brewpub serves its brew along with burgers, fries, and the like. The bar is one of the city's few remaining old saloons aglow with stained-glass windows, tile floors, skylit ceiling beveled glass, a mahogany bar, and a massive overhead fan running the full length of the bar—a bizarre contraption crafted from brass and palm fronds. There's music most evenings.

20 Tank Brewery. 316 11th St. (at Folsom St.). ☎ **415/255-9455.**

Right in the heart of SoMa's popular strip, this huge, come-as-you-are bar is known for serving good beer at fair prices. Pizzas, sandwiches, chilis, and assorted appetizers are also available. Live jazz is performed two nights a week. Other nights you can amuse yourself with darts, shuffleboard, and dice.

NORTH BEACH BARS & CAFES

San Francisco in general—and North Beach in particular—is loaded with Italian-style cafes where patrons are encouraged to linger.

Caffè Greco. 423 Columbus Ave. (between Green and Vallejo sts.). ☎ **415/397-6261.**

Doing the North Beach thing is little more than hanging out in a sophisticated but relaxed atmosphere over a well-made cappuccino. You can do it here, and grab a bite, too. The affordable cafe fare includes beer, wine, a good selection of coffees, focaccia sandwiches, and desserts (try the gelato or house-made tiramisu).

Caffè Trieste. 601 Vallejo St. (at Grant Ave.). ☎ **415/392-6739.**

One of San Francisco's most beloved cafes is very down-home Italian, with only espresso drinks, pastries, and indoor and outdoor seating. Opera is always on the jukebox, unless its Saturday afternoon, when the family and their friends break out in operatic arias from 2 to 5pm. Drinks cost $1.95 to $3.75, except during performances when they're $3.50.

Savoy Tivoli. 1434 Grant Ave. ☎ **415/421-4112.**

Euro- and wanna-be Euro-trash crowd the few pool tables and indoor and patio seating to smoke cigarettes and look cool at this popular trendy bar.

Specs' Adler Museum Café. 12 Saroyan Pl. (off Columbus Ave.). ☎ **415/421-4112.**

Specs' is one of the liveliest and most likable pubs in North Beach. Maritime flags hang from the ceiling, while the exposed brick walls are lined with posters, photos, and various oddities.

Vesuvio. 255 Columbus Ave. (at Broadway). ☎ **415/362-3370.**

This is one of North Beach's best beatnik-style hangouts. Popular with neighborhood writers, artists, songsters, and wanna-bes, Vesuvio also gets its share of longshoremen, cab drivers, and business people. In addition to well-priced drinks, Vesuvio has espresso.

COCKTAILS WITH A VIEW

The Carnelian Room. 555 California St., in the Bank of America Building (between Kearny and Montgomery sts.). ☎ **415/433-7500.**

This 52nd-floor room offers panoramic views of the city. In addition to cocktails, sunset dinners are served nightly, for about $45 per person. Jackets and ties are required for men. The restaurant has the most extensive wine list in the city: 1,275 selections to be exact.

✪ **Crown Room.** In the Fairmont Hotel, 950 Mason St., 24th Floor. ☎ **415/772-5131.**

Of all the bars listed here, the Crown Room is definitely the plushest. Reached by an external glass elevator, the panoramic view from the top will encourage you to linger. In addition to drinks, dinner buffets are served for $31.

Harry Denton's Starlight Room. Atop the Sir Francis Drake Hotel, 450 Powell St., 21st Floor. ☎ **415/395-8595.**

Tourists and locals sip cocktails at sunset and boogie down to live swing and big-band tunes after dark. The room is classic 1930s San

Francisco, with red-velvet banquettes, chandeliers, and fabulous views. Like Harry's SoMa dance club, early evening is more relaxed, but come the weekend, this place gets loose. Jackets recommended.

✪ **Top of the Mark.** In the Mark Hopkins Intercontinental, 1 Nob Hill (California and Mason sts.). ☎ **415/392-3434.**

One of the most famous cocktail lounges in the world. During World War II, it was considered de rigueur for Pacific-bound servicemen to toast their good-bye to the States here. The spectacular glass-walled room features an unparalleled view. Sunday brunch, served from 10am to 2pm, costs about $32.

4   Gay & Lesbian Bars & Clubs

As with straight establishments, gay bars and clubs target varied clienteles. The major lesbian community is in Oakland, though there are a few hangouts in the city.

Check the free weeklies, the *San Francisco Bay Guardian* and *San Francisco Weekly,* for listings of events and happenings. The *Bay Area Reporter* is a gay paper with comprehensive listings, including a weekly community calendar.

Alta Plaza. 2301 Fillmore St. (at Clay St.). ☎ **415/922-1444.** No cover.

Pacific Heights's wealthy gays flock to this classy Fillmore establishment, with both bar and restaurant. It's especially festive on Friday and Saturday during happy hour.

Badlands. 4121 l8th St. (at Castro St.). ☎ **415/626-9320.** No cover.

This popular hangout is decorated with license plates from practically everywhere. Neon throws a stream of multicolored light on Levi-clad patrons.

Castro Station. 456 Castro St. (between 17th and 18th sts.). ☎ **415/ 626-7220.** No cover.

A well-known gay hangout, this bar is popular with the leather and Levi's crowd; trendy boys from around the country show up here looking for action.

The Cinch Saloon. l723 Polk St. (near Washington St.). ☎ **415/776-4162.** No cover.

Among the popular attributes of this cruisy neighborhood bar are the outdoor patio, Sunday barbecue or buffet, and progressive music and videos. Forty-niner fans also gather here for televised games. The bar attracts a mixed crowd of gays, lesbians (now that there are almost no exclusively lesbian bars left in San Francisco), and gay-friendly straight folk.

Detour. 2348 Market St. (near Castro St.). ☎ **415/861-6053.** No cover.

Right in the heart of gay San Francisco, this bar attracts a young, often hot crowd of boys, with its low lighting and throbbing house music. Chain-link fences seem to hold in the action, while a live DJ spins a web of popular hits. Special events, including the Saturday go-go dancers, keep this place jumping.

The Eagle. 398 12th St. (at Harrison St.). ☎ **415/626-0880.**

One of the city's most traditional leather bars, The Eagle boasts a heated outdoor patio and a popular Sunday afternoon beer fest.

The End Up. 401 6th St. (at Harrison St.). ☎ **415/543-7700.** Cover varies.

It's a different nightclub every night of the week, but regardless of who's throwing the party, the place is always jumping with the DJ's blasting tunes. There are two pool tables, a flaming fireplace, outdoor patio, and a mob of gyrating souls on the dance floor. Some nights are straight, so call for gay nights.

Metro. 3600 16th St. (at Market St.). ☎ **415/703-9750.** No cover.

With modern art on the walls, the Metro provides the gay community with high-energy dance music and the best view of the Castro District from its large balcony. The bar seems to attract people of all ages who enjoy the friendly bartenders and the highly charged, cruising atmosphere. There's also a Chinese restaurant on the premises.

The Mint. 1942 Market St. (at Laguna St.). ☎ **415/626-4726.** No cover.

Come out of the closet *and* the shower and into The Mint, where every night you can sing show tunes at this gay and lesbian karaoke bar. Along with song, you'll encounter a mixed 20- to 40-something crowd who like to combine cocktails with do-it-yourself cabaret.

Nightshift. 469 Castro St. (between 17th and 18th sts.). ☎ **415/626-5876.** No cover.

Deep in the heart of the Castro District, young men and their pursuers show up here, enjoying the low lighting, the sexually charged atmosphere, and even the occasional exhibition of a local artist's work. The age group ranges from the early 20s to the 50s, and it's a convivial place with sometimes exciting shows. For would-be Jeff Strykers, "The Battle of the Bulge" (a jockey underwear contest) takes place on the second Sunday of the month.

Rawhide II. 280 Seventh St. (at Folsom St.). ☎ **415/621-1197.** Weekend cover charge includes two free drinks.

Gay or straight, this is one of the city's top country-western dance bars, patronized by both men and women. Free dance lessons are offered Monday through Friday from 7:30 to 9:30pm.

The Stud. 399 Ninth St. (at Harrison St.). ☎ **415/863-6623.** Cover $2–$6 weekends.

The Stud has been around for 30 years, is one of the most successful gay establishments in town, and is mellow enough for straights as well as gays. Music here is a balanced mix of old and new, retro-disco for boys on Wednesdays and women's nights on Thursdays and Saturdays.

Twin Peaks Tavern. 401 Castro St. (at 17th and Market sts.). ☎ **415/864-9470.** No cover.

Right at the intersection of Castro, 17th, and Market streets is one of the Castro's most famous gay hangouts, which caters to an older crowd and is considered the first gay bar in America. Because of its relatively small size and desirable location, the place becomes fairly crowded and convivial by 8pm, earlier than many neighboring bars. Drinks run from $2 to $5.

5 A Classic Movie House

Castro. 429 Castro St. (near Market St.). ☎ **415/621-6120.**

One of the largest and funkiest theaters in the city, the Castro is known for its screenings of classics and for its Würlitzer organ, which is played before each show. There's a different feature here almost nightly, and more often than not it's a double feature. Bargain matinees are usually offered on Wednesday, Saturday, Sunday, and holidays. Phone for schedules, prices, and show times.

Easy Excursions from San Francisco

*T*he Bay City is, without question, captivating, but don't let it ensnare you to the point of ignoring its environs. They contain a multitude of scenic communities like Tiburon and Sausalito. If you have time, venture across the bay for a half- or full-day excursion.

1 Angel Island & Tiburon

8 miles N of San Francisco

A federal and state wildlife refuge, **Angel Island** is the largest of the San Francisco Bay's three islets (the others being Alcatraz and Yerba Buena). The island has been, at various times, a prison, a quarantine station for immigrants, a missile base, and even a favorite site for duels. Nowadays, though, most of the people who visit here are content with picnicking on the large green lawn that fronts the docking area; loaded with the appropriate recreational supplies, they claim a barbecue, plop their fannies down on the lush green grass, and while away an afternoon free of phones, televisions, and traffic. Hiking, mountain biking, and guided tram tours are also popular options.

Tiburon, situated on a peninsula of the same name, looks like a cross between a fishing village and a Hollywood western set—imagine San Francisco reduced to toy dimensions. This seacoast town rambles over a series of green hills and ends up at a spindly, multicolored pier on the waterfront, like a Fisherman's Wharf in miniature. But in reality it's an extremely plush patch of yacht-club suburbia, as you'll see by both the marine craft and the homes of their owners. **Main Street** is lined with ramshackle, color-splashed old frame houses that shelter chic boutiques, souvenir stores, antiques shops, and art galleries. Other roads are narrow, winding, and hilly, and lead up to dramatically situated homes. The view of San Francisco's skyline and the islands in the bay is a good enough reason to pay the precious price to live here.

The Bay Area

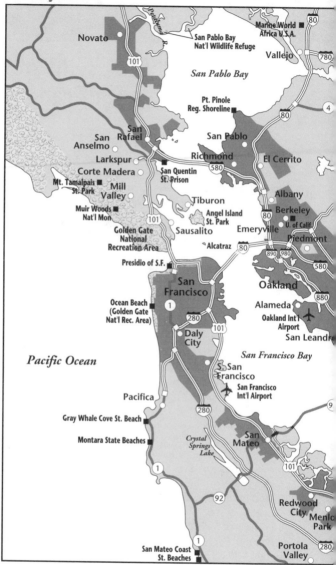

San Pablo Bay Nat'l Wildlife Refuge

Marine World Africa U.S.A.

Vallejo

Novato

San Pablo Bay

Pt. Pinole Reg. Shoreline

San Pablo

Richmond

El Cerrito

San Rafael

San Anselmo

Larkspur

Corte Madera

San Quentin St. Prison

Mt. Tamalpais St. Park

Mill Valley

Tiburon

Angel Island St. Park

Albany

Berkeley

U. of Calif.

Emeryville

Muir Woods Nat'l Mon.

Golden Gate National Recreation Area

Sausalito

Alcatraz

Piedmont

Presidio of S.F.

San Francisco

Oakland

Ocean Beach (Golden Gate Nat'l Rec. Area)

Alameda

Oakland Int'l Airport

San Leandro

Daly City

San Francisco Bay

Pacific Ocean

S. San Francisco

San Francisco Int'l Airport

Pacifica

Gray Whale Cove St. Beach

Montara State Beaches

Crystal Springs Lake

San Mateo

Redwood City

Menlo Park

Portola Valley

San Mateo Coast St. Beaches

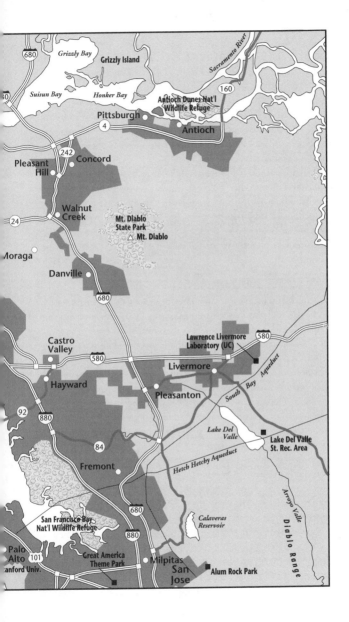

ESSENTIALS

Ferries of the **Red and White Fleet** (☎ **415/546-2700** or 800/
229-2784 in California) leave from Pier 43¹/₂ (Fisherman's Wharf)
and travel to both Angel Island and Tiburon. Boats run on a seasonal schedule; phone for departure information. The round-trip
fare is $9 to Angel Island, $11 to Tiburon; half price for kids 5 to
11. (*Note:* The Red and White Fleet is slated to be converted into
the Blue and Gold Fleet by 1997, but will probably keep the same
schedule and fares.)

By car from San Francisco, take U.S. 101 to the Tiburon/
Highway 131 exit, then follow Tiburon Boulevard all the way into
downtown, a 40-minute drive from San Francisco. Catch the
ferry (☎ **415/435-2131** or 415/388-6770) to Angel Island
from the dock located at Tiburon Boulevard and Main Street. The
15-minute round-trip costs $5 adult, $3 children 5 to 11, and
$1 for bikes.

WHAT TO SEE & DO ON ANGEL ISLAND

Passengers disembark from the ferry at Ayala Cove, a small marina
abutting a huge lawn area equipped with tables, benches, barbecue
pits, and restrooms. Also at Ayala Cove is a small store, gift shop,
cafe (with surprisingly good grub), and overpriced mountain bike
rental shop (helmets included).

Among the 12 miles of Angel Island's hiking and mountain bike
trails include the **Perimeter Road,** a partly paved path that circles
the island and winds its way past disused troop barracks, former gun
emplacements, and other military buildings; several turnoffs lead up
to the top of Mount Livermore, 776 feet above the bay. Sometimes
referred to as the "Ellis Island of the West," from 1910 to 1940
Angel Island was used as a holding area for Chinese immigrants
awaiting their citizenship papers. You can still see some faded Chinese characters on the walls of the barracks where the immigrants
were held. During the warmer months you can camp at a limited
number of sites; reservations are required.

Also offered at Angel Island are guided sea kayak tours. The all-
day trips, which include a catered lunch, combine the thrill of pad-
dling stable one-, two-, or three-person kayaks with an informative,
naturalist-led tour that encircles the island (conditions permitting).
All equipment is provided, kids are welcome, and no experience is
necessary. Rates run about $110 per person. For more information,
call **Sea Trek** at ☎ **415/488-1000.**

For recorded information about Angel Island State Park, call
☎ 415/435-1915.

WHAT TO SEE & DO IN TIBURON

The main thing to do in Tiburon is stroll along the waterfront, pop
into the stores, and spend an easy $50 on drinks and appetizers be-
fore heading back to the city. For a taste of the wine country, stop
in at **Windsor Vineyards,** 72 Main St. (☎ **415/435-3113** or 800/
214-9463)—their Victorian tasting room dates from 1888. Thirty-
five choices are available for a free tasting. Wine accessories and
gifts—glasses, cork pullers, gourmet sauces, posters, and maps—are
also available. Carry-packs are available (they hold six bottles). Ask
about personalized labels for your own selections. The shop is open
daily from 10am to 6pm.

WHERE TO DINE IN TIBURON
MODERATE

Guaymas. 5 Main St. ☎ **415/435-6300.** Reservations accepted. Main courses
$12–$18. AE, CB, DC, MC, V. Mon–Fri 11:30am–9:30pm, Sat 11:30am–
10:30pm, Sun 10:30am–9:30pm From U.S. 101, exit at Tiburon/Hwy. 131;
follow Tiburon Blvd. 5 miles and turn right onto Main St. The restaurant is
situated directly behind the bakery. Ferry: Walk about 10 paces from the landing. MEXICAN.

Guaymas offers authentic Mexican regional cuisine and a spectacular
panoramic view of San Francisco and the Bay. In good weather, the
two outdoor patios are almost always packed with diners soaking in
the sun and scene. Inside, beige walls are hung with colorful Mexican artwork, illuminated by modern track lighting. Should you be
feeling chilled, to the rear of the dining room is a beehive-shaped
adobe fireplace.

Guaymas is named after a fishing village on Mexico's Sea of
Cortez, and both the town and the restaurant are famous for their
camarones (giant shrimp). In addition, the restaurant features
ceviche, handmade tamales, and charcoal-grilled beef, seafood, and
fowl. Save room for dessert, especially the outrageously scrumptious
fritter with "drunken" bananas and ice cream. In addition to a good
selection of California wines, the restaurant offers an exceptional
variety of tequilas, Mexican beers, and mineral waters flavored with
flowers, grains, and fruits.

Sam's Anchor Café. 27 Main St. ☎ **415/435-4527.** Reservations accepted.
Main courses $8–$16. AE, MC, V. Mon–Thurs 11am–10pm, Fri 11am–10:30pm,
Sat 10am–10:30pm, Sun 9:30am–10pm. From U.S. 101, exit at Tiburon/Hwy.

131; follow Tiburon Blvd. 4 miles and turn right onto Main St. Ferry: Walk from the landing. SEAFOOD.

Summer Sundays are liveliest in Tiburon, when weekend boaters tie up to the docks at waterside restaurants like this one, the kind of place where you and your cronies can take off your shoes and have a fun, relaxed time eating burgers and drinking margaritas outside on the pier. The fare is pretty typical—sandwiches, salads, and seafood such as deep-fried oysters—but the quality and selection of the food is inconsequential: beers, burgers, and a designated driver are all you really need.

INEXPENSIVE

Sweden House Bakery-Café. 35 Main St. ☎ **415/435-9767.** Reservations not accepted. Omelets $6.50–$7; sandwiches $6–$8. MC, V. Mon–Fri 8am–6pm, Sat–Sun 8am–7pm. From U.S. 101, exit at Tiburon/Belvedere; follow Tiburon Blvd. 5 miles and turn right onto Main St. Ferry: Walk from the landing. SWEDISH/AMERICAN.

This small, cozy cafe with gingham-covered walls adorned with copperware and kitchen utensils is a local favorite. On sunny mornings there's no better seat in the Bay Area than on the bakery's terrace, where you can nurse an espresso and pastry while gazing out over the bay. Full breakfasts are served, too, all accompanied by toasted Swedish limpa bread; skip the eggs and bacon routine and go with the tasty Swedish pancakes: lingonberry, blueberry, and apple. At lunch, there's typical American fare plus traditional openface sandwiches, including avocado and bacon or asparagus tips rolled in Danish ham. Beer and wine are available.

2 Sausalito

5 miles N of San Francisco

Just off the northern end of the Golden Gate Bridge is the eclectic little town of Sausalito, a slightly bohemian, nonchalant, and studiedly quaint adjunct to San Francisco. With approximately 7,500 residents, Sausalito feels rather like St. Tropez on the French Riviera—minus the starlets and the social rat race. It has its quota of paper millionaires, but they rub their permanently suntanned shoulders with a good number of hard-up artists, struggling authors, shipyard workers, and fishers. Next to the swank restaurants, plush bars, and antique shops and galleries, you'll see hamburger joints, beer parlors, and secondhand bookstores. Sausalito's main touring strip is **Bridgeway,** which runs along the water, but those in the know make a quick detour to **Caledonia Street** one block inland;

not only is it less congested, but there's a far better selection of cafes and shops.

ESSENTIALS

Ferries of the **Red and White Fleet** (☎ **415/546-2700** or 800/ 229-2784 in California) leave from Pier 43½ (Fisherman's Wharf) and cost $11 round-trip, half price for kids 5 to 11. Boats run on a seasonal schedule; phone for departure information. (*Note:* The Red and White Fleet is slated to be converted into the Blue and Gold Fleet by 1997, but will probably keep the same schedule and fares.)

By car from San Francisco, take U.S. 101 north, then first right after the Golden Gate Bridge (Alexander exit). Alexander becomes Bridgeway in Sausalito.

WHAT TO SEE & DO

Above all, Sausalito has scenery and sunshine, for once you cross the Golden Gate Bridge you're out of the San Francisco fog patch and under blue California sky (we hope). The town's steep hills are covered with houses that overlook a forest of masts on the waters below, but almost all the tourist action, which is almost singularly limited to window shopping and eating, takes place at sea level on Bridgeway.

Bay Model Visitors Center. 2100 Bridgeway. ☎ **415/332-3871.** Admission free. Winter, Tues–Sat 9am–4pm; summer, Tues–Fri 9am–4pm, Sat–Sun 10am–6pm.

The U.S. Army Corps of Engineers uses this high-tech, 1½-acre model of San Francisco's bay and delta to resolve problems and observe what impact any changes in water flow will have. The model reproduces (in scale) the rise and fall of tides, the flows and currents of water, the mixing of fresh- and saltwater, and indicates trends in sediment movement. There's a 10-minute film that explains it all and a tour, but the most interesting time to visit is when it's actually being used, so call ahead.

WHERE TO SHOP

Sausalito is a mecca for shoppers seeking handmade, original, and offbeat clothes and footwear, as well as arts and crafts. The town's best shops are found in the alleys, malls, and second-floor boutiques reached by steep, narrow staircases on and off Bridgeway. Additional shops are found on Caledonia Street, which runs parallel to and one block inland from Bridgeway.

Village Fair, at 777 Bridgeway, is Sausalito's closest approximation to a mall. It's a complex of 30 shops, souvenir stores, coffee bars, and gardens. Among them, **Quest Gallery** (☎ 415/332-6832) features fine ceramics, whimsical chess sets, contemporary glass, hand-painted silks, woven clothing, art jewelry, and graphics. The shop specializes in celebrated California artists, many of whom sell exclusively through this store. The complex is open daily from 10am to 6pm; restaurants stay open later.

Burlwood Gallery. 721 Bridgeway. ☎ **415/332-6550.**

Visit this gallery for one-of-a-kind redwood furniture plus fine jewelry, metal sculptures, hand-blown glass, Oriental rugs, and other interesting gifts. It's well worth browsing. Open daily from 10am to 6pm.

Pegasus Leather Company. 28 Princess St. (off Bridgeway). ☎ **415/332-5624.**

Pegasus is a vendor of beautiful leather clothing and accessories. Along with jackets, coats, skirts, and blouses, there are handsome belts, gloves, and purses made from ultrasoft, richly colored leathers. Clothing can be custom made and altered for a perfect fit at no extra charge. Open daily from 10am to 5:30pm.

The Sausalito Country Store. 789 Bridgeway. ☎ **415/332-7890.**

This place sells oodles of handmade, country-style goods for the home and garden. Many of these items—ceramic, stuffed, and painted-wood animals, aprons, baskets, birdhouses, embossed quilt prints, and lithographs—are made by local artists and artisans. Open daily from 10am to 6pm.

WHERE TO DINE
MODERATE

Guernica. 2009 Bridgeway. ☎ **415/332-1512.** Reservations recommended. Main courses $10–$17. AE, MC, V. Daily 5–10pm. From U.S. 101 north, take the first right after the Golden Gate Bridge (Alexander exit); Alexander becomes Bridgeway in Sausalito. FRENCH/BASQUE.

Established in 1976, Guernica is one of those funky old kinds of restaurants that you'd probably pass up for something more chic and modern down the street if you didn't know better. What? You don't know about Guernica's legendary Paella Valenciana? Well now you do, so be sure to call ahead and order it in advance, and bring a partner cause it's served for two but will feed three. Begin with an appetizer of artichoke hearts or escargots, and be sure to try the wonderful homemade bread. Other main courses are grilled rabbit with a spicy red diablo sauce, a hearty Rack of Lamb Guernica, and medallions of pork loin with baked apples and Calvados. Rich desserts include such in-season specialties as strawberry tart and peach Melba.

Horizons. 558 Brideway. ☎ **415/331-3232.** Reservations accepted weekdays only. Main courses $9–$15, salads and sandwiches $6–$8. AE, MC, V. Mon–Fri 11am–11pm, Sat–Sun 10am–11pm. SEAFOOD/AMERICAN.

Eventually, every San Franciscan ends up at Horizons to meet a friend for Sunday Bloody Marys. It's not much to look at from the outside, but it gets better as you head past the funky dark wood interior toward the waterside terrace. On warm days it's worth the wait for alfresco seating if only to watch dreamy sailboats glide past San Francisco's distant skyline. The food here can't touch the view, but it's well portioned and satisfying enough. Seafood dishes are the main items, including steamed clams and mussels, freshly shucked oysters, and a variety of seafood pastas. In fine Marin tradition, Horizons has an "herb tea and espresso" bar, and is a totally non-smoking restaurant.

INEXPENSIVE

Feng Nian Chinese Restaurant. 2650 Bridgeway. ☎ **415/331-5300.** Reservations accepted. Lunch specials $4–$5.50; main courses $6.55–$14. AE, DISC, MC, V. Mon and Wed–Thur 11:30am–9:30pm, Fri–Sat 11:30am–10pm, Sun 12:30–9:30pm. From U.S. 101 north, take the first right after the Golden Gate Bridge (Alexander exit); Alexander becomes Bridgeway in Sausalito. The restaurant is located near the intersection of Bridgeway and Harbor Drive, before downtown Sausalito. CHINESE.

A pretty restaurant serving fine quality Chinese food, Feng Nian has such a wide selection of appetizers that a combination of several would make a delicious meal in itself. The crispy roast duck is a personal favorite, but if you'd like an assortment, try the flaming combination (enough for two) that includes egg roll, fried prawn, paper-wrapped chicken, barbecued ribs, fried chicken, and teriyaki. There are nine soups, including a truly exceptional, rich crabmeat/shark's-fin soup with shredded crab-leg meat.

Choosing one of the chef's suggestions isn't easy. The Peking duck requires about a half hour of preparation, but it's always delectable. If you enjoy seafood, try the twice sizzling seafood, with prawns, scallops, squid, and fresh vegetables in oyster sauce; it's prepared at your table. Beef dishes are prepared in a variety of ways: Mongolian, Szechuan, Hunan, Mandarin—with ginger, curry, and broccoli, just to name a few. The restaurant offers more than 90 main dishes, including a number of main courses for vegetarians.

PICNIC FARE & WHERE TO EAT IT

Even Sausalito's naysayers have to admit that it's hard not to enjoy eating you way down Bridgeway on a warm, sunny day. If the crowds are too much or the prices too steep at the bay-side restaurants, grab a bite to go for an impromptu picnic in the park fronting the marina.

Café Soleil. 37 Caledonia St. ☎ **415/331-9355.** No credit cards. Daily 7am–6:30pm.

Small, clean, cute, and cheap, Café Soleil whips up some good soups, salads, and sandwiches along with killer smoothies. Order to go at the counter, then take you goods a block over to the marina for a dock-side lunch.

Caledonia Kitchen. 400 Caledonia St. ☎ **415/331-0220.** No credit cards. Daily 8am–8pm.

Caledonia Kitchen is the sort of place you wish were just around the corner from your house—a beautiful little cafe serving a huge assortment of fresh salads, soups, chili, sandwiches, and inexpensive entrées like herbed roast chicken or vegetarian lasagna for only $4.95. Continental-style breakfast items and good coffee and espresso drinks are also on the menu.

Hamburgers. 737 Bridgeway ☎ **415/332-9471.** No credit cards. Daily 11am–5pm.

Like the name says, the specialty at this tiny, narrow cafe is juicy flame-broiled hamburgers, arguably Marin County's best. Look for the rotating grill in the window off Bridgeway, then stand in line and salivate with the rest (chicken burgers are a slightly healthier option). Order a side of fries, grab a bunch of napkins, then head over to the park across the street.

Venice Gourmet Delicatessen. 625 Bridgeway. ☎ **415/332-3544.** AE, DC, DISC, MC, V. Daily 9am–6pm.

This classic old deli has all the makings for a superb picnic: wines, cheese, fruits, stuffed vine leaves, mushroom and artichoke salad, quiche, delicious sandwiches (made to order on sourdough bread), olives, and fresh-baked pastries.

Index